The Feuding Truth
James M. Vance and Family

Barbara Vance Cherep – Janice Vance
Terry Vance - Elaine Vance Looney

DEDICATION

Dedicated to the families of James and Mary Vance
with our sincerest appreciation.

James M. Vance with his wife Elizabeth Barbour. He is the son of James Vance Jr. and wife Vicey Stepp, and grandson of James Vance Sr. and Mary Collins.

Used with permission of James Vance, a direct descendant of James Vance Sr. and Mary Collins Vance

CONTENTS

INTRODUCTION

Jim Vance, who is he, and why is he included in the Hatfield and McCoy books and folklore? When we started researching the life of Jim Vance, we uncovered a very different person than the one portrayed in previously written feud stories. The Jim Vance that emerged in our research revealed a respectable, dedicated, family man. The records will show that Jim Vance was educated and served in Kentucky as a deputy sheriff. He was elected to the position of constable in West Virginia. Jim Vance, who has been referred to in previous writings as being "the most desperate man in the valley", ran a successful timbering business and was never arrested for a single crime in his life. He was appointed to the position of Justice of the Peace in the Magnolia District of Logan County, West Virginia. We hope to introduce you to the Jim Vance that we have discovered. That is why we are writing this book. We hope to give you a better understanding of this family. It is not our intent to exclude the feud, but, it is our intent to show that what has been written was done without much study or research of the records regarding Jim Vance. We realized there would be challenges, perhaps, because the Hatfields and McCoys have, up until now, solely presented their version of the feud, with regard to protecting their legacies, their own reputations, and their family folklore.

As Vance family researchers, we had already compiled a nearly 600-page history on the early Vance family in America. Initially, we thought that the research of Jim Vance's life would be minor in comparison. Well, we couldn't have been more wrong. To research Jim meant that we would have to research every feudist individual and his or her neighbors, each person named in relevant documents, including the feud related books and documents. There was nothing minor about this feud research. So, you might ask, why do we care? Who are we to attempt such a feat? Who are we to confront what's been written?

We are not heirs of Jim Vance, but distant cousins, other branches of the Vance tree. We are researchers and genealogists; we care how history is written. This is why co-authors *Elaine Vance, Terry Vance, and Janice Vance*, with myself, believe that Jim and his family deserved a credible, well researched written history. We felt that Jim deserved his moment to show who he was, as well as who he was not. We desire to tell his story based on facts and the records, **good or bad**. We hope to dispel the myths and change the perception of what has been iniquitously portrayed in movies and books regarding James M. Vance.

1

Chapter 1
VANCE FAMIY – THE EARLY YEARS

The Vance family lineage is Irish in origin, and begins in America with Matthew and Anne (Jones) Vance, the great grandparents of Jim Vance and the great, great grandparents of Anderson Hatfield. Matthew and Anne married in the First Presbyterian Church of Philadelphia on June 5, 1746. After their marriage, the young couple migrated down into Augusta County, VA, where his name is listed for three large parcels of land, surveyed by James Tremble in 1751. This land was previously owned by Col. James Patton. Matthew and Anne lived in Arnolds Valley, on Opossum Creek, for 17 years and 5 months. Anne gave birth to three sons while in Arnolds Valley; those are John, Abner, and Matthew Vance Jr. There is at least one unknown daughter according to the 1790 census.

Survey made by Jam. Tremble, land of Jam. Patton, surveyed for Matthew Vance in April 1751[1]

Moving further south, Matthew and Anne moved to Pittsylvania Co., Virginia in 1766. They lived on Straight Stone Creek for the next ten years on 400 acres of land. By 1778, the family took those early roads into Surry County, NC., where the second son, Abner Vance, met Susannah Howard, and would soon start a family. By 1783, Matthew, with sons John and Matthew Jr., moved on to Spartanburg, SC, and then over to Greenville, SC. This is where Matthew left his last known documented sale of goods, in 1798.

John Vance, the eldest son was born in May of 1753. After John's Revolutionary War service, he went to Spartanburg SC., in 1783. By 1794, he settled in Carter County, TN., then moved to Burke County, NC., in 1805, living there until his death in May of 1830. John's descendants dispersed from Burke in 1835, moving into Russell County, VA. Later, some settled in Wise, Buchanan, and Dickenson Counties, VA., while some moved into WV.

Matthew Vance Jr. and his family lived in Greenville until 1817, and then moved over to Burke County, NC. to join his brother John. Matthew

---

[1] Patton Papers, Virginia Library

2

Jr. served in the War of 1812. Many of his descendants still live in the same area of Burke, Avery, Yancey and surrounding counties in N.C., making Avery, Burke and surrounding counties their home for nearly 200 years.

Abner Vance, Grandfather to Jim Vance

Abner Vance is the brother who is scrutinized by feud writers, showing Abner as the reason Jim Vance was of a desperate character. This is an example where FOLKLORE is used to illustrate that the apple does not fall far from the tree. Abner's ill-fated mistake is used in feud books as an example to make all of his heirs appear unprincipled and undisciplined. That simply is not so. Abner and Susannah settled in Russell County, VA. They lived there peaceably until Abner was hanged for murder in 1819. Soon after, Susannah and most of the children moved into Logan and surrounding counties.

Not proven a revolutionary soldier, Abner did supply grain for the

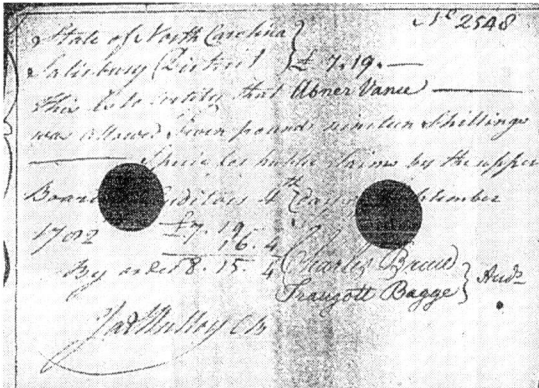

troops in NC., during the Revolutionary War. Abner is listed in the N.C. Army Accounts Vol. III, Book 6 on Sept. 4, 1782. Abner was allowed 7 pounds, 19 shillings from Charles Bagge and Traugott Bruce, who were the auditors in the Salisbury District, for grain delivered to the troops. His name is also found with his father's name, Matthew, in Pittsylvania in 1776, as swearing his allegiance to America.

Abner lived a quiet life in Russell County up until 1817, as a farmer and road builder. Then, his life was turned upside down because he shot a man by the name of Lewis Horton. See, Lewis Horton was the brother of Daniel Horton, who Abner swore to kill, according to Judge Johnson, who stated that the Hortons had threatened the life of Abner during testimony in Chancery Court. Now, Abner in 1817 would have been near 57 years of age. He was an older, long timed settled man. Lewis Horton was passing through the ford of the creek near the home of Abner. There, Lewis raised his voice to Abner, because of that previous deposition in chancery, and yelled, "be dammed and shoot!" As Lewis was riding steadily away, enraged, the old man did shoot at him, hitting Horton squarely in the back. Abner spent two years in jail during the two trials, and then was hanged in 1819.

However, not before a law was written so that Abner could be tried in the city of Abingdon, VA, in Washington County. There, the second and final trial was held in court. The first trial in Russell resulted in a guilty verdict. There was an appeal with the first trial and a second trial was granted in Russell County. However, the court was unable to yield enough jurors for a second trial in Russell. The sheriff swept the county, but no one wanted to sit on that jury, because most admitted to having formed a previous opinion. Judge Johnson, during this time, had written a news article demeaning Sylvanus Brewer and Abner Vance, calling them savages. The judge exhibited his influences stating that Abner was guilty, writing that article under an assumed name. It became a problem for Russell County. During this time, Judge Johnson asked for a new law from the Virginia Legislature, stating that when the jury in such cases couldn't find enough men to sit, that the trial could be moved to another county. The second trial officially moved to Washington County. We call this law "Change of Venue". Abner was hanged for the murder, but his case set a precedent. Abner fully admitted to his crime and took his punishment with utmost dignity. He stood and faced his accusers from the hangman's platform. Abner talked, some say preached, for many hours. The newspapers said he addressed nearly 5000 people for nearly 5 hours. Before taking his last breath of life, Abner sang a song on the gallows that he had written for his family and friends, which is still popular among family members today. (See Appendix A)

Elizabeth the Mother of Jim Vance

Elizabeth, the daughter of Abner, and the mother of Jim Vance, was "thought" to be the reason for the shooting of Lewis Horton for which Abner Vance was hung. This is unproven. The legendary story passed down says that a daughter had a rendezvous with Horton. People assumed it was Elizabeth, because she was an unmarried daughter with children. Elizabeth may have been unmarried, but she was readily committed to John Ferrell, with whom she had a number of children. Folklore says after this weekend excursion, Lewis rode his horse over the ford, where Abner was waiting. Horton dropped Elizabeth off by horseback after having his way with her. It was dishonorable for a man to treat a woman with such indignity. What do the court records tell us? Not to listen to folklore. The judge said that the reason for the shooting was because Horton threatened to kill Abner. The judge's document does not stipulate the reason for making that threat. It could have very well been over land, or boundary lines, or even a daughter. To draw conclusions on history, is not our job, but to write it from the records. What we know, is that Elizabeth was having children with John Ferrell long before Abner killed Horton. The feud authors take the story of Abner Vance and make egregious errors by enveloping folklore. Even so, this is the perfect venue to correct many of the wrongs written in the Hatfield and McCoy books.

The court records tell us that Abner never posted bond at his trial. He is led to the bar by the sheriff. Abner said in his own words, that he was kept in "yon stone walls". During the second trial in Abingdon, Abner was sick, and was examined by a doctor in order to stand trial. This can be proven in court records; the Letter to the Legislature by Judge Johnson; the Journal of the House of Delegates for the Commonwealth of VA; and again in the Abingdon trial, written about in VA Cases/or Decisions of the General Court of VA. (See Appendix A)

Elizabeth Vance and the Ferrell Connection

After the trial and hanging, Abner's wife and children moved into Logan County, VA. (At that time it was known as Cabell, County). John Ferrell moved along the Tug River Valley. John Ferrell and Charles Canady are mentioned in KY *Civil Case #8*, in 1822, against Robert Scott, by his attorney one James Fuller, over land recently purchased of Scott. John Ferrell, in 1822 lived in Cabell per this case, whereas, Scott and Fuller were said to be citizens of Virginia. John Ferrell, while still living in Russell, had procured a portion of this land in 1814/1815, originally in Floyd County, KY, (now Pike)[2]. By 1822, a deed had not been secured, so John Ferrell sued Scott for the deed. By 1823, the deed was acquired in his name legally. The Reverend James Madison had once owned this land in 1796 on the Tug.

---

[2] This Indenture of bargain and sale made this 3 day Nov. 1823. Between James Fuller Attorney for Robert G. Scott, and John Ferrell of the other part. Witness that the said James Fuller by virtue of on the 20th day of January 1814, and recorded in the county Court of Russell on the 5 day of September 1815, for and in consideration of the sum of two hundred dollars to him in hand paid. The receipt whereof is hereby acknowledged hath granted bargained and sold. And by these present doth grant bargain and sell unto the said John Ferrell and Charles Canady a certain tract or parcel of land lying and being in the county of Floyd [later Pike] and state of Kentucky, on the waters of the Tug of Sandy River. Being part of land tract of land granted to Reverend James Madison by patent, bearing date on the 28th day of January 1796 and containing 164 acres.

By January 6, 1839, John Ferrell owned a mill, as well, on the Kentucky side mentioned in a Warrant No. 2805, next to land secured by Joseph Hatfield.

Warrant No. 2805 - Governor of Commonwealth of Kentucky - To all to who these presents shall come, Greetings: Know ye that by virtue and in consideration of a warrant from the Pike County Court, there is granted by the said Commonwealth, unto Joseph Hatfield a certain tract of parcel of land. Containing one hundred and fifty acres by survey bearing the date the 17th day of April 1839. Lying and being in the county of Pike on the Tug Fork of Sandy River, beginning at a beech standing on the hillside opposite John Ferrell mill. Thence S79 E6 poles to a hickory standing on the bank of the Tug Fork of Sandy River. Thence N39 E174 poles to a Spruce Pine and beech standing on a cliff of rocks. N75 SW66 poles to a beech on a point, thence D76 W60 poles to two beech S68 W62 poles to a dogwood and beech N52 W103 to a beech in the head of a hollow thence N89 poles to two beeches S80 W21 poles to a maple and gum S165 poles to a stake S57 E190 poles to the beginning.

By the census records, we estimate that Elizabeth was born about 1796. Elizabeth gave birth to several children with John Ferrell[3]. John and Elizabeth were never legally married. John Ferrell was already a married man and had a legal family. Some would call Elizabeth Vance a common law wife during this period. Both families were close, nonetheless. They lived as neighbors, signed marriage bonds, and sold land to one another.

As already stated, Elizabeth was having children with John Ferrell long before the shooting of Lewis Horton. Daughter, Nancy Vance, married Ephraim Hatfield in 1828 in Pike County, KY, with bond by John Ferrell, and Andrew Ferrell, his proxy, and also signed by Elizabeth Vance. Nancy Hatfield gave birth to Anderson "Anse" Hatfield. Another daughter, Sarah, married Azandra Taylor, with Andrew Ferrell as witness. Daughter, Phoebe Vance, married Ephraim Hatfield, son of Joseph and Martha Evans Hatfield. Daughter, Mary Vance, married Valentine Hatfield. Elizabeth Vance also gave birth to a son Richard F. Vance, who married Mary Staton. Richard died during the Civil War in the year of 1863. This has been proven by notations in the family bible and by Logan County Minutes and tax lists[4].

---

[3] Ragland wrote that Nancy and Jim were children of John Ferrell. History of Logan County
[4] McDowell County Tax Records 1863, Vance, Richard Estate of, McDowell, 134, On the Dry Fork

James Vance (Sr.), our subject, was born about 1830 by the census, and died Jan. 8, 1888. James married Mary Collins, who died in Cabell County, Sept. 19, 1894, of flux. In a loving manner, they were commonly called Uncle Jim and Aunt Mary. James Vance's grave marker says he was born in 1832 and died in January of 1888. There are no known family Bibles or court records stating the exact dates of birth or death. When visiting the gravesite, the old gravestone had no markings.

After leaving Russell and Logan Counties, Elizabeth purchased fifty acres at the mouth of Blackberry Creek on April 1, 1834, in Pike County, KY. The grantors were James and Jane (Hatfield) Justice. By 1840, the family was living on Mate Creek., Logan County, VA[5]

---

[5] 1834 - James Justice and wife To Deed E. Vance} This indenture made and entered into on the year of our Lord 1834 between James Justice and his wife Jane of the Co. Logan and State of VA of the one part and Elizabeth Vance of the County of Logan, County and State of VA of the other part. Witnessed that the said James Justice and his wife Jane in consideration of the sum of 150.00 dollars, money of Virginia, to them in hand paid by the said Elizabeth Vance...a certain tract of land containing 50 acres lying and being on the Tug Fork of Sandy River in the County of Pike and State of Kentucky.

1840 - Andrew Ferrell to Elizabeth Vance, Richard Vance} Deed Logan Bk B pg. 256-257 - This indenture made the 7th day of March 1840 between Andrew Ferrell of the one part of the Co. of Logan and State of VA, and Elizabeth Vance and Richard Vance of the other part of the same Co. and State. Witnessed that I, said A. Ferrell, in consideration of $200.00 to him in hand paid by the said Elizabeth and Richard Vance....do delivery of these present the receipt in hand. Convey unto said Elizabeth and Richard Vance...a certain tract of parcel of land lying...County of Logan and State of VA on Mates Creek. Beginning at John Murphy's line and running down said creek....each side 100 poles from the ridge to a conditional line made by the said A. Ferrell between the house and the little field up the upper side of the creek. The creek to be the line from the rock house on the said creek containing 75 acres .... Andrew Ferrell and Polly Ferrell.

1842 - Vance from Ferrell} Deed – This indenture made this 6th day of Jan. in the year of our Lord 1842 between John Ferrell Sr. of the one part of the Co. of Logan and State of Va., and Elizabeth Vance of the other part of the same Co. and State. Witnessed that the said John Ferrell in consideration of $300.00 lawful money of the commonwealth. Paid by the said Elizabeth Vance.....To hold the said land with it appurtenances unto said Elizabeth Vance...and the said John Ferrell...unto the said Vance, her heirs.... whereof I have hereunto set my hand and the day and year above written. Jn & Nancy Ferrell

In 1842, John Ferrell and wife sold property to Elizabeth, and by 1851,[6] we can see that the sons of Elizabeth were growing into men when Elizabeth sold land to her eldest son, Richard, and his wife, Mary (Staten) Vance. The family makes many land deals in the 1850s, moving from upper Logan to lower Logan County in 1854, when Richard, Jim, and Elizabeth leave the Tug to live on property on the Bradshaw Mountain area of Virginia (WV).

February of 1854[7], Elizabeth deeded one acre of Tug property in upper Logan County to Randolph McCoy and H.H. Williamson for $20.00. The same day she sold to Randolph McCoy other property joining H.H. Williamson. Only one deed will be shown. This is not Randal McCoy of the feud.

Elizabeth, with sons Richard and Jim Vance, left the Tug to move to Bradshaw Mountain, an area now in McDowell County, WV. One of the properties has an old graveyard where Richard Vance is buried, and is owned by Charlie Vance, who comes down the line of John Vance, brother to Abner.

The 1860 census shows that Elizabeth and son James came back to the KY side of the Tug for a short time, before going back into lower Logan when the war moved into Kentucky.

---

[6] 1851 - Elizabeth Vance to Richard Vance} Deed - This indenture made and entered into this 3rd day Oct. 1851 by and between Elizabeth Vance and Richard Vance both of the Co. of Logan and State of VA. Witnessed for and in consideration of the sum of $100.00, paid in hand, the receipt whereof is hereby acknowledged. The said Elizabeth Vance now sold unto the said Richard Vance a parcel of land lying and being in the Co. of Logan State of VA on the Tug Fork of Sandy River. Bounded as follows to wit; beginning at a chestnut on the ridge thence square out a straight line to the back line of John Greens 30,000 acre survey. Thence with the line of said survey to John Ferrell's line thence with said line to a stake 8 poles to a stake on the river bank thence up with the meandering of the river to the beginning supposed to be 100 acres..... Elizabeth Vance Attest W. Straton Clk.

[7] Elizabeth Vance to Randolph McCoy) This deed the 11th day of Feb. 1854 between Elizabeth Vance of the first part and Randolph McCoy of the second part. In consideration of $300.00 paid in hand by cash and note from the second party to the first party. The first party do grant unto the said party of the second part all his lands except the land sold to H.H. Williamson and Wm A. Dempsey lying and being in the Co. of Logan. Beginning at a cucumber tree in the bank of the river in the lower edge of the road below the Mill seat. Thence running up the river with the meanders of the river to the upper end of the Island below Little Blackberry Creek to a lynn sugar and ash. With the conditional line between the said Elizabeth Vance and John Ferrell to the ash gap in the Horse Ridge, down back Horse Ridge the conditional line between the said Elizabeth Vance and Richard Vance to a white oak on the hill side thence with a cross fence to a chestnut tree on the bank of the river.... 11th day of Feb. 1854. Pleasant McCoy J.P.

Prior to McDowell becoming a county, records prove that the taxes were paid as part of Logan County. The properties warrant and first deed were recorded in Tazewell in 1854, before the war. Jim acquired land in Tazewell Deed Book 12, page 274[8]. The warrant given for that land was #18187, on Nov 29, 1854.

Found in my Vance family book published in 2012, is the data, (listed below), on sons Jim and Richard, with mother Elizabeth. This McDowell Land Book started in the year of 1859, just prior to the civil war. The book gives landowner, taxable amount and acreage. The data in this book is much like a census record in showing that Jim, Richard and Elizabeth owned land on the backside of Bradshaw Mountain, (an area known today as Paynesville), until 1869.

1859, Vance, Richard, McDowell, 134, On the Dry Fork
1859, Vance, Elizabeth, McDowell, 180, Ground Hog, Oosley Br. Panther
1859, Vance, James, Logan, no quantity, On Panther and Bradshaw Ridge
1859, Vance, James, Logan, 130, On Panther and Bradshaw Ridge
1859, Vance, James, Logan, 54, On Dividing Ridge
1860, Vance, Richard, McDowell, 134 acres on Dry Fork
1860, Vance, Elizabeth, Logan, no quantity Panther and Bradshaw Ridge
1860, Vance, James, Logan, 54 on the Dividing Ridge
1861, Vance, Richard, McDowell, 134, On the Dry Fork
1861, Vance, Elizabeth, McDowell, 180, Ground Hog, Oosley Br. Panther
1861, Vance, James, Logan, no quantity, On Panther and Bradshaw Ridge
1861, Vance, James, Logan, 130, On Panther and Bradshaw Ridge
1861, Vance, James, Logan, 54, On Dividing Ridge
1862, Vance, Richard, McDowell, 134, On the Dry Fork
1862, Vance, Elizabeth, McDowell, 180, Ground Hog, Oosley Branch
1862, Vance, James, McDowell, no quantity, On Panther Creek
1862, Vance, James, McDowell, 130, On Panther Creek
1862, Vance, James, McDowell, 54, On Dividing Ridge
1863, Vance, Richard Estate of, McDowell, 134, On the Dry Fork
1863, Vance, Elizabeth, McDowell, 180, Ground Hog, Oosley Branch

---

[8] Deed Bk 12, pg. 122 Tazewell Co. VA., 11th Sept. 1856- James Vance from H.A. Harman Deed} Know men by these present that H.A. Harman of the aforesaid county and state doth bargain and part unto James Vance of the aforesaid county and state said title as is vested in me. In and to a certain parcel of land lying in the aforesaid county and state on the divides between Big Slate Creek of the Levisa Fork of Sandy River and Bradshaw Creek of the Dry Fork of Tug River. About one mile southerly from top of the divide between Panther Creek of the Tug and said Slate and Bradshaw and containing 54 acres more or less, the grant to said Harman calls for 54 acres which is called the Rife or Payne place, the said Vance has it in possession now conveyed by a rents. The above day and date as witness my hand and seal. H.A. Harman; Witnessed by Polly Aldridge and Richard Vance

1863, Vance, James, McDowell, no quantity, On Panther Creek
1863, Vance, James, McDowell, 130, On Panther Creek
1863, Vance, James, McDowell, 54, On Dividing Ridge
1866, Vance, Elizabeth, McDowell, 180, Ground Hog, Oosley Branch
1866, Vance, James, McDowell, no quantity, On Panther Creek
1866, Vance, James, McDowell, 130, On Panther Creek
1866, Vance, James, McDowell, 54, On Dividing Ridge
1869, Vance, Elizabeth, Month of Oct. for non-payment of taxes for the year 1865-66;
Delinquent Land Sale Book 1 – Elizabeth Vance 180 acres
1870, Vance, Richard Estate of, McDowell, 134, On the Dry Fork

McDowell Land Survey of the land of James Vance Sr., Richard Vance, and Elizabeth Vance, mother of James and Richard.

Chapter 2
FOLKLORE AND THE RECORDS

The Hatfield and McCoy feud has captivated a region of Appalachian geography for nearly 130 years and is still the most talked about feud in this nation's history. As fabulous as the Hatfield-McCoy feud is, records located in the archives and courthouses are unacceptably ignored, when it comes to previous writings about Jim Vance. The source for the written history of the feud was a newspaper-generated event, mostly for human-interest, and was folklore driven. Large city newspapers helped the spiraling of misinformation by causing a flood of small city newspapers across America to pick up the by-line. True or not, with exaggerated jargon, reporters were eager to print the stories. Reporter, John Spears led the pack with his storybook version, which drew his circulation. The most noted article was called *"The Dramatic Story of a Mountain Feud"*, setting the precedent for what would become feud history in many Hatfield and McCoy books. Then from the New York Sun, an article appeared on December 28, 1892, *The Story of a Desperado*, written about Frank Phillips. The article appeared in the Cincinnati Courier, with the writer of the article, depicting Frank as a gallant, and yet so destructive person. Once a mere farmer-turned gun master, Frank killed several people, according to this article. If you read the hundreds of articles, you start to notice how the feud eclipsed into people dying several times within a few-year period. Frank died several times, as well as Johnse, Cap, and Anse. Let us address how this happened.

In the mountains, most news traveled by word of mouth. Reporters back then were not held to the same standards as they are today. The early reporters did not verify the stories or the sources, which accounts for many of the false legends that persist as a result of what was presented in the newspapers during that time. Newspaper reporters formed opinions, sometimes because of the source, and sometimes because of politics, or even religious views. And at this time, yellow journalism was getting its start. Yet, there are some articles proven to be incredibly accurate. Newspaper accounts should match what is in the actual records in time and substance. Unless the newspaper articles that were printed during that time can be substantiated by other records, they should not be used as the venue to speak of how history should be written.

Not to say that all feud books didn't look into the actual records, but....if they had looked at Jim Vance in the records, they should have seen what you will read here, but, alas, that didn't happen.

So, how do we know what happened in the feud? I'm not sure that anyone will ever know, or will be able to tell the feuding truth. It's certain if Randal McCoy or Anse Hatfield were standing before us today, we would never know the entire story.

Both men were married, yet caught, according to court records, entertaining women. Randal McCoy had an ongoing affair with Nellie Pinson[9], while Anse was caught in bed with the wife of John France[10]. The legal affairs or the morality of these men didn't seem to affect their wives. According to records, no one divorced. Nancy E. [Smith] Hatfield, wife of Cap, finally fed up with Cap's adulterous affairs, eventually brought divorce charges in Logan[11]. These records are undated without an outcome, none the less, charges were brought for divorce. Now, Johnse Hatfield, credited with four wives over his lifetime, was apprehended in Logan County, WV, charged in Pike County, KY, and the case was moved to Floyd County and tried in 1899. He would divorce Nancy McCoy Hatfield, his first wife, in 1891, stating Nancy had committed adultery. This was substantiated in Pike County Criminal Records[12]. In Logan County records, case 080-00021, Johnson Hatfield

---

[9] Microfiche 7040489 Pike Circuit Court - Commonwealth vs Randolph McCoy and Nellie Pinson} Adultery - This day came the parties and therefore came a jury to wit – Lewis Runyun, Wm. A. Hatfield, Wm. A. Taylor, Edward Maynard, John Charles, H.S. Carter, Jam. Burris, Nathaniel Blackburn, Asa Runyun, Lewis Sturgel, Samuel Brewer. Who was selected and sworn to will and truly try the issue as to Randolph McCoy who returned the following verdict – we of the jury find the defendant guilty and assess the fine twenty dollars. Lewis Runyun one of the jury. - It is therefore adjudged by the court that the commonwealth of Kentucky of the defendant Randolph McCoy the sum of twenty dollars find for cost herein expensed and upon the failure to pay, he will be confined in the jail of Pike County for ten days and filed away as to Nelly Pinson.

[10] KY Archives File 3296 - Anse, while living in Pike, took a fancy to the Polly France, the wife of John France in 1873. Jacob Cline (Jr. as Sr. was dead) in testimony said this "I know of her laying out after night with other men besides her husband several different times and I saw her laying on the bed under the cover with a man named Anderson Hatfield".

[11] WV Archives File 080-00001 - The plaintiff complains and says that heretofore, to wit, or the _day of 18__, she intermarried with the defendant Anderson Hatfield Jr., in Logan county WV, and since that time they have both resided in the said county and until quite recently, as man and wife and as the fruits of said union they have children aged respectively and named. The plaintiff further complains and says that since the said marriage she has been a constant, dutiful and loving wife to the said defendant, but that he, the said defendant has been unkind, cruel, and harsh in his treatment of her and that he has been guilty time and again of the act of adultery, within the last five years; that the said act of adultery were not committed with the consent of the plaintiff.

[12] Microfiche 7040489 Pike Criminal Court – March 10, 1891 - Commonwealth vs Frank

was named in the divorce suit brought by Henry Daniels against Jane Daniels, as her counterpart. Henry and Jane was said to be married in 1880 in this suit, of 1886. Henry said he had not lived with Jane for five years, since the infidelity.

The court recorded years of the Hatfield and McCoy feud is put to rest by Jim McCoy, when he made it clear under testimony that the feud began in 1882 and ended with the killing of Deputy Dempsey, of Logan County, VA in 1888. The only two feud events of 1882 were the killing of Ellison Hatfield and the retaliatory shooting of the three McCoys.

During the trial of Johnse Hatfield, he stated that on New Year's Eve 1887, there was a dance held at Anse's house, at which he attended. Johnse admitted to drunkenness with a cast of individuals. Some of these men were of questionable character, and possibly wanted in other counties. The only time these men were mentioned was during this trial.

The murders on that eve of Alifair and Calvin McCoy set off a rage in Pikeville, and the Hatfields realized they had overstepped the boundaries of the law. Killing an unarmed woman had just gone too far. Eight days later, the murder of the elderly Jim Vance was carried out by an illegal posse. Soon after, at the battle of Grapevine in 1888, the death of the duly appointed deputy, William Dempsey, occurred. The Battle of Grapevine, according to Jim McCoy and Johnse Hatfield, was very much a part of the feud. Johnse in testimony said, *"I did not see Jim McCoy there"* when asked about the Grapevine raid, which was perpetrated by the unlawful Phillips-McCoy posse. Jim McCoy, on the other hand, admitted he was there.

C.S. Lewis said; *"What you see and what you hear depends a great deal on where you are standing. It also depends on what sort of person you are."*

Lewis is the son of a magician. His words are applicable in explaining the discrepancies surrounding the feud folklore. What you see and hear depends on "where you are standing" in connection to the people involved or even slightly involved. Court cases became part of the feud legend because of local gossip. Bill Staten had an affair with a McCoy girl, and then was killed by Paris and Sam McCoy. The pig story, as told, holds no relevance, according to Jim McCoy under testimony, and has

---

Phillips and Nancy Hatfield} Adultery - Bench warrant awarded as to Phillips bail $50.00 summons awarded vs. Hatfield

been added, even though the McCoy constituents from the trial never speak of it. Now, the beating of Mary Daniels has credibility, since Cap Hatfield and Tom Wallace were summoned in Pike County on Sept 6, 1887 for assault and battery, with a $100.00 Bench Warrant issued. Even if this assault can be proven to be for the Daniels women, neither Jim nor Randolph mentioned the assault in testimony as a feud event. These events were added to the feud to enhance hatred for the Hatfields and to show cause for the Kentucky governor to take steps for arresting the Hatfields. Mary Daniels never brought charges and no one to date has located "that" pig trial in the records. There are several trials after the civil war which involve farm animals, but no one has been able to conclude if the pig story transformed from one of those Kentucky civil files.

The death of Jim Vance and his story regarding the feud morphed from someone who was "thought" to be involved in the New Year's raid on the McCoy home, to him being accused of beating Nancy McCoy Hatfield and killing Asa Harman McCoy. In the Costner movie, Jim was described as a ruthless pauper, who would stop short of nothing, including killing someone, if he felt threatened. Hatfield and McCoy feud books say that he owned no land, that Jim Vance was of **desperate character**. Randal McCoy blatantly mislead the newspapers, and Sam Hill regarding Jim and his life. Randal responded to those inquiries that Jim owned no land. We know that Jim owned land. Randal stated that Jim had a love interest. This is untrue to our knowledge and is totally unsupported in the records to date. Jim was devoted to his wife, Mary, and a great supporter of his mother, Elizabeth. There were rumors that a love child may have come about. There was no love child with Jim as the father. This was never mentioned in court papers, and never mentioned in the lawsuits that came of the family after Jim died. At this time in history, state laws ensured that even "a love child" had rights to an estate. The letter written Jan. 8, 1888, by John A. Sheppard shows that Randal McCoy was barreling down the first shots without provocation, causing the killing of Jim Vance, while looking for Cap Hatfield. Randal wanted to cut a slice of meat from Cap's body, broil and eat it. Randal was angry over the deaths of his children, Alifair and Calvin. He was angry over his home burning. More than likely, he was equally as angry at himself for leaving them to fend for themselves, while saving himself. After putting up a good volley of shots, Randal ran from the New Year's attack, leaving his wife and children behind, while he sought refuge at his neighbor's home until the next day. People may have thought of him as a coward for leaving his beaten wife, two children who were shot, and the other young children to take care of the injured and dead, at night in the December winter. It was said that Alifair's blood had frozen to her neck. Randal is aged at this time, his mountaineer days were behind him, and he probably felt that he had no chance against the men who were trying to kill him.

Jim McCoy admitted during testimony in 1899 that he and the Phillips-McCoy men traveled first to Anse Hatfield's home, where no one was found. After taking hostages along the way, they proceeded toward Thacker Creek looking for Cap Hatfield. Randolph only knew of three men being in the raid on his home. One by sight (Johnse) and two by hearing his daughter, Alifair speak their names, mere seconds before she was shot (Cap and Hense), per his own testimony. It was only after Jim Vance was murdered that he would be called a **desperate character** in his nearly sixty years of life.

Death of Jim Vance - This letter was sent to KY. Gov. Buckner from John Sheppard
Extract from Letter of John A. Sheppard
*On the 8th (hard to distinguish which date from the original found in the KY Archives) of this month, 30 men came from KY with Frank Phillips and John Rite [Wright] as the head, took charge of Anderson Hatfield's family. Drove the women and children before them down the river to the mouth of Grapevine Creek where they took L.P. Smith and every member of his family and Cap Hatfield's wife and children and drove them like beasts before them some four or five miles down the river to Wm. Ferrell. There they made Ferrell and another man go with them as guides and started for where old man James Vance lived telling them, women and children, all the time that they would leave them at Ferrell's, and if one of them told of their being in the country they would kill them as they returned to Pike. Then with the guides above referred to, they proceeded up Thacker Creek to Vance's where they found old man Jim Vance and pursuant to a threat made sometime before that, **old Randolph McCoy fired on him and that was followed by repeated shots until the body of the old man was torn into shreds. And as I understand with no earthly provocation. All that they could say, I suppose, was that he was a relative of and friend to the Hatfield's.** From there they came to the head of Island Creek and we can't tell what they will do next. The reward offered by Governor Buckner has put on the trail of the Hatfield's, a set of lawless men who not only have no respect for men, but brute-like, will destroy women and children. The whole country is alarmed and everyone feels that there is not security to life and property. We are listening all the time to hear of other horrible deeds.*
Later news just from the scene, and it is true, says that Vance's wife and Cap Hatfield were with old man Vance when he was killed. They told Vance and Cap to throw up their hands and fired simultaneously. Cap made his escape with a

slight wound in the hand. Frank Phillips, the officer walked up and crowed while two of the McCoys shook hands over the dead body of Vance. They then turned and went back to Vance's house, broke his trunk open, took what money he had and a box of cartridges he had together with his pistol and gun. They threw his beds into the yard, cursed his daughter, the only person in the house, and told her if she offered to raise her hand they would kill her, and from there they went back to KY. The men they made guide them through the mountains say that <u>old Randall McCoy, said he intended to kill Cap,</u> cut a slice of meat from his body and broil and eat it. This trouble is ruining this country. I tell you that good, quiet men are growing desperate over the <u>brutal murder</u> of old man Vance.

Civil Cases in Pike County

Many Pike County civil cases are located at the Kentucky Archives and Library, and are some of the most significant cases one can read if interested in the Tug Valley people. Pike County has some of the most incredible history-driven civil cases from the county's early formation, and includes at least a dozen cases that speak of the civil war. Most of the ones we will bring forward will be life event causes, where the plaintiffs in these causes brought an action against the defendants. Some would lose land, thereby losing their livelihood. John Dills Jr. had no less than 31 civil cases as the plaintiff. When John Dils Jr. died, he left his wife Anne with an abundance of legal actions to pursue. Those cases can be found in the University of Kentucky, in the Harkins' files. Walter Harkins was not only the lawyer for John Dils' estate, but was also one of the attorneys on the cases of Alex Messer, Valentine Hatfield, the Mahons, and later for Johnse Hatfield. All were convicted. Perry A. Cline had 14 cases as the plaintiff. Both Dils and Cline had many others cases as defendants. The Hatfield families (not just the feudists) had nearly 90 case files as plaintiffs, and slightly over 150 as defendants. The McCoy families had no less than 75 case files as plaintiffs and about 110 as defendants. These cases span up until 1920. These civil cases weren't always about the taking of land or money, but about real life events, like adoptions, estates, or divorces.

Starting in about 1890, we see an increase in the number of suits in the Tug region concerning land, its acreage, and its uses. The Big Sandy and Cumberland Railroad sued Pike residents in 1902 with nearly 24 cases, with another 17 cases being brought against citizens by the Chesapeake Railroad Company. The Yellow Poplar Lumber Company had brought 24 cases to the Pike county courts, with various other suits over the use of land and minerals. Logging and cultivating timber was a lucrative source of employment. Coal mining and timber became crucial to the economy of the region. The demand for coal and timber was greatly stimulated with the expansion of the American railroad industry. Most of the earlier pioneers, like Jim Vance, floated those log rafts on the Tug River up to Catlettsburg, KY, where the timber was sold. With the expanding railroad in the region, coal and timber could go out in larger loads, as well as bring into the area other goods not easily accessible to the mountain region.

All of these civil cases are legal, even though some were an elaborate ruse in order to obtain wealth, gain land, or after the civil war, to get even-steven with their war opposition. For example, a neighbor could bring a cause against another neighbor because the defendant spoke a bad word against the plaintiff. One could lose their property, and be forced to pay large fines. Suing was profitable for the plaintiff. If someone stole a pig, the person could be forced to give up $50.00 (civil case 2589) for a $4.00 to $10.00 porker, depending on the size. If you witnessed a fight on the neighbor's property while pregnant, indeed bring a cause for $5,000.00 (civil case 3417). Incredibly, if someone witnessed men brawling, that person could file a lawsuit.

The cases initiated after the civil war show that men were under direct order from a commanding officer, to capture horses or food for the soldiers, and in most cases, it was considered an act of "unlawful taking with arms." If a suit was brought against a soldier in the Union forces, it was a "legal necessity authorized by the President". If a person sued a confederate soldier, they were considered armed rebels of the so-called Confederate States. Kentucky Civil case 2092 proved Pikeville, KY was a Confederate stronghold until April of 1863, after that, Pike County became Union held ground. In one case, Mitchell Clay[13] was testifying that Allan Maynard was in the Pike Home Guard and that the rebel forces had control of the Pike County. Prior to that, Confederate Colonel A.J. May, who also testified, had held the Territory of Pike County, and that his troops were camped on Johns Creek.
Col. A.J. May was said to be with the 10th KY Mounted Rifles.

---

[13] KY Archives Civil Case 2092

Chapter 3
THE FEUD EVENTS

According to Randal and Jim McCoy, during testimony in 1899, the feud years are 1882 to 1888. This can be backed up with the trial of Plyant and Doc Mahon in 1889, when it is stated that the feud began in 1882[14]. There are only four significant feud related events as already stated. The first is the killing of Ellison. The second is the slaying of the McCoy brothers. These two events started the ill-feeling between the families of Randal McCoy and Anse Hatfield. Tolbert was 31 years old, Farmer was 19 years of age, and Randal Jr., was a supposed 15 year old young man, according to their mother. In the given testimonies, they refer to the three McCoys forever as "boys". Back in the hills, boys grew to be men at a very young age. These young men knew what it meant to stab a man numerous times, and then point a gun and fire. What we fail to remember, the killing of Ellison Hatfield was not a misdemeanor crime.

Randal focused on the injustice done to his sons and was fixated on the fact that they did not have a legal trial. There was no regard for what these three McCoys had done to Sarah Hatfield, the wife of Ellison. Not only did they brutally kill Ellison Hatfield, they left a grieving widow with several children, without a father, and without an income. Randal and Jim McCoy only focused on getting revenge in Pike County Court.

---

[14] KY Archives Case 19601 Commonwealth vs. Plyant and Doc Mayhorn Appellants against The commonwealth of Kentucky Appellee - This is a trial of Appellants, (two brothers) and by consent the trial had jointly under an indictment found against, and about twenty others; charging them with the willful murder of Tolbert McCoy, and they further charge, that they did each conspire together to do said murder. This trial grew out of the noted Hatfield-McCoy feud, and murderers; that had its inception in Kentucky on Blackberry Creek, on the election day in August 1882. These Appellants not being present. But first time we find the was on Blackberry the day after the election trouble, and then it appears they were there for the purpose of assisting, or caring for their Uncle Ellison Hatfield, as they had been informed that he had been killed or mortally wounded. When they got to Blackberry Creek from their homes they for the first time learned, that Ellison had been taken out of the state, then they hear that the parties accused of the crime were to have a trial that day, and they went up Blackberry Creek to hear it. When they found that there was no trial, they returned back down Blackberry Creek, and went down the river to Anderson Ferrell's, where Ellison Hatfield was. They being son in law of Wall Hatfield, by marriage, nephews to the wounded man. Neither one of Appellants were back in Kentucky, until long after Tolbert McCoy was killed. This being a statement of the case for part of the facts: reference to the proof referred to in the brief for Appellant, in the case of Valentine Hatfield; sent with this case.

While in Logan court records[15] , Sarah Hatfield, wife of Ellison, is shown losing her land, because she was not able to pay county land taxes. Sarah relied on family and friends for help with everyday necessities to raise her children. Sarah was a feud victim! These are two of the questions, with answers from that case when E.H. Simpkins and Joseph Simpkins testify:

2nd question; what is the financial condition of the widow of Ellison Hatfield and his children?
Answer; I do not think that her personal property would exceed $100.00 in value, and if she has anything else I know nothing about it. I think she has a very hard time in keeping something for her, for her family to eat and wear.
Same question another answer: Land would not exceed one hundred dollars in value. If she has, anything else except what interest. She as widow of Ellison Hatfield in his real estate, I know nothing about it. And I don't think she has. I think she has considerable difficulty in keeping something to eat and clothe her family.
6th question: Do you know in what manner the taxes against said lands have been paid?
Answer: the taxes I think have often been paid by Joe Simpkins, have often been returned delinquent and redeemed again, and I have been informed that it sold once for taxes; which has never been paid by them.
Same question another answer: The taxes have been paid by other parties. I don't think that the widow or heirs of Ellison Hatfield has been able to pay the taxes on the said land for the last 8 years and further this deponent sayeth not. Joseph Simpkins

Pike County authorities took relatively little to no course of action for five years after 1882. Since these three McCoy men were killed by Anse and friends, there was no legal action for the murderers of Ellison Hatfield. Anse had executed these three McCoys by tying the men to bushes, then shooting them. Anse with the others were then indicted for murder. Anse Hatfield never answered a Pike County court summons during several terms of court. He flatly ignored them, and no one seemed to care, except J. Lee Ferguson, Perry Cline, Randal McCoy, and

---

[15] WV Archives Logan County Court Chancery Case 29 Anse Hatfield against Ralph Steele. Anse Hatfield, Ralph Steele, Andrew Varney, and L.P. Smith co-owners in the company Anderson Hatfield and Co. The suit was over timber and mentions timber on the land of Sarah – Sarah Hatfield guardian and petitioner would most respectfully represent that sometime in the year 1882, Ellison Hatfield departed this life, intestate, leaving the said petitioner, as his widow, and the defendants Mary Varney, Emma J. Hatfield, Nancy Hatfield, Lydia Hatfield, Lewis Hatfield, Andrew Hatfield, Floyd Hatfield, who are al infants under 21 years of age, and Valentine Hatfield and Elliott S. Hatfield, the only children and heirs-at-law of the said Ellison Hatfield.

Jim McCoy. The word "extradition" was well known to men on both sides of the river. If they were to commit a crime in West Virginia, they would run to Kentucky to avoid prosecution. If a crime happened in Kentucky, they would run to West Virginia.

The Hatfields had lucrative bounties issued by Gov. Buckner. During that time period, we can prove Perry Cline had been in Frankfort visiting the Governor. The "Frankfort Roundabout in August 20, 1887", wrote that Perry was a visitor to Frankfort. Those who visited the capital were always of special note to the press, just as it is today. Perry had been in Frankfort in order to get the "**rewards**" rolling in August, as is shown in the KY Governors Journal Book page 57 [Appendix G]. Confirming that visit was a letter by Judge John M. Rice[16], on Sept. 6, where he makes note of that confirmed visit by Perry and Kinner, the State Attorney. By Sept 10th, the KY Governor made his requisitions for a $500.00 reward of Anse Hatfield, Cap Hatfield, Johnse Hatfield, and Thomas Chambers.

KY Archives – Governors Journals Requisitions page 7
The Governor this day issued his requisition on the Governor of West Virginia for the surrender to Frank Phillips appointed agent on the part of the state to receive and deliver them to the jailor of Pike County of Anderson Hatfield, Johnson Hatfield, Cap Hatfield, Valentine Hatfield, Elias Hatfield, C. Carpenter, Joseph Murphy, Doc Mayhorn, Pleasant Mayhorn, Selkirk McCoy, Albert McCoy (Kirks son), L.L. McCoy (Kirks son), Thomas Chambers, Lark Varney (Henderson son), Anderson Varney (Henderson son), Daniel White, Samuel Mayhorn, Alex Messer, John Whitt, Elijah Mounts Beach Creek fugitives charged with murder.
The governor this day offered rewards of $500 each for the apprehension and delivery to the jailor of Pike County of Anderson Hatfield, Cap Hatfield, Johnson Hatfield, and Thomas Chambers, fugitives, charged with murder.

---

[16] Office of S.G. Kinner - Attorney at Law - Pikeville, Ky., Sept 6, 1887 - S.B. Buckner, Governor of Kentucky - Dear Sir, Mr. Kinner & Hon. P.A. Cline a reliable gentlemen and their visit to you is in the intended of law and order who true statement made to you by those connection with or reference to the matters relating to the petition of Judge Waggoner can be relied on implicitly. From all accounts received through trustworthy sources it has resolved itself into the simple question of either apprehending these partied, or else turn over the east side of this County to utter (?). I trust the visit of Mr. Kinner & Cline will not be veined of results. Very Respectfully, John M. Rice

THE PAROLE BILL, in which Mr. Dickerson is chiefly interested, was discussed until almost the time for adjournment and went over till to-morrow.

A message was received from the Governor recommending that something should be done in the way of satisfying Perry Cline for his services to the State in the Hatfield cases.

On March 17, 1888, the Courier Journal printed that Kentucky Gov. Buckner, is recommending a Parole Bill (funds) for Perry for his services in the Hatfield matter. Yet, we see in the records, Perry had blackmailed the Hatfields. Now, politician Perry told the Hatfields that he had the Governor in his pocket, and proceeded with extorting money from the Hatfields. Perry claimed that he would be able to get the indictments against them dropped for the killing of Tolbert, Farmer and Randolph Jr. Instead, Perry used the money to help with the cost of the West Virginia extraditions and indictments of the 1882 men who killed the McCoys. The $52.00 filing fees was much less than what was extorted. Bucker, in the most condescending tone, wrote to Governor Wilson stating that Cline did come to him with this "cool" proposition. Buckner said he turned it down[17]. Then, Buckner proceeded to say that it was the Hatfields who asked Perry to reconcile the proposition with Buckner. However, Gov. Buckner wanted to explain it away, there was no love, per Buckner, between Anse and Perry at this time. They were "former" enemies. Yes former, Perry had sometime during this whole endeavor, decided to take on the Doc and Plyant Mahon, and Valentine Hatfield as their lawyers.

Noted in Logan Deed Book K, Perry Cline and others secured a bond from Doc and Plyant Mahon, and Valentine Hatfield for his services, dating all the way back to August of 1888, along with Walter S. Harkins, J.S. Cline, and W. Mayo Connolly[18]. Prior to this, Connolly petitioned

---

[17] Senate Legislative Doc. #2 March 6, 1888 - Correspondence of the Governors of Kentucky and West Virginia Jan 30, 1888 - Before receiving your letter I had been fully apprised of the efforts on the part of P.A. Cline to secure a withdraw of the requisition and rewards in this case; in fact, the cool proposition made to me by the indicted parties through their attorney, Mr. Auxier, to the effect that they would obligate themselves not to come again into Kentucky, provided I would withdraw the requisition and rewards named, was indorsed by Mr. Cline, who had previously shown an active interest in their apprehension. But this proposition I, of course, declined even to entertain, much less to agree to; and even admitting the truth of the affidavit enclosed by your Excellency, which charges in terms that the friends of the indicted parties succeeded in bribing Cline, their former enemy, to urge the acceptance of their cool proposition.

[18] KY Archives - W. Mayo Connolly, Attorney at Law - Nov 18, 1887 - Dear Sir, I have been informed that one Mr. Auxier has a petition to you aksing you to call in the reward offered for Anderson Hatfield and others, on a statement made that the parties agree to lay down arms become quiet citizens, - and remain out of the State of Kentucky. I just knowing all the facts – that in order to secure peace and the suppresion of riots and the presistance of bloodshed that it would be a grave thing for you to do. If you could only know the true situation, I do not think you would hestitate to do so. This is an old feud and while we know that these men have violated the law, but taking into consideration the fact – that

Buckner in November of 1887 not to let the Hatfields off the hook, even if they swore no blood going forward. August 1887, Cline and Kinner visited Gov. Buckner to get the rewards on these same men. In December 1887, Frank Phillips sent Gov. Wilson of WV the paperwork for extradition. Wilson said those papers were in Perry Cline's handwriting, and that he had Auxier's sworn word that he gave Cline the money to get the charges dropped against the Hatfields, using his political influence over Buckner. This is only a very small fraction of the implications that the same lawyers who were asking Governor Buckner for indictments and bounties for the Hatfields were also taking bond on the defendants' homes in February 1889, dating back to August of 1888. These are also the same men who would be representing Valentine Hatfield, and the Mayhorn's in court.

Logan County Deed Book K – A.J. Auxier & to M.A. Ferrell} Power of Attorney Know all men by these present that we, Andrew J. Auxier, Richard M. Ferrell and W. Mayo Connelly composing the firm of Auxier, Ferrell, and Connelly and P.A. Cline and J.S. Cline, composing the firm of P.A. Cline & J.S. Cline of Pikeville, Kentucky and Walter S. Harkins of Prestonsburg, Kentucky hereby appoints…M.A Ferrell Esq., of Logan County, WV, our true and lawful agent, and attorney in fact, to receive for us the amount of the indebtedness of Valentine Hatfield, D.D. Mahorn, Plyant Mahorn, and Samuel E. Mayhorn, to us, which is as follows. To Walter S. Harkins from Plyant Mahorn, Samuel E. Mayhorn and D.D. Mayhorn joints notes for three hundred dollars with interest at 6% interest from Aug. 15th 1888.

To said Harkins from Valentine Hatfield one note for one hundred dollars with 6% interest from Aug. 15th, 1888.

To Auxier, Ferrell, and Connelly from Valentine Hatfield one hundred dollars with 6% interest from Aug. 15, 1888.

To Auxier, Ferrell, and Connelly a joint note from Plyant Mahorn, Samuel Mayhorn, and E. Mayhorn for six hundred dollars, with 6% interest thereon from Aug. 15th, 1888.

To P.A. Cline and J.S. Cline from Valentine note for two hundred dollars with 6% interest thereon from Aug. 15, 1888, to P.A. Cline & J.S. Cline note from Plyant Mahorn, D.D. Mayhorn, and E. Mayhorn for two hundred dollars with 6% interest thereon from Aug. 15th 1888. - Which said amounts are secured by mortgage or real estate in Logan County WV, fully described in a deed of mortgage to us from Plyant Mayhorn, D.D. Mayhorn, and Samuel E. Mayhorn and their wives and a deed of mortgage from Valentine Hatfield and wife to the above named parties of even date, with the execution of said promissory notes.

---

there is great danger to our people arising from the dangers growing out of the capture of these men say that - it could be done. I freely recommend that you do this and let us try them. Yours truly W. Mayo Connolly

We further empower our said agent and attorney in fact, hereby created to relinquish our liens upon said land, upon the payments to him for all the amounts of said indebtedness, herein before set out. In testimony whereof we have this day affixed our seals and signatures, done at Pikeville, Kentucky the 28th day of Feb. 1889. Andrew J. Auxier, R.M. Ferrell, Wm. Connelly, P.A. Cline, J.S. Cline, Walter S. Harkins

In 1885, Perry Cline is shown as the democrat candidate[19] elected to represent the counties of Pike, Knott, Letcher, and Martin Counties, KY, for the term of 1886 and 1887. The book, "History of Kentucky", tells us that Perry Cline was a staunch, union democrat. A later court case in Logan, told by Harry Weddington, shows Cline was a mason, and that Perry died March 19, 1891 at 7:00PM as recorded in the Masonic Temple Book. Harry stated he was there to help with his burial, being that he was an officer of the Masonic Lodge. Perry wrote his estate Nov. 7th, 1890, he never mentioned his West Virginia stake over the Grapevine land. Martha Adkins and Perry Cline were married by Bill Blankenship, with Jane McCoy, John Dils, and Green Taylor in attendance, on the 3rd day of September 1868[20].

The Cline or Grapevine 5000 acre tract in Logan, as it was called, purchased by Anse Hatfield in 1877, was the source of contention for Anse Hatfield and Perry Cline. After Perry passed away in 1891, his wife Martha Cline was still arguing cases in Logan. The Ellison versus Torpin[21] case shows Perry sold his land to Anse, and Martha signed her dower rights in 1877. That was hardly the end of the lawsuits. Martha won a suit, however small, and however clever in the way she engineered it. Her fight wasn't with Anse in the Torpin case, since she and Perry had signed over their portion of the land. This, though, was an ongoing argument of its own over resources. We know this because Martha kept suing in Logan County court, telling that Perry had sold the land to Anse, for far less of its real value of $16,800, during this court case in 1893 she states its worth $80,000[22].

---

[19] The Courier Journal July 15, 1885
[20] WV Archives case 026-00044 Logan County Chancery
[21] WV. Archives Case 10058, Box 471-7
[22] WV Archives case 026-0044 Logan County

For Martha, now, it was in question if Jacob Cline (brother to Perry) had signed over his ½ portion of the 5000 acres. The court didn't side with Martha on dower, since she nor Perry ever claimed the other half of the 5000 acres, for many years, or paid taxes. Wayne and Jacob Cline (sons of deceased Jacob, nephews of Perry) were approached by J.B. Ellison, when he purchased their rights to the other half of the land for $200.00, remembering this land had traded hands since.

Martha in 1893 filed this suit *"Martha Cline versus Richard Torpin Jr."*, wherein Martha was asking for dower rights to that ½ portion of land. Case 037 file 00044, Martha in 1893 also sues the N&W Railroad. Both cases are mentioned in Ellison vs. Torpin. Since Martha bought out the deed of her attorney, J.B. Ellison, she claims rights under her brother in law's ½ portion of the 5000 acres of land. Ellison had purchased from the Jacob Cline Jr. heirs, their potion of Grapevine.

Getting back to the feud, Frank Phillips was appointed special agent of Gov. Buckner of Kentucky. Frank was threatened with his job in a letter written Nov. 28, 1887. Prosecutor S.G. Kinner wrote that Frank was not the right man for the job. Kinner was right. Frank was not the right man to make the arrests in a peaceable manner. Frank in the Dec. Term of Pike Court, was released from the role of deputy sheriff. Shortly after that, he invaded West Virginia with his illegal posse. [Appendix D]

Col. William Smith told a story of his meeting Frank Phillips, during his testimony in the Johnse Hatfield trial. He stated that Phillips had introduced himself bluntly saying, **"Do you know who I am?"** The Colonel responded with, **"No I do not."** Frank said to the Colonel, **"I am Bad Frank Phillips."** He tried to kill the Colonel that very evening. Frank accused the Colonel, while in the civil war, of sending his father to prison where Frank's father subsequently died. That night, Phillips tried to creep into the room of Smith to kill him, shooting only to graze the hair on his skin. Frank ran up the side of the hill, while Smith watched him run. Phillips was also once sued for hitting a man in the head with a hammer and trying to murder him [KY Civil Case 4349]. Frank and Bud McCoy are listed in Pike County court records because allegedly, Bud shot and killed Frank's horse. Notorious for his escapades in his personal life, and now public life, he earned the name of Bad Frank. During that brief encounter, according to Colonel William Smith, Frank wore that badge of honor proudly. January 30, 1888, Gov. Buckner wrote to Gov. Wilson that he had Frank's reputation wrong, stating this; *I am satisfied that Frank Phillips, the agent appointed by me to receive the fugitives named in my requisition, is not the murderous outlaw your Excellency seems to suppose; but as he has undertaken to arrest some of these parties in West Virginia without your warrant, and is, therefore, objectionable to you..."*

Gov. Wilson of WV, refused to sign the extradition warrant of the Hatfields in Dec. 1887. Undaunted, and without extradition, the Pike faction organized a squad of men who were ready to strike. The illegal gang was headed by two men, Bad Frank Phillips and Devil John Wright. With bounty on the Hatfields, bounty hunters were looking to collect. John Wright was one such man, causing the Hatfields to lay out in the mid of winter to avoid being captured. Therefore, the pressure on the fugitive Hatfields was building to a white-hot breaking point. Being hunted and feeling threatened, the Hatfields resorted to the unthinkable feud event on New Year's Eve. In the trial of Johnse Hatfield, several witnesses testified that alcohol was consumed prior to the raid on the McCoy home. Johnse repeated to a few witnesses *that if he had not been drunk, he would not have gone on that raid to the McCoy home.* If that is the truth, and I suspect it partly is, alcohol was the fire in the bellies and the explanation for much of the Hatfield and McCoy behavior in the killing of Ellison Hatfield and the killings of Alifair and Calvin McCoy.

Jan. 8, 1888 [Appendix C], Frank Phillips took it upon himself, along with Jim McCoy and others, and raided on the West Virginia side of the Tug River. This resulted in the murder of the once Justice of the Peace, Jim Vance. Shortly thereafter, once again, Frank invaded West Virginia and killed the duly appointed deputy sheriff who was part of a legal posse, sworn by Logan County officials, to arrest the murderers of Jim Vance. Frank Phillips showed neither man mercy. Frank Phillips and the McCoy posse were indicted for the murders of both James Vance and William Dempsey.

The two men Frank killed were neither indicted for any crimes in Kentucky, nor were these men part of the 1882 killing of the McCoy brothers. The Pike County, KY warrants for 1882, which were never signed by Gov. Wilson, was the pretense to invade West Virginia. A week after Vance was killed, J. Lee Ferguson, Pike County Attorney, admitted that he was searching for the names of those involved in the New Year's affair. When Vance and Dempsey were killed, no one in the McCoy family knew who was involved in the McCoy home raid except for three names; Hense Chambers, Johnse Hatfield, and Cap Hatfield according to Randal's own testimony in Commonwealth vs. Johnson Hatfield.

Jim McCoy said the raid was New Year's Eve 1887, and that he went to the home after the raid on New Year's Day, Jan. 1, 1888. These young bucks forged into Kentucky serving notice upon Randolph that the rewards offered by the Kentucky Governor were not going to sway them from moving about as they were accustomed. They were not going to stay in the woods avoiding men like John Wright, or other bounty hunters forever. The Pike County Court *Summons, which* had been in the Hatfield minds as largely ignored for five years, had now come full circle and landed at the McCoy cabin front door. This seven and a half mile jaunt over to the home of Randolph McCoy would have profound consequences for both families. Calvin and Alifair McCoy were murdered and the family home burned. Both Governors' refusal to work together to bring peace to the families and peace to the region is an outcry of injustice. All of this could have been brought to some resolution prior to the house burning. In fact, in a letter from Gov. Buckner to Gov. Wilson, dated January 30, 1888, Buckner laid that blame squarely on Gov. Wilson for not signing the extradition orders in December 1887, when sent for his signature by Frank Phillips. Bucker said if Wilson had done his duty as Governor, the New Year's night raid quite possibly wouldn't have happened[23]. There are always two sides to any

---

[23] Senate Legislative Doc. #2 March 6, 1888 Correspondence of the Governors of Kentucky

story. Wilson felt the truth had been blurred by Cline and Phillips. They wanted to arrest two men, Elias Hatfield and Andy Varney, who could prove they were nowhere near the 1882 murders of the McCoy brothers, and Wilson wanted their names removed from the requisition. He also wanted time to investigate the matter. Buckner wanted Elias and Andy to stand trial, even if they were innocent of being at the paw paw murders. None the less, these two Governors failed the states and didn't intervene soon enough.

In December of 1887, Perry Cline sent a letter to Gov. Buckner stating that the Hatfields had killed his nephew[24], and that the rewards needed to stand. This letter was in response to a letter which R.M. Ferrell, Pike County Clerk, wrote in Nov. 1887. Ferrell, stating that the rewards would bring trouble and harmful to investor money in the area. He asked that the rewards on the

---

and West Virginia - The forgoing account, which differs so widely from that received by you, was obtained from the County Attorney of Pike county, who claims to have taken great pains to ascertain the real facts, and who seems to have no doubt about its correctness; but I, of course, understand how difficult it is to arrive at exact facts in an affair of this kind from the statements which he may have heard from the parties of either side. **I regret exceedingly that my portion of the citizens of Pike county should have attempted, under any circumstances, to arrest citizens of West Virginia for crimes committed in this state, without first obtaining the requisite authority therefor.** But if the forgoing account of this affair be anything like correct, I am sure your Excellency will agree that it is not surprising that the people of Pike County, having employed every legitimate means for the apprehension and delivery of these men, and failing therein, should have determined to resort to such other steps as might be necessary to bring to justice the desperate characters who were not only burning homes, but killing unoffending men and helpless women in their midst. I feel assured that your Excellency has, from your standpoint, done in the case what you conscientiously conceived to be your duty in this premises, but I cannot concur in the views which seem to be entertained by your Excellency, as to your right to investigate the circumstances under which my demand was made, or to inquire into the guilt or innocence of the fugitives therein named, and if, instead of stopping to inquire into these questions, your Excellency had though proper to take the necessary steps for the apprehension and delivery of the fugitives demanded. I respectfully submit that in all probability, the disturbance above referred to would not have occurred.

[24] KY Archives Dec 30, 1887 - Member The Davis Bar and Collection Association - Office of Perry A. Cline - Attorney and Counselor At Law - Office back of Court House - Pikeville, KY. Dec 30, 1887 – To Hon. G.M. Adams Secretary - Dear Sir, In closed find $8.50 paid for requisition for Cap Hatfield and Thos. Wallis. We had Wallis [Wallace] in jail & he escaped and is now in W.VA. We have got a detective to locate him and say he will bring him if we will send him a requisition. Please send me the requisition affording W.G Balden [Baldwin], as agent to receive the party's, the charge is sure they shot & killed one of my nephews. Please send the requisition forth with to me & I will send to the Detective as asked, hope you are well. Your Friend, P.A. Cline

Hatfields be reconsidered[25]. Even Gov. Buckner was warned of further trouble if those rewards stood, without some reconciliation. While Gov. Buckner blasts Gov. Wilson for not acting sooner on the requisitions for the Hatfields, Gov. Buckner also had his fair warning of further trouble.

These politicians wanted to bring in outside investors to buy the rights to the minerals in the area prior to this feud. Proctor Knott said as much in his statement in the Kentucky Superior Court opening remarks[26]. Regarding the battle between KY and WV over the kidnapping of WV citizens without proper extradition, Knott said, "*...the court should not assume authority to twist the well-settled principles of law gone awry in order to promote the development of marvelous minerals...* " There was so much at play in the counties, states, and families, that later, the only people who would win the battle over resources would be the big firms of the north, who had been buying out the mineral rights from many. Some were buying land for back taxes, pennies on the real value, which can be read about in more detail in the WV Archives Chancery cases for Logan County.

---

[25] Kentucky Archives - Office of R.M. Ferrell - Pikeville, Ky, Nov 18, 1887 to Gov. S.B. Buckner, Frankfort, Ky - Dear Sir, The bearer Mr. Auxier of our place visited your Excellency at the request of many good and lawbiding citizens to have something done to quiet an old feud in our county and citizens of WV. It had grown to an alarming state on the border of our county. So as to prevent intercorse among the best people and paralyzing industry. I think, I express the wished of a large numner of our business men and best citizens when I beg of your Excellency that the offer of rewards be withdrawn on the condition of the chiefs of one of the feud never again appearing in our State – if it were practicable without bloodshed to bring the Hatfield party to trial and punishment. I do not believe it would end the trouble. I think it would only tend to widen the trouble among the followers of the opposing parties and resulting in further bloodshed and injuries to our County – hoping you may give this matter your favorable consideration. I am truly yours, R.M. Ferrell Pikeville Ky. I was with you at Donalson but my opportunities were much better for knowing the Commanding General than his knowing me. I therefore beg to refer you to Hon. G.M. Adams. R.M. Ferrell.

[26] Proctor Knott Feb. 28, 1888- I have not the time, therefore, even if I had the inclination, to follow the learned counsel who opened the case for the prisoners, in his excursions beyond the legitimate domain of the present inquiry, either to discuss questions which the court has already expressed its determination not to consider; or to argue a supposititious case of murder upon an imaginary state of facts; or to insist that the court should not assume authority to twist the well-settled principals of law awry, in order to promote the development of the marvelous mineral resources which lie on either side of the line between this state and WV.

So, a broad net was cast and many people were accused, or believed to have aided in the McCoy home raid, but the Pike County court needed time to investigate. Just a week later, after the McCoy home was torched, court prosecutor J. Lee Ferguson (Appendix E) wrote to the Gov. Buckner, telling him, *we are attempting to find the names of those involved in the home raid.* Ferguson had not yet determined who had done the deed upon Randal McCoy's home. Now, in testimony, Randal said he could see very well that night. Randal testified that the moon was shining bright and the fire of his home lighted the area. He and Sarah, his wife, differ on the evening setting. In the telling of Randal's testimony, he heard Alifair, his daughter, tell the names of Cap Hatfield and Hence Chambers, saying, *"Cap Hatfield and Hence Chambers you wouldn't kill a woman would you?"* Randal said the only man he saw that night was Johnse Hatfield, who he shot in the shoulder.

Back to the Governors, on January 21, 1888, Wilson responded to Buckner regarding the Hatfield extraditions. Wilson stated that as soon as Kentucky submitted the appropriate papers to his office, that he would issue the indictments against the Hatfields for extradition to Kentucky. On the 28th of January, Gov. Wilson also issued papers for the arrest of the Phillips-McCoy members for the deaths of Jim Vance and William Dempsey. Buckner and Wilson were at odds, and it was a dance between the states. The political cronies had made a bad situation worse by not allowing due process on each side of the WV/KY border. The West Virginia governor called what happened in the arrests of the Hatfield members "a kidnapping across borders." Politically, that was correct, spoken by Judge Barr of the Kentucky Supreme Court. He said, no such case had ever been heard and there is no precedence. Tactically, this had helped to compound the situation. In the same context, KY Governor, Buckner, did the same thing by not sending the Phillips-McCoy supporters back to West Virginia to stand prosecution for two murders. So, using the same reasoning outlined in Buckner's letter to Wilson on Jan. 30, why didn't Buckner send these KY men back to WV to stand trial and prove their innocence, as he expected Wilson to do for the state of Kentucky? Instead, Frank Phillips and Jim McCoy, along with members of their gang were charged only with a misdemeanor crime of unlawfully banding and confederating, according to court papers dated March 6, 1888, in Pikeville, KY. These were such minor charges when one contemplates the ruthless, cold blooded murders of two WV citizens, neither man having ever been charged with crimes in their lives. Buckner said, Jan 30th, he regretted that Frank had entered WV illegally.

With all of the political dancing between the governors, and the delay of legal opportunities, justice was not served. After writing letters and failing to sway Gov. Wilson to extradite the Hatfields, Frank Phillips knowingly, without the warrant of extradition, illegally entered WV to make good on the killings of Randal McCoy's son and daughter. This raid had nothing to do with the 1882 murders, and was more about the New Year's Eve tragedy, per Buckner. In books of the past, the gang had always been referred to as "The Phillips Posse", removing the McCoy name from the appearance of complicity. On Jan. 25, 1888, Gov. E.W. Wilson indicted 27 men for murder, based on eyewitness testimony, and the sworn affidavits from John R. Thompson, Nancy L. (McCoy) Hatfield, and Richard Blankenship.

THE STATE OF WEST VIRGINIA - EXECUTIVE DEPARTMENT
To his Excellency the Governor of Kentucky Whereas, It appears by copy of warrant, issued by J.M. Jackson a Justice of the Peace of Logan County, State of West Virginia, hereto attached and which I hereby certify to be duly authenticated in accordance with the laws of this State, that Frank Phillips, John Phillips, James McCoy, Samuel McCoy, Lark McCoy, "Big" Sam McCoy, Sam Miller, George McCoy (of Johns Creek), Sam King, Randolph McCoy, Paris McCoy, Jasper McCoy, Dave Plymer, Bill Saunders, Jacob Hurley, David Straton, John Swords, James Swords, Bud Hurley, Curtis Luster, John Luster, John S. Cline, Jake Mounts, Jasper Coleman, Moses Maynard, John Chappel and John Mounts, stand charged with the crime of Murder committed in the county of Logan, in this State, and it has been represented to me that they have fled from justice, and have taken refuge in the State of Kentucky. Now therefore, pursuant to the provisions of the constitution of laws of the United States, in such case made and provided, I, E.W. Wilson Governor of the State of West Virginia, do hereby request that

the said Frank Phillips, John Phillips, <u>James McCoy, Samuel McCoy,</u>
<u>Lark McCoy, "Big" Sam McCoy,</u> Sam Miller, <u>George McCoy, (of Johns</u>
<u>creek),</u> Sam King, <u>Randolph McCoy, Paris McCoy, Jasper McCoy,</u> Dave
Plymer, Bill Saunders, Jacob Hurley, David Straton, John Sowords,
James Swords, Bud Hurley, Curtis Luster, John Luster, John S. Cline,
Jake Mounts, Jasper Coleman, Moses Maynard, John Chappel and John
Mounts <u>be apprehended and delivered to Alf W. Burnett</u> who is hereby
authorized to receive and Convey them to the State of West Virginia,
there to be dealt with according to law. In witness whereof, I have
hereunto affixed my name and the Great Seal of the State of West
Virginia, at the City of Charleston this <u>28th day of January in the year of</u>
<u>our Lord 1888</u> and of the State the 25th. E.W. Wilson

On May 26, 1888, Gov. Wilson issued ***rewards*** on the following
men for the murders of James Vance and William Dempsey[27]. In
all, 22 men were named in the indictment for Vance and 14 men
were named in the indictment for the murder of Dempsey. Yet,
feud writers often speak of the "Battle of Grapevine" as the major
Kentucky raid, when in fact, the killing of Vance exposed more
men to murder warrants than that of Dempsey in the "Battle of
Grapevine". Of the 14 men named in Dempsey's murder, 7 are
McCoys. Of the 22 named in the murder of Vance, again, 7 are
McCoy names. Randal McCoy was named in January for murder,
but did not make the list for the May rewards. Witnesses to the
event put old Randal McCoy right there at the murder of Jim
Vance. He was named in the murder of Dempsey. Those
witnesses said that Randal fired upon Vance, without asking for
anyone to give themselves up. Jim McCoy, in testimony, stated
that there were **29** men on this first trip of their invasion into West
Virginia. But, **only 22** were ever indicted for murder!

---

[27] Jan 24, 1888 Logan County, to-wit; To any constable of said County: Whereas, John R.
Thompson, Nancy L. Hatfield, and Richard Blankenship, have this day made complaint
and information on oath before me, J.M. Jackson, a Justice of the said County, that Frank
Phillips, John Phillips, James McCoy, Samuel McCoy, Bud McCoy, Lark McCoy, "Big" Sam
McCoy, Sam Miller, George McCoy, (of Johns creek), Sam King, Randolph McCoy, Paris
McCoy, Jasper McCoy, Dave Plymer, Bill Sanders, Jacob Hurley, David Straten, John
Swords, James Swords, Bud Hurley, Curtis Luster, John Luster, John S. Cline, Jake Mounts,
Jasper Coleman, Moses Maynard, John Chappell, and John Mounts, did on the 19th day of
January, 1888 in the County aforesaid, feloniously, willfully, maliciously, deliberately, and
unlawfully, slay, kill, and murder one William D. Dempsey.

WV Archives – Executive Journal #5 - May 26, 1888 - Whereas it appears from a certified copy of indictment found at the April Term of the Circuit Court of Logan County, W.VA. That Frank Phillips, Bud McCoy, Jasper McCoy, Lark McCoy, James McCoy, Samuel McCoy (son of Randal McCoy), Samuel McCoy (son of Samuel McCoy), Samuel King, David Straton, John Norman, William Saunders, Joseph F. Smith, John B. Dotson, and George McCoy are charged with the willful murder of William D. Dempsey committed in said county. And whereas it appears from a certified copy of another indictment found at the same term of said court that Frank Phillips, Bud McCoy, Joseph Hurley, James McCoy, Big Sam McCoy, Sam McCoy (son of Randal McCoy), Lark McCoy, Andrew King, Ed Stuart, George McCoy, Curtis Smith, David Smith, John Yates, John Sowards, John England, Rans Maynard, Sam Miller, James Jones, Londo Harden, William Saunders, Minis Sowords, and James Sowords, are charged with the willful murder of James Vance committed in said county. Whereas it is for the best interest of society that the parties committing such grave offenses against the law should be apprehended and brought to justice. Therefore, I, E.W. Wilson Governor of the State of West Virginia do offer a reward of five hundred dollars for the said Frank Phillips. And one hundred dollars each for the said Bud McCoy, Jasper McCoy, Lark McCoy, James McCoy, Samuel McCoy (son of Randal McCoy), Samuel McCoy (son of Samuel McCoy), Samuel King, David Straton, John Norman, William Saunders, Joseph F. Smith, John B. Dotson, George McCoy, Joseph Hurley, Andrew King, Ed Stuart, Curtis Smith, David Smith, John Yates, John Sowards, John England, Rans Maynard, Sam Miller, James Jones, Londo Hardin, Minis Sowords, & James Sowords. To be paid out of the State Treasury for the apprehension and delivery of the aforesaid parties to the jailor of Logan County, W.Va., at the jail thereof to await a trial on said charges. And the reward for each of the aforesaid parties will be paid to the party entitled thereto upon the certificate of the jailor of said Logan County, certifying to the delivery of the said party or parties (as the case may be) as aforesaid. By the Governor E.W. Wilson - Henry S. Walker Secretary of State

Frank Phillip, Johnse Hatfield and Nancy McCoy

So, who was Franklin Phillips, alias, Bad Frank Phillips? Frank was an interesting sort of plucky fellow, according to Kentucky Adjutant General, Sam Hill. He married Nancy McCoy, the ex-wife of Johnse Hatfield. Nancy McCoy Hatfield Phillips fell in love with two men of debatable character. Her gravestone called her a *flower,* which is why these two men fell for the lovely woman. Nancy wasn't the first Mrs. Frank Phillips. Frank first filed for a divorce from Matilda in 1879. The divorce proceedings continued on until 1883. Frank then was under 21 years old, having only been married for a short period. Matilda accused Frank of abuse in 1879. Wm. Phillips testified against Frank, stating that he had never provided for Matilda, that she had been sick, and the separation had been no fault of Matilda. Frank accused his wife of wanting his money. Frank's inheritance was in the hands of his guardian, Col. John Dils Jr. Testimony states that Frank took the mattress from beneath a sick Matilda when he left. Testimony also shows that Matilda was not able to walk from the bed to warm by the fire[28].

Nancy may have been Frank Phillips's true prize, taken from Johnse Hatfield within a short period of Johnse leaving to go west to avoid the long arm of the law. In Logan,[29] Johnse was suing Nancy for divorce in 1895, stating that Nancy had committed adultery. Per this case, Johnse and Nancy married May 14, 1881. Johnse stated, *"While we were married, I was kind to her, an affectionate husband."* Johnse also stated that in the year of 1888, he was forced to leave his home, that shortly after, Nancy had abandoned his home, leaving to Kentucky to live with Frank Phillips and diverse other lewd and lascivious persons. He stated that he had co-habited with Nancy until March 8, 1888, the same date Johnse will use in testimony, in 1899. Now this case for divorce was in 1891. Johnse left Logan to go west in March of 1888, which tells us Johnse was telling the truth in his testimony in 1899, in his own trial. Johnse had no way of knowing that he would later be captured. This also tells me that our colorful William Smith, who will tell the court in 1899 that he met Johnse in May of 1888 at the home of Anse Hatfield, where Johnse supposedly told Smith the story of the New Year's Eve fire and killing, made inaccurate statements in court. The good Col. Wm.

---

[28] KY Civil Cases 3928, 4063 and 4464.
[29] WV Archives 033-00035, Johnson vs Nancy Hatfield

Smith had lied, perjured himself, or just didn't remember correctly, take your choice. Whatever the case may be, Johnse had told the truth when he stated that he didn't speak with the good Colonel Smith in May of 1888. The last of Johnse's divorce statements was that in December of 1889, Nancy delivered a child, but that the child was not of his blood, he had not had intercourse with Nancy since he left to go west.

January 18, 1888, just days after the death of Jim Vance, we find a newspaper article, wherein it points out that Gov. Wilson had failed to sign warrants for the arrests of the Hatfields. This article stated that Jim Vance was killed near Beeck Creek in a shoot out, where Cap ran and escaped. Others tell it was Thacker Creek, where Jim was murdered. Who released this artilce is unknown, though, it would seem only a politician would turn a deadly scene into a political agenda and talk about roads, railroads, education, and lawlessness. The article did not say that Jim Vance was part of any Hatfield party, just that he was killed. By a moral choice of words, this shows that even up to Jan. 18, no one had indicated that Vance was involved in the New Year's eve raid. In the Johnse trial, niether Randal nor Jim McCoy knew who was part of that New Year's raid when Jim Vance was murdered. The article was spun in the best possible light for the purpose of keeping the McCoys, and perhaps Pike County leaders, out of prison for allowing, and knowing they had sent the Phillips-McCoy posse into West Virginia illegally. Connecting Vance to the feud was brilliant, legally, for the McCoys, in the event that they would ever be brought to trial for murder. In the trial of Commonwealth of Kentucky vesus Johnson Hatfield, it becomes clear, the McCoys would answer no direct questions about the killings of Dempsey or Jim Vance. Now, in saying this, we know that Kinner and Cline are the men who procured the rewards. The article states "so says the man who was instrumental in procurring the rewards."

Jan. 18, 1888 Big Sandy News (Louisa Kentucky) - *A Review - Of the Troubles in Pike County - Railroad Development Badly Needed - Pikeville, Ky, Jan 15th 1888. - In the first place about twenty three men were indicted in the Pike Criminal Court, charged with the crime of murdering three McCoy boys, (a history of these crimes having long* *since been given to the public through the press) and about Oct 1ˢᵗ, 1887 the Governor of Kentucky offered a reward of $500 each for the delivery to the jailer of Pike County; Ans Hatfield, Cap Hatfield, Johnson Hatfield, and one Thomas Chambers, the latter being rewarded by mistake;* **so says the man who was instrumental in procurring the rewards**, *and that it was intended for one Tom Mitchel, who is sometimes called Tom Chambers. In December, Tom Chambers found by Frank Phillips and a party at home in Logan County, W.Va., and brought to the jail at this place. An attempt was made by counsel for Chambers to have an investigation of the charges made against him as to his probable guilt or innocence, with a view to obtaining bail for him. They applied to the County Judge and obtained a writ of habeas corpus, and when Chambers was brought before him he (Chambers) by oath removed the Judge. There the sheriff returned the writ before T.O. Marrs, Judge of Pikeville, and he refused to hear the case. The officer then returned it before a Justice of the Peace, who decided that Marrs was the man to try the case. Then the Counsel applied to Judge Rice for a new habeas corpus, but no answer to the petition was received.*

On the night of Jan. 1ˢᵗ, 1888, the House of Randall McCoy was burned and one son and daughter of McCoy killed and their mother badly wounded. (She has been removed to this place and is recovering.)

Soon after this, a posse of 25 or 30 men from this county, well armed and led by Frank Phillips, made a raid into the enemies country, and found in the gap at the head of Beech Creek, James Vance and a woman and Cap Hatfeild. After a lively exchange of shooting Vance was killed and Cap was shot in the wrist and back. Cap ran after just a few shots. The pursuing party then started home and back to the head of Johns Creek. then with a reinforcement party they returned to West Virginia where they arrested Valentine Hatfield (called Wall), Andrew Varney, Doc Mahon, Pleasant Mahon, Sam Mahon, and L.D. Mccoy, all of who are indicted; but they were found at home and their is not reward for them. They are now in jail. There have been many reports about men killed, but here is the best authority we can get. Vance is the only dead man. Johnson Hatfield was wounded in the shoulder, *and Cap in the back and arm. There may be others killed, but we do not know it; hence we will not state. At the time the reward was offered, the Governor of this State issued his requistion on the Governor of West Virginia for the surrender of these violators of the law; just now we are credibly informed that the Governor of West Virginia refused to issue his warrant for their apprehension or to do anything in the matter. This is as full a history of the facts as we may have them told without exaggeration, that the public may know only the truth; for God knows, the truth is bad enough.* **We want more railroad development of the country, better education and more enlightenment, less killing, less lawlessness, less idleness and fewer crimes; and a development of the resources of the country is the road to these and the driving away of lawless and worthless characters.**

Sam Mahon/Mayhorn, mentioned above, when released from prison, went back to Logan County. He then found out that his wife Mary Ann had left and had abandoned his children with the neighbors. These children became feud victims. Sam, who was 39 years old, then proceeded to divorce his wife in 1894. In this divorce, it mentions that Sam was taken against his will and kidnapped to Pike County. Sam also stated that he was charged as part of the Hatfield-McCoy Feud. Thereby, if these men who were part of the feud, state that it was a feud, then, who is to argue with them. After some long exhausting research, we happen to agree. In the divorce of Leland Smith[30], during the depositions by E.H.

---

[30] WV Archives File 024-00037 – S.L. Smith vs R.M. Smith - Testimony of E.H. Simpkins - Q. Please state in what community the plaintiff and his father and mother live. A. They live in the Hatfield settlement on Island. Q. Are you acquainted with the general reputation of that community and the people who live in for being a peaceable and quite community and people a lawless community and people? A. I am acquainted with its general reputation. Q. According to that reputation is that community and people peaceable and quiet or is it lawless? A. It has the general reputation of being a lawless community and people. Q. Is it not a fact that most, if not all of the people who live in that community, go armed with Winchesters and pistols at all times. A. From the personal knowledge that I have of that community they do. Q. Would you not regard that a very bad community in which to rear a boy? A. Under all circumstances and influences, I would not think it an appropriate place. Q. Is the father and mother of the plaintiff in any way related to the Hatfields or if so what is that reputation? A. The mother of the plaintiff is a sister to Anse Hatfield and the mother in law of Cap Hatfield. Q. Which community, the one where the plaintiff lives, or the one that the defendant lives, would you regard as the better community in which to raise a boy? A. I would consider the place where the defendant resides as the better community. Q. Is it not also true, that one of the Hatfield gang, French Ellis, married one of the daughters of plaintiffs father and mother and now lives in that community? A. It is.
Testimony of Alexander Varney - Q. Are you acquainted with the wives of Cap Hatfield and French Ellis, the daughters of Mr. and Mrs. Smith, and if so, how long have you known them? A. I reckon I have known them 10 or 15 years. Q. What is the reputation in the neighborhood where they live and have lived? A. I never heard anything else but that they were respectable nice women.
Testimony of Sam Varney - Q. Can you not state any trouble that you have ever heard of him being in? A. No sir. I don't know of him being in any trouble or difficulty that I recollect of at all. Q. Is it not a fact, that he has been engaged in the feud between the

Simpkins, Sam Varney and Alexander Varney, the lawyers in this case use the same term....Hatfield and McCoy feud. Leland was thought to be in the mountains with the Hatfields during this feud. S.L. (Leland) Smith is the son of Emma Hatfield Smith, a sister to Anse Hatfield. The other interesting fact of this divorce and child settlement, Sam Mahon stated that "*he remained under charge of conspiracy with the Hatfields in the Hatfield-McCoy feud for about six years, trying, but ever failing to get a trial of his case, until at last through sympathy of some of the officials, the court was induced to release him, the Commonwealth being unable to make any case whatsoever against him.*"[31] So what we have coming out of Pike County is that they held a man, under conspiracy, without a trial for six long years! Pike County tried to bring Sam into court to stand trial. Those entries shown in the Pike Criminal Book up until 1893, at which point many witnesses decided they would not testify, forfeiting their bonds[32] and warrants attached. Sam was said to be ill in many of these court entries ranging from 1891 to 1893, stating he was not able to withstand a trial. Sam was never legally convicted.

With those illegal raids, the arrests and incarceration of the

Hatfields and McCoys carrying deadly weapons and that he now lives in the immediate neighborhood of the Hatfield parties and is identified with them in their troubles? A. As to him being engaged in that feud, I know nothing of that. And as to him being identified with the Hatfields, I know nothing of that, but I suppose he is working for some of them over there. Q. Have you not heard of his being with the Hatfields when they were staying in the mountains? A. I have no recollection of hearing he was staying in the Mountains. Q. Your recollection is bad, is it not? A. I think I have a pretty good recollection and am able to tell the truth. Q. So you pay very much attention to neighborhood reports. A. Not more so sir, that can possible help.

[31] WV Archives Case File 038-00055 Logan County

[32] March 6, 1893 - Commonwealth vs A. Hatfield and others} Murder - Continued for the commonwealth as to Sam Mayhorn and set for the first day of the next term of the Pike Circuit Court which convenes after Jan 1st, 1893 and James McCoy, Sam McCoy, W.A. Hatfield, Joseph Hatfield, J.M. McCoy, Tolbert Hatfield, James Hatfield, Dan Whitt, John Hatfield, Sarah McCoy, and Randolph McCoy witnesses for plaintiff and John Hatfield, W.A. Hatfield, and Tolbert Hatfield witnesses for defendant appeared in court and acknowledged themselves indebted to the commonwealth in the sum of $100 each to be void on condition that they each appear in the Pike Criminal Court on the first day of its next term held June term to testify in said case and to depart without leave of the court and on motion of plaintiff the recognizance of W.A. Ratliff, Lewis Farley, A.J. Ferrell, and William Daniels, ordered forfeited summons attached awarded against them bail $100.00 each and on motion of the defendant the recognizance of A.J. Ferrell ordered forfeited summons and attachment awarded against him bail $100.00. Alias bench warrant awarded against those not found.

men engaged in the 1882 troubles, it takes us into the criminal charges resulting from the so-called feud. The Commonwealth versus Johnson Hatfield is by far the most illuminating of the case files.

Chapter 4
COMMONWEALTH VS. JOHNSON HATFIELD

In 1898, Johnse Hatfield was arrested by H.E. Ellis[33] and Dan Cunningham just below his father's home, in Logan. Johnse will tell you in testimony that he was kidnapped from West Virginia and taken to Kentucky against his will. Johnse states that it was "without papers", meaning that a warrant and extradition papers were not signed in West Virginia.

We have studied the testimony of Sarah McCoy, wherein she described the house burning, during which her two adult children were killed, and Sally was beaten [Appendix B]. Now, we will show what Randal and Jim McCoy tell about that night, during Johnse Hatfield's trial, held in Floyd County Court ten years later. The trial was moved from Pike County because Johnse was unable to get a fair or an impartial jury trial, which is part of the trial transcripts. Rightly so, Johnse had no chance of getting an impartial jury in Pike County, per Pike residents. We have included full testimony of Jim and Randal McCoy, and only partial testimony of some witnesses, if interested in the whole transcript it can be located at the KY Archives.

The case starts out with the indictment of *Commonwealth vs. Cap Hatfield, Johnse Hatfield, Ellison Mounts, French Ellis,* Elliott Hatfield, Charles Gillespie, and Thomas Mitchell. Stating *on January 1st, 1888, in the county circuit court aforesaid, did feloniously of their malice, aforethought, kill and murder Alifair McCoy by shooting her with guns and pistols. Each of the*

---

[33] H.E. Ellis is whom Elias Hatfield shot, over the claim made by Doc, that he had arrested Johnse; in The State of WV versus Elias Hatfield, Jr. an indictment for murder in Mingo County. This case can be ordered from the WV Archives.

defendants was present and willfully and feloniously and of their malice, aforethought aided abetted persisted and encouraged each of his co-defendant to kill and murder Alifair McCoy as before stated and to do this the said defendants did conspire together.

Note, that in this indictment, the name of Jim Vance is excluded as a participant in the raid. On Sept. 3, 1898, Johnse asked for the deposition of several people to be taken: Sanford Hatfield, Harrison Hatfield, Leander Hatfield, Elliott Hatfield, Robert Hatfield, Anse Hatfield, Elias Hatfield, French Ellis, Troy Hatfield, Cap Hatfield, Nancy Hatfield and Emma Smith. It was also ordered that Johnse be assigned two guards for protection, the court deeming it necessary. Unable to get a fair trial in Pike, Johnse was moved to Floyd County and from there, he was transferred to Lexington, KY, until his trial date.

On September 27, 1898, an order was given to call witnesses. For the Commonwealth was James McCoy, J.S. Cline, Andy Scott, J.W. Scott, Dr. A.D. Spears, William Daniels, J.W. McCoy, Sam McCoy, Nancy Phillips, J.B. Polly, Thompson Phillips, G.W. Pinson, F.C. Hatcher, George Syck, L.D. Marrs, and John A. Dils. For the defendant: Vicy Hatfield, Bettie Hatfield, Jane Scott, Nancy A. Farley, J.A. Dils, F.J. Williamson, James L. Dotson, Andy Scott, Jeff Davis, S.H. Keel, and Henry Harrison. On October 4, 1898, Randolph McCoy, J. Scott, Bill Scott, Aly Farley, D.S. Spears, and Sam and J. McCoy are summoned to appear for the commonwealth. As well, Mary Simpkins and Nancy Bell Vance were summoned to appear for the defendant. On the 24th day of December 1898, it was ordered by the court that Dan Cunningham, Mose Mounts, Mrs. Sam Cisco, Vicy Whitt, Leander Hatfield, and Robert Mitchell were important witnesses and were material to the commonwealth.

By January 10, 1899, there was an order to impanel the jury in Floyd. On the 10th, the affidavit of Johnse was submitted to the court; *where he claimed to be a citizen of West Virginia, and without due process of law was abducted from that state.* It further stated that Pike Circuit Court identified his family as "The Hatfield Gang", therefore, he would not receive a fair trial. And, that James McCoy, upon finding out that Johnse was being transferred to Prestonsburg, *James McCoy, who was active in this prosecution, mounted his horse, hastened to Prestonsburg with the former Sheriff, arriving there in advance of this defendant, made pretense and gave out a speech to the authorities of Floyd County, stating that there was danger and that Johnse would be released by force, which was untrue and known to be untrue by James McCoy. His purpose was to keep him far from his family and his attorneys.* While in Lexington, Johnse claimed he was not allowed to write his family, nor submit to his attorneys. When he was finally able to file by mail the names of his witnesses, as shown above, the order was taken to Mayo of Floyd County, and copies were made for A.B. Stephens the County Attorney; two copies to the sheriff of Martin County, and two copies went to A.J. Kirk, Commonwealth Attorney. The defendant asked to proceed with depositions, which the clerk of Floyd County refused to order several times. After three months of incarceration in Lexington, KY, only then was he allowed to confer with his attorney. Johnse filed other wrongdoings in his trial.

Johnse further stated that on the night of the New Year's Eve, that he can prove he was at his father's home at a dance and the witnesses would prove that, if called on for interrogatories. He stated that these interrogatories would prove that before Christmas, he was accidentally shot in the back by his brother Robert, while hunting rabbits. It could also be proven by his sisters and others that three days after the house burning and murder of Alifair, Randolph was in Pikeville trying to secure warrants of persons whom "he believed" to have been engaged in the fight. Randolph then disclosed to Sam King that he was not sure who he recognized, and only later, he made mention of Johnse being present. When in fact....it was Hense Chambers he recognized. He stated that Sam King would testify to this and that Randal made no mention of shooting Johnse or anyone else that night. It was also revealed that Johnse wanted to call Ned Chapman, who was the Justice of the Peace when Randolph made his warrants. According to Johnse, Randal had made no mention to Ned of shooting Johnse or that he had seen Johnse at his home the night of the New Year's raid.

On Jan. 13, 1899, after days of testimony, the jury deliberated and found Johnse Hatfield guilty of murder. While in court, Johnse believed he was being represented by three lawyers, N.J. Auxier Jr., James P. Marrs, and Walter S. Harkins. He said that Auxier and Marrs had abandoned the case as his attorneys without notice. These two lawyers made claim of receiving no funds for service, and therefore had no obligation to defend him, leaving Harkins, who was appointed by the court. Harkins said he only once tried a murder case. That case, from what I now know, was the case of Alex Messer, who was sentenced to life in prison during his trial. The trial lawyers were Auxier and Harkins[34]. Harkins was mentioned as counsel with Cline, Cline &

---

[34] Feb 27, 1889 Pike Co. Court - Commonwealth Vs. Anderson Hatfield & others} Willful Murder - Continued for the Commonwealth as to Elijah Mounts, Dock Mayhorn, Plyant Mayhorn, Sam Mayhorn, and the case of Alexander Messer being next called and he being poor and unable to employ counsel the Court appointed A.J. Auxier and W.S. Harkins as

Harkins in the trial of Valentine Hatfield. Harkins had participated, and a bond was taken in Logan against the properties of the plaintiffs, Valentine, and the Mahon murder cases, which are not disclosed in the court papers relating to this case. Earlier I presented the bond for the lands of the accused in the 1882 murders of the three McCoy men, where Harkins was named as their lawyer along with P.A. Cline, J.S. Cline and W.M. Auxier. These lawyers, shown in Logan County Deed Book K, are noted as giving M.A. Ferrell of Logan "power of attorney" to collect on the lands of Valentine, Plyant, and Samuel Mahorn money with 6% interest of the money on their lands paying for their legal services. Harkins was involved in a legal firm that handled property sales and negotiated contracts with rich investors of the north in Prestonsburg. None the less, Harkins did maintain the seat in the court room during the trial next to Johnse.

Jim McCoy was the first witness called by the commonwealth to give testimony. Jim McCoy, who was present the next morning after the raid, told what his role was in the discovery of blood on the trail. Jim gives us an account that he and Andrew Scott made the initial investigations, because they were the first ones on the scene. Jim McCoy was the fighting spirit of the McCoy family. When reading between the lines, Jim gets his revenge on the Hatfields for this raid. Jim McCoy was called first because the commonwealth wanted Jim as second chair, even though he was not a lawyer. Jim McCoy was also wanted for murder in WV, and was heavily involved with the indictments. When Johnse's trial was moved to Floyd County, Jim had raced on his horse to alarm the people in Floyd County that there would be armed men, the Hatfields, coming to break Johnse out of jail. That never happened, as Jim seemed to be a bit anxious. Jim claimed to have gone to Logan County many times while he was sheriff, but anyone involved in the raids who would have crossed that KY border into WV., would have been risking arrest for the murders of Vance and Dempsey. Jim McCoy's arrest would have been imminent. He was under an indictment of Governor Wilson from ten years earlier. Murder is a serious charge. Jim McCoy didn't know the man Bill Dempsey, but by leading the posse along with Frank Phillips, allowed the murder of Dempsey during this raid. James McCoy was well aware of his surroundings. He could name how many men were on the raid, which was a far different number than that of Gov. Buckner. Jim McCoy also claims that there were no problems between the families between 1882 and the night of the New Year's raid. There was no

---

counsel for him. And the Deft filed affidavit and made motion for continuance and cause continued for him.

feuding between those years, per James McCoy, only that he and Randal were pushing for the arrests of the men who killed his McCoy brothers on the August 1882[35] election day. The civil war never came up in testimony in the first trial of Valentine Hatfield, or this trial with Johnse, which again proves that the Asa Harmon McCoy story was a fabrication used by the press to fuel hatred of the "Hatfield gang" and create bias in the minds of the readers. This was also a tool to absolve the McCoy gang from any fault in the murders of Vance and possibly to relieve the others in Kentucky (i.e. Ferguson, Cline, and possibly others) from their responsibility or role in the two murders. They had knowingly made those raids without Gov. Wilson's signature.

James McCoy

Q. Mr. McCoy do you know the defendant, Johnson Hatfield? A. Yes Sir. Q. How long have you known him? A. For twenty years, I guess. Q. What relation are you to Randolph McCoy? A. He is my father. Q. What kin are you to Calvin McCoy and Alifair McCoy? A. Brother and sister. Q. Where did Calvin McCoy live during his lifetime? A With my father. Q. In Pike County? A. Yes sir. Q. How old was Alifair McCoy? A. I believe she was 22 (29?) years old, maybe a little older. Q. Did she live with your father? A. Yes sir, she was a consumpted girl.

Q. Tell the jury about the time Alifair McCoy was killed, if she was killed. A. On the night ending of 1887, or the coming in of 1888. Q. On New Year's night? A. I think it was the night before New Years. Q. How soon after she was dead did you see her? A. I never saw her until New Year's morning. Q. What wounds did you find on her, and in what condition? A. Shot in the breast, or near the left breast. Q. Did the bullet come out? A. Yes sir. Q. What kind of a bullet was it? A. 33 Winchester it looked like.

Q. Was she dead when you got to her? A. On a bed at the mouth of the branch, some distance from where the house was burned. Q. Who else was there with her when you found her? A. My mother, a little boy a grandchild of my fathers, two sisters. They were all in the same place. Q. Were the wounds dressed? A. No sir. Q. Did they have on their night clothes? A. Yes sir. Q. Was it cold? A. Rather cold. Clear cold night, ground frozen hard. Q. You said you had two sisters, how large were they? A. One was in her 16th year, the other in her 18th year. Q. Where are they now? A. One is dead, and the other is near Pikeville. Q. Was she

---

[35] Those indicted for the killing of the McCoy brothers - Pike Cir. Ct 10th day of Sept Term, 14th day of Sept 1882 - The Grand Jury report in the following indictments is ordered to be filed} Charge of Willful Murder; Anderson Hatfield, John Hatfield, Cap Hatfield, Valentine Hatfield, Elias Hatfield, Charlie Carpenter, Joseph Murphy, Doc Mayhorn, Plyant Mayhorn, Selkirk McCoy, Albert McCoy (Kirk's son), L.D. McCoy (Kirk son), Thos. Chambers, Lark Varney (Henderson son), Andy Varney (Henderson son), David Whitt, Samuel Mayhorn, Alex Messer, John Whitt, Elijah Mounts (Beech Creek), Bench warrant awarded

a witness and why did she not come? A. She has a little child and could not come. Q. Who else was there? A. Some neighbors. Q. Was any of the boys or men of the family there? A. No sir. Q. Where was Calvin? A. Laying on the ground dead. Q. What time of the day did you arrive? A. In the morning early. Q. Did you see your father, Randolph McCoy before leaving? A. **Yes sir, at Johnse Scotts.**

Q. When you got there did you make any investigations as to who had committed this offense? A. I do not know whether I did or not. I went up the creek about a quarter of a mile and tracked across the fence._Q. Did you find some tracks? A. I saw a dozen or more. I followed about a quarter of a mile. I found plenty of blood and did not go any further. Q. How soon after that did you make another investigation? A. I ask my mother when she got able to talk about it.

Q. Where did you go to? A. I left and came to Pikeville. Q. Then where did you go? A. Frank Phillips and others and myself went to West Virginia to Anderson Hatfields. Q. Did you go to their home? A. We went to Andersons house first. Q. Did you find them or any of the parties? A. No sir. Q. Where did you go next? Did you find Cap or Johnse on that trip? A. Yes sir, we found Cap. Q. Where did you find him? A. On the ridge at Thacker. Q. Was he in the woods, and who was with him? (Objected to by counsel)

Q. Did you find any of the other parties mentioned in the indictment? A. No sir. Q. How if you found or discovered anything while at Anderson Hatfield, the father of the defendant, tell what it was. A. We did not discover anything there. Q. Did you find some beds? A. Yes sir. Q. Did it have anything on it? A. Not at the house.

Q. Where was your father, Jim, on the night this occurred? A. On the evening before he was at home. Q. Was Calvin McCoy at home? A. Yes sir. Q. How far is it from your father's home to that of Anderson Hatfield's home? A. Seven and a half miles. Q. How far did you live from your fathers? A. A mile. Q. In what part of Pike did he live? A. On Pond Creek, in Pike County, Kentucky. Q. What kind of house did he live in? A. A hewed log house with petition between, two doors, and one chimney to each house. It was a double log house.

Q. Did you see the defendant, Johnson Hatfield, after he was arrested and brought to Pikeville? A. Yes sir. Q. How come you to see him? A. I went into the jail. Q. State what he said. (Counsel for the deft objects, sustained) Q. Did you at any time make or promise him any reward to make to you any statements on the occasion? A. None at all. Or any promises to get make it.

Q. What did he say to you? (Counsel for deft objects. Overruled witness permitted to answer) A. He shook hands with me, and said, **"Jim, I saved your life once, you can save mine now if you will."** I said "I do not know." He said "that ain't what I mean. I am not prepared to die and I will take a life sentence in the penitentiary, and square off with the commonwealth." (Deft counsel objects) I said I cannot promise that. I do not know what the commonwealth attorney will do about it. I said "you need not be uneasy, a fair *and impartial trail." He said, justice was not what he wanted, that mercy was what he wanted. (The attorney, Mr. Harkins moved the court to exclude from the jury the above statement, which was made in the jail. (Overruled - Deft excepts).*

Q. Upon at your father's house that morning did you notice any signs of foulness, other than your brother and sister being dead? A. Yes sir, I found some cartridge shells in the yard, and bullet that had been shot in the chimney and the house burned down. Q. Did you examine your brother that was shot and state whether or not, any wound were on him? A. A bullet had entered the back of his head. Come out over the eyebrow, it was a very large hole. Q. Any other wounds on him? A. None that I know of.

Q. How far was it from where your sister and mother from where the house was burned? A. 40 or 50 yards. Q. Were they in the field or in the woods? A. In the field. Q. What were they on? A. Nothing but at straw bed. Q. What did you find the matter with your mother? A. Her head was cut all to pieces by being struck with something hard. Deft counsel objects. Overruled. Deft Excepts. Q. Was she conscious? A. No sir. Her hair had frozen to the ground from the blood from her head. Q. Is your mother living now or dead? A. She is dead. Q. Were you ever over the river to where Johnson Hatfield stayed and Cap Hatfield in the neighborhood before this time? A. Yes sir, I had been there lots of times.

Q. Had there been any trouble before this? A. Yes sir

Q. How long before the killing occurred? A. The trouble began at the August election 1882.

Q. Now from the time of the first trouble had there been a continual ill feeling, between your family and the Hatfield family? A. Yes sir, we had been trying to have them arrested, but had not had any trouble. Q. During that time and up to the last killing, was you along and saw these parties banded together? State where, and who they were. A. Yes sir, I saw them several times myself. *Q. State how and what they were in? A. I do not know. I saw them coming down and up the road. Q. How many? A. Nine. Q. Tell what resulted, if you know, or what trouble occurred after the August election, and the parties named. (Counsel for defendant objects. Sustained)*

Q. Did you know Ellison Mounts, Mr. McCoy? A. Yes sir. Q. Where is he now? A. He is dead. Q. Are you a brother to Tolbert, Randolph Jr., and Farmer McCoy? A. Yes sir. Q. Are they living or dead? A. Dead. Q. Did their killing occur in Pike Co., and before the finding of this indictment? A. Yes sir.

Cross Examined by Mr. Harkins for the defendant.

Q. When was the last time you were in West Virginia Mr. McCoy? A. Last fall, I think at Williamson. Q. How long were you there? A. About an hour and a half. Q. How long had it been before that, that you were in West Virginia? A. I was a deputy sheriff and went over there frequently?

Q. Did you go whenever you wished? A. Yes sir.

Q. **On the occasion of the visits you made to West Virginia after the death of your sister Alifair McCoy, who went with you? A. Frank**

Phillips, and I, and others, was 38 that went. Q. For making arrests? A. Yes sir. Q. What kind of arms did they have? A. All kinds.

Q. Who did you see on the occasion of your first visit over there and how long were you there? A. We went in the evening, and at twelve o'clock came back. Q. Who did you see on that trip? A. I saw Anse Hatfields family. Q. On the other trips, did you see a man named Bill Dempsey? A. I did not know him. They called him that. Q. Which trip was that? A. I am not certain; I think it was the second trip. Q. How many was together on that trip? A. 33 I think. I am not certain. Q. Then you saw Bill Dempsey? A. They called him that. Q. Where is he now? A. Dead. Q. On another one of these trips did you see <u>James Vance</u>? A. Yes sir, the first trip.

Q. How many was there that trip? A. 29 Q. Do you know where he is now? A. He is dead.

The commonwealth attorney, Mr. Kirk, asks that he be permitted to retain James McCoy in the courtroom to assist in the prosecution, that his presence would aid him in bringing out the evidence; which was granted. Counsel for defendant objects. Overruled. Deft. Excepts.

Randal McCoy was called next, and spoke of the memories of that night. He makes no quarrel that he saw Johnse bending down fixing his rifle after shooting at his son Calvin. Randal tells that Johnse had just fired at Calvin upon his exit from the burning house. Never does Randal, in his testimony, mention Jim Vance. Randal's testimony in this trial does not match what he told the Justice of the Peace Chapman, or what Ferguson relayed to the Governor of Kentucky on January 13, 1888, shortly after the raid on the McCoy home. It hurts Randal's credibility to know that his testimony differs from what he told Ferguson and the Governor through the Sam Hill letter, 10 years prior. No one agrees as to what happened, who was there, how it happened, including Governor Buckner, who received his facts from J. Lee Ferguson and conveyed them to Gov. Wilson[36] in a letter dated January 30, 1888. After this letter, Gov.

---

[36] Senate Legislative Doc. #2 March 6, 1888 Correspondence of the Governors of Kentucky and West Virginia Jan 30, 1888 - Thus matters stood until the latter part of December, when Frank Phillips, named as agent in the requisition for these parties, having sent the required fees, and being unable to hear anything from your Excellency, went into West Virginia in company with two others, and without any disturbance or conflict of any kind, succeeded in capturing Thomas Chambers, Selkirk McCoy, and Moses Christian, three of the persons named in the indictment for the murder of the McCoy brothers, who were brought to Kentucky and lodged in the jail of Pike county. This so incensed the Hatfield party that on the night of January 1st a company of twelve men, headed by Capt. Hatfield and James Vance Sr., came from West Virginia into Pike county, and having surrounded the house of Randolph McCoy, the father of the three McCoy brothers, who had been murdered in 1882, commanded him to surrender, saying they were the Hatfield crowd. They then forced their way into a room where his three daughters were sleeping, shot one of them through the

Buckner sent Sam Hill to the McCoy home and those facts are different than those of Bucker's letter! In this letter, we start to see why there are so many discrepancies throughout the feud; it clearly changes in each telling by those who were in communication with the Kentucky Governor. Randal says there were 3 dozen men at his home on New Year's Eve, while Buckner is stating 12 men. Ali Farley will state in his testimony only 7 men walked by his home that night after the burning of Randal's home. Buckner states that Sally was picked up and thrown back into the burning home. Never in any testimony does it state that happened. Buckner says the men went to the McCoy home because they had arrested three men, (i.e. Selkirk McCoy, Moses Christian, and Thomas Chambers) while others would testify that it was because they wanted to quiet Randal McCoy and prevent him from pushing the indictments. During the death of Jim Vance, Sam McCoy says Jim Vance was firing at Phillips with a pistol. Buckner says Vance had a repeating rifle in his hand when killed. The depositions of the witnesses that were taken hostage by the Phillips posse state that Jim was standing when Randal fired the first shots, without as much as a "give yourself up". Sam McCoy said Jim would not have been hurt if he had stood still. Sam intimated he went with Randal McCoy and the posse in order to keep people from being hurt. In Shepard's letter, he told that Phillips and his gang stole Jim's guns and money from the house, throwing his beds into the yard, after killing him. They also threatened Jim's daughter with death. The incredible part of this letter, is that Buckner stated that Randal was not with the invading party who crossed into WV., and there would

---

heart, and set fire to the house. The old man and his son Calvin, seeing that they intended to kill them, made the best defense they could, but the flames soon drove them from the house. The son, in his efforts to escape, was riddled with bullets, and the old man, who ran in an opposite direction, was fired upon by several of the party, but escaped unhurt. His wife had, in the meantime, come out of the house and begged for mercy, but was struck in the head and side with a gun, breaking her ribs and knocking her senseless to the ground, after which she was thrown back into the house to be burned, but was dragged out by her two daughters as they left the burning building. Some days thereafter twenty-six men armed themselves and went into West Virginia in pursuit of the perpetrators of this atrocious crime, and on reaching the house of Anderson Hatfield, so far from abusing or mistreating his wife, as has been represented to your Excellency, they treated her kindly, and at her request left some of their party with her to quiet her fears but after leaving there in search for the men they were fired upon by James Vance Sr., Capt. Hatfield and others, and in the fight which followed James Vance Sr., was killed, having two pistols on his person and repeating rifle in his hand when killed. Old Randolph McCoy was not with the pursuing party, as has been represented to your Excellency, but was at the time in Pikeville, Kentucky, as the citizens of that place will all testify. The pursuing party then returned to Kentucky and being reinforced by ten additional men, went to the next day and succeeded, without the firing of a gun, in capturing six more of the men indicted for the murder of the McCoy brothers in 1882, bringing them back to Kentucky, where they were lodged in the jail of Pike county.

be plenty of witnesses in Pike County who would attest to that! No one did. Again, so many discrepancies, and who is to say. Randal McCoy was named in January 1888 for murder, but was not named in May of 1888, when rewards were being signed in WV, by Gov. Wilson. One thing is for sure, Kentucky's Gov. Buckner and Adjunct-General Sam Hill don't agree with the story taken directly from Randal himself, at his home. Nor will they agree with the number of men on the raids, given by Jim McCoy as twenty-nine and thirty eight. Jim McCoy, with Phillips, led the raid to kill the Hatfields for the New Year's Eve murders of Alifair and Calvin. Now, with Vance and Dempsey murdered, everyone was covering up with some type of story, or being released from prosecution[37], or were promised leniency in their trials if they testified. Pike County Attorney, J. Lee Ferguson, clearly had not talked directly to Randal or Jim McCoy before presenting the facts to Buckner as of Jan 30.

Randal stated, "*I could see very well, because of the burning home, and the night was a clear cold night, the moon was bright.* Let's face it, a burning log home would make for a tremendous fire. He said that Sarah was beaten by Johnse Hatfield, and that the house was ablaze and well-lit near, where Randal says, Alifair fell in the doorway of the attached second home.

Now compare what Ellison Mounts said in testimony [Appendix B], that the men were wearing false faces (masks). If in fact the men had masks, how did Alifair recognize Cap and Hense? How did Randal recognize Johnse? The whole mask introduction in the confession of Ellison Mounts draws on an inference of untruths. With Aly Farley testifying to seeing seven men, and not nine as previously written in books, this exposes that they shot a man without any proof he had been to Randal' home. Later, testimony will say, that when the men left Randal's on New Years Eve, they went to the home of James Vance. Johnse testified he was at a dance at his fathers. His father had then left and went to Vance's home that night of the dance, which tells us that Anse and Jim were not at this dance with these men who were getting drunk on New Years Eve. That's if......you believe there was a dance at Anse's home the night of New Years Eve, 1887. Men testified during the trial that there was a dance.

---

[37] Jeff Whitt testified: I am the same Jeff Whitt mentioned in the letters from S.G. Kinner Commonwealth Attorney, and I had his promise that I shall not be indicted in this case. Testimony of Daniel Whitt: I am staying with Uncle Randall McCoy's house, have talked but little with him or Aunt Sallie about this case.....The only promises I have is that, that Indictment should be dismissed and that I should be protected if I would come and testify in this case.

The confession of Ellison Mounts was written on Nov. 5th, 1888, almost 1 year after the raid, under dubious circumstances. The confession took place in the presence of some of the same politically connected people who had enlisted Governor Buckners help in securing bounties for the Hatfield gang's capture. (Appendix B). This confession was found in the Kentucky Archives. This confession was not with the trial case but found inside Gov. Buckner's correspondence files, and not spoken of as part of the sentencing trial records for Mounts. It was later spoken of when Mounts' case went to the KY Supreme Court. A first confession, secured by bounty hunter, Dan Cunningham, was written on Oct. 29, 1888. The first is less detailed, and was written for newspaper exposure. In both confessions, there are discrepancies, but in both, Mounts testified that Jim Vance was present the night of the raid. Mounts believed he was offered leniency and that Sarah McCoy would not testify, or he would not have agreed to "make his mark" on this confession. But, Sarah did testify in Mounts' case, reinforcing the atrocious acts of the New Year's raid and creating anger and justification for a death sentence. Her testimony had the desired result. Mounts was sentenced to hang. All of these promises made by the men in the room (i.e. Dils, Cline[38], York, Cunningham, Gibson), were broken. Thereby, his attorney filed an appeal, which was decided by the Kentucky Supreme Court, and overruled. Mounts trial was a sentencing phase because Mounts had pleaded guilty, so there was no elaborate trial in his defense. Mounts believed that if there was no testimony, he would get life in prison, not an execution by hanging. Many believe Mounts may have been challenged in some way effecting his judgement. I've not seen any proof of this. In the case of Wm. Ratliff vs. Rebecca Jane (Blankenship) Ratliff[39], for divorce, nineteen year old Mounts was deposed in 1885. He stated that he knew William and Rebecca all of his life. Mounts knew of Rebecca having intercourse three times, and names the places these rendezvous occurred. Mounts said he was living on the Kentucky side of the river at that time, and his occupation was farming. In this case it's said that Wm. Ratliff had been in an interlude with on Patsy Mounts, now Patsy Crockett.

Randolph McCoy

---

[38] Interesting fact: As of Nov. 5, 1888 Perry Cline is in the room with Mounts when he gave his confession. When you look at the Property Bond, securing Perry's attorneys fee from Pliant and Doc Mahon in February of 1889, he charges the Mahons, with interest, back to August of 1888. Prior to the arrest and confession of Ellison Mounts.
[39] Logan County File 038-00018, WV Archives

Q. Is your name Randolph McCoy? A. Yes sir. Q. How old are you? A. I was born in 1825. Q. Where do you live? A. In Pike Town. Q. How long have you lived in Pike County? A. Fifty years. Q. Do you know Johnson Hatfield, and what relation are you to Alifair McCoy? A. She was my daughter. Q. What relation were you to Tolbert McCoy, Farmer McCoy and Randolph McCoy? A. They were my sons.

Q. Do you know Cap Hatfield, Anderson Hatfield, and the parties named in this indictment? A. I do know that, I would know them all. Q. Do you know Johnson Hatfield? A. Yes sir.

Q. Begin in your own way and tell all about the case that you know?

A. The first I knew of it was the dogs woke me up. My boy came to the bed and said "Pa they are coming on us, get up" and by the time I was up on the floor they had surrounded the home, and I heard one of them say "God d*** you, come out and surrender yourself a prisoner of war." We never (unreadable next line) We got behind the door that broke; they fired a volley each way into the house, and I moved, for I say I could not stay there, and next I went to the fireplace; and Calvin to the back of house. They shot cross shots from the side of each door through the doors. I stayed there a good while. They kept up shooting and finally I went in the loft. The firing kept up a long time. I thought it a long time. Finally, they fired the house. The room I was in, my wife, Calvin, and little Melvin was in the same room. I took a cup, and when the blazing would come through the room, I would throw water on it and put it out. Finally the water gave out. The boy had gone up in the loft, and I went to where he was. I stayed in the house until three of the joist had burned and end of the joist fell down before we attempted to leave the house. The boy then came to me and said "Pa you stay here, I can outrun you. Said I will go to the barn and try to attract their attention in that direction and maybe I can save you." He started and got past the corner of the house, when they began firing again. He never got to the barn. The little boy hung on to me, but I shoved him loose at the door, and went out among them. I stepped out of the house, and saw Johnson standing 8 or 10 steps from the rets [rest], and just as I stepped from the house his gun fired, in the direction of the way Calvin was running. I discovered that his gun had caught foul and he was humped down working on it. I fired into the crowd and then I turned and fired at Johnson. I aimed to shoot him in the neck, and aimed to low and shot him in the shoulder. The burning house made it as light as day, and I know it was Johnson. Q. What did you do when you shot Johnson, the defendant? A. I run down the creek. Q. Where did you go then? A. I crawled into a shuck pen. Q. Did you have on your night clothes? A. Yes sir.

Q. What time of night was it? A. About nine o'clock when they come. I do not know when they left. We had all gone to bed when they came. Q. What kind of night was it? A. The moon was shining very pretty. Q. When you come out and saw Johnson standing there, was there any light? A. Yes sir, very bright from the house burning and the moon.

Q. Where was Alifair McCoy? A. She was in the house – the upper house when

they came past where she stayed. They did not fire it until the shots fired at the other of the room we were in.
Q. What did you hear at that time? (Deft objects overruled and the deft excepts)
A. I heard Alifair McCoy say "Cap Hatfield and Hence Chambers, you wouldn't shoot a poor innocent woman would you?" Then they said shoot her, God dam it shoot her down, spare neither man nor woman, and then shot her in the left breast. I heard her fall and struggle near the door. This was before I came out of the house and before Calvin came out. Q. Where did you stay that night? A. At Johnse Scotts. Q. When did you go back? A. At daylight. Q. What did you find? A. I found my son lying there dead, my daughter dead with her hair frozen in blood to her breast. Q. Was the house there? A. No sir, it was burned up. The little girls had dragged their sister off the house.
Q. How far from the house? A. About thirty yards. Q. Is your girls living? A. One of them is. Q. How old was she at the time, and why is she not here? A. She was [blank space} she has a family of children, and on account of the river tide could not come. Q. What wounds if any did you find on the boy? A. He was shot in the back of his head through the eyebrows. Q. How many shots did they fire? A. No man could count them. They came in volleys and platoons. Q. Did you have a gun too? A. Yes sir. Q. Your wife in her night clothes? A. Yes sir, they thought they had killed her no doubt or I think they would have done so.

Cross examination of Mr. Harkins

Q. You say that on that night, your daughter named the names of Cap Hatfield and Hense Chambers. Did you see them? A. No sir. Q. How many men there that you saw? A. I could not tell, several. Q. How many would you guess? A. There looked to be about 3 dozen.
Q. You tell the jury that you recognized Johnse Hatfield the defendant? A. Yes sir, as I passed the corner of the house I looked at him. He was down working with his gun. After the shot in the direction of Calvin. Q. How many feet were you from him? A. About six feet. Q. How far were you from the other men? A. Twelve or fourteen feet. Q. Was the moon shining bright enough for you to see clearly? A. Yes sir together with the light from the burning building. Q. How was he dressed? A. He had on an overcoat; I do not know the color. Q. Did any of the balance have on overcoats? A. I do not know. Q. Did you see Hense Chambers there? A. No sir. Q. How long had you at that time been acquainted with Hense Chambers? A. [blank] Q. How old a man was he? A. Near thirty years old. Q. Did you know Anderson Hatfield? A. Yes sir. Q. How old a man was he? A. I do not know. Q. How far did you live from him? A. About seven and one half miles.
(The witness was excused and left the room and was recalled by Mr. Kirk Commonwealths Attorney and the examination of the witness proceeded by Mr. Harkins cross examining as follows)
Q. Mr. McCoy was you before the Grand Jury of the Pike Circuit Court, which convened in August 1888? A. I was not there. Q. At that the time, were you or before that time acquainted with Ellison Hatfield? A. Yes sir. [note: he knew

French Ellis, did not know Elliott Hatfield, Charles Gillespie, or T.R. Mitchell]
Q. I believe you told the commonwealth attorney that you knew Cap and
Robert? A. Yes sir. Q. What kind of a looking man was French Ellis, how old a
man was he? A. 25 or 30.

Re-examined by Mr. Kirk Commonwealth Attorney
Q. Mr. McCoy what kind of gun was used when you shot the defendant? A. A
shotgun. Q. In which shoulder did you shoot him? A. The right shoulder. Q.
What time or what year was it – give the date? A. It was New Year's night
1888, I reckon. Q. What was your gun loaded with? A. Small shot, squirrel
shot.

Melvin McCoy is not listed in the 1880 census, which matches his trial
transcripts of about 6 years of age at the time of the New Year's raid in
1887, and 17 years old at the time of his testimony in 1899. Later, his age
listed in census records would vary. There is also an issue with the age
listed on his death certificate.

Throughout his testimony, Melvin never named his parents, but did
say Randal and Sarah are his grandparents and that he had a little hunch
back sister. Cora would be that little girl. He mentioned Aunt Alifair and
Uncle Calvin. Randal told Sam Hill, that Tolbert's two children were
present during the New Year's raid. Melvin adds to the trial as he
believes them to be. Sarah was hit in the head, unconscious for a short
time, and cracked in the ribs. Sarah told Melvin that it was Johnse
Hatfield who hit her, not Jim Vance, as feud authors write. Melvin
remembered very little himself, only repeating what his grandparents
told him. Also included are the testimonies of Andrew and William
Scott, and Ali Farley, who will testify to the number of men seen walking
by their homes. They stated that they believed the men had guns, and
was part of the New Year's Eve raid. Seems that they come forward, but
this testimony went against what Jim McCoy would have wanted,
because it lays doubt to the number of men on the raid, where Calvin
and Alifair are killed.

Melvin McCoy
Q. How old are you? A. Seventeen years is about my age. Q. What kin are you
to Randolph McCoy? A. He is my grandfather. Q. Were you at his house at the
*time Alifair McCoy was killed? A. Yes sir. **Q. Now Melvin, do you know***
***how old you were at the time? A. Six years was about my age.** Q. Now*
tell the Jury if you remember what occurred; tell what occurred in your own
way? A. On New Year's 1888 (Counsel for defendant objects to the
introduction of the witness, on the grounds that he was of such a tender age at
the time of the killing that he is incompetent – overruled, and the defendant

excepts) or about that time, the Hatfields come to my grandfather's house, and surrounded the house. The first words I remember was they said "God Dam you we have got you. We are going to take you to Logan County, you shant be hurt." Then they fired into the house and shot a right smart through the house, then you know one of my aunts Alifair McCoy came and told them not to burn the house down, and they shot her down. Then from that time you know the house was burned, and we all left the house.

Q. Now Melvin, which room was you in? A. With my grandfather. Q. Who else was in the room with you? A. One of my Uncles, Calvin. Q. Who else? A. My grandma. Q. Who was in the other room? A. One of my aunts that was killed and another one of my aunts. Q. Which room was the fire set to? A. The one my grandfather was in. Q. Do you know who went out of the house first? A. My uncle and grandmother, grandmother first. Q. Who went next? A. My Uncle Calvin went next. Q. Who went next? A. Grandfather. Q. Who went next? A. They told me to come in the house where grandma was, I turned and went and got my clothes, and went back in the room where they were.

Q. What did you discover? A. I saw a man. Q. Did you know any of the parties? A. No sir, I did not. Q. Did you see your aunt? A. Yes sir. Q. Where was she? A. Laying there dead in the door or near the door. Q. What was her name? A. Alifair McCoy. Q. At the time you found her laying in the door, was the house on fire? A. Yes sir. Q. Where did Calvin go, and did you see him anymore? A. Not until the next morning and we found him dead. Q. When you went into the house did you see your grandmother? A. No sir, not until we got into the other room. Q. You found her then? A. Yes sir. Q. Did you find that your grandfather gone out? A. Yes sir.

Q. Did you see your grandmother any more that night? A. Yes sir, I stayed with her all the time. Q. Was there anything that was to matter with your grandmother? A. Yes Sir, she had been struck with something on the head. **Johnson Hatfield struck her with a Winchester.**

Q. Did the house burn down? A. Yes sir. Q. Where did you go? A. Up the branch from the house. Q. Who went with you? A. My two aunts and myself dragged my dead aunt up there. Q. How far from the burning building did you get? A. Two or three hundred yards. Q. Did you have any fire? A. No sir. Q. What kind of night was it? A. Cold. Q. How cold? A. It was freezing cold. Q. Was the ground frozen up? A. Yes sir. Q. Where did you stay the rest of the night? A. Up the branch until daylight. Q. How many up there was there? A. My grandma two aunts little sister and myself and my dead aunt. Q. How far was Calvin away from you all? A. I do not know how far it was – three or four hundred yards I guess. Q. Did you lay Calvin on anything? A. No sir, we did not know he was killed until next morning.

Q. Was your aunt that got killed dressed or in her night clothes? A. She had her clothes on. Q. How was your grandmother dressed? A. I do not remember. Q. Was your sister dressed? A. I think she had her clothes on. Q. Did you examine your dead aunt to see if she had any wounds? A. Yes sir. Q. Did she have any wounds? A. She was shot through the left breast.

Q. How long had you been acquainted with her? A. She raised me. Q. Do you remember who come there the next morning first? A. Yes sir, but I have forgotten who it was. Q. What did you do with the sled? A. They hauled my grandmother and my dead aunt in it. Q. What was the matter with your grandmother (deft objects – overruled and the deft excepts) A. She was hit in the head with a pistol and over the back with a gun; her ribs were broken on one side. Q. Was she in unconscious condition? A. Yes sir.

Cross examined by Mr. Harkins

Q. You say Mr. McCoy that you were then six years old when that occurred. A. Yes sir. Q. I will ask you if you heard them say the words you have repeated? A. That is all I heard them say. Q. Were you in the same room with your grandfather? A. Yes sir. Q. Did you see but the one man you have mentioned? A. No sir, I did not. Q. Have you been living with your grandfather since that time? A. Yes. Q. During that time have you frequently talked about what occurred there that night? A. Yes sir. Q. Very often? A. Not a great deal. Q. Have you heard it talked some? A. Yes sir. Q. You say your grandmother was hit on the head with a pistol and over the back with a gun? A. Yes sir that is what she said he did. I do not know only what she said. I do not know that myself. Q. Did not Mr. Kirk ask you what you recollected about it? A. Yes sir.

The next three witnesses called were Andy Scott, William Scott[40], and Aly Farley, who testified to a difference of opinion as to how many were in the party the night of the raid, none said nine. One could make out four or five, the other, NO MORE than seven. Aly Farley said seven were walking single file, and was confident of that number. Only after ten years' people were willing to testify to the number of men on the New Year's raid.

Andrew Scott

Q. Where do you live Mr. Scott? A. On Pond Creek. Q. Do you remember of hearing the occurrence of old man McCoy house being burned and the persons killed there? A. Yes sir, I was there the next morning. Q. How far did you live from him at that time? A. About a mile and three quarters. Q. How come you to go there the next morning? A. Jim McCoy came and told me what had happened and wanted me to go out see what was done. Q. Tell the Jury what you found. A. I found Calvin McCoy lying dead shot, and the house burned. I found the girl and the old lady, and two little children, something like fifty yards up the branch from – above where the house stood. They had got a bed up there and the old lady was lying in the bed. The dead girl was also in the bed, and the two

---

[40] Pike County Court May Term 1868 - Upon motion of Perry Cline to have John Dils Jr. appointed his guardian said Cline being under fourteen years old said Dils being in Court and extend into bond with the Commonwealth of KY with William Scott as is hereby and took the oath according to law.

little children were covered up between them. The old lady pulled the cover over their heads. I ask her if she knew me and she said she did.

William Scott

Q. Mr. Scott do you know Randolph McCoy? A. Yes. Q. Do you remember of the occurrence of his house being burned and his family killed? A. Yes. Q. Where did you live, how far from him? A. About a quarter a mile. Q. Did you live in the direction leading toward Anderson Hatfields from Randolph McCoys? A. Yes sir. Q. Did you hear some one pass that night? A. Yes sir. Q. What direction were they coming? A. Up the creek toward Blackberry. Q. Did you hear them talking, about how many? A. Four or five.

Aly Farley

Q. Do you know Randolph McCoy? A. Yes sir. Q. Did you hear of the occurrence of his house burning and some of his family killed? A. Yes sir. Q. How far did you live from it at that time? A. About a mile and a quarter. Q. Did you live on the road toward Blackberry form Randolph McCoy? A. Yes sir, I saw some parties coming up the creek toward Blackberry. Q. How many? A. As well as I remember there was seven. Q. What time of night was it? A. Between one and two o'clock. Q. Where they making any fuss as they passed? A. No sir, I heard no talk. Q. Did these parties have guns? A. I think they did, they looked like guns, I am not sure. Q. What kind of night was it? A. The moon was shining bright and it was freezing cold weather. Q. Was that the same night you learned the house was burned? A. Yes sir. Q. Did you go somewhere the next morning? A. Yes sir, after the house burned I came on down to the creek to where the houses were burned.

Crossed examined by Harkins Attorney for defendant

Q. How far did you live from the road? A. I lived by the side of the road not further than the width of this room. Q. You say that the men had guns? A. I am not sure. Q. What opportunity did you have to see? A. Only from the light of the moon. Q. How were you looking? A. Out the window. Q. You counted seven? A. Yes sir. Q. How were they dressed? A. I cannot tell? Q. Did you know any of them? A. No sir. Q. How were they walking close together or in single file? A. In single file.

In the testimony of the defendant, Johnson (Johnse) Hatfield, Johnse said that on the night of the New Year's Eve, he was at the home of Anse, his father. Johnse was not the only person who stated that they attended that dance, but the jury didn't buy it. Johnse said it was his brother Robert, not Randal McCoy, who shot him in the shoulder. He admitted that he ran for 32 months, as far away as Canada. Was there a dance held at the log hewed home of Anse Hatfield? We know that Anse did in fact live in a log home, and the property is depicted with some description. With Anse being a distributor, people knew he would have the corn liquor, so stopping by his home for shine was not out of the question. It seems to have been a very popular occurrence, even spoken of in other testimonies not given here.

The commonwealth attorney, Mr. Kirk made a statement about Vance with no other information provided. Counselor Kirk to Johnse; **Q. When your father left and went back to Vance's, did you go to bed at the dance? A. No sir.** When they asked Johnse about who was hiding out from John Wright and the Kentucky gang, Johnse admits Jim Vance was with them in the woods, with himself, Cap and Anse at times. What we now know from the divorce suit of Leland Smith[41], is that he and others were possibly in the mountains with the Hatfields. I suspect that others were there as well. At another time Johnse says only himself, Cap, and his father Anse were in the woods. Though, I can understand that reasoning, and Uncle Jim Vance might have been with them. With men like Devil John Wright and Bad Frank Phillips, with a squad of bounty hunters along with them, some protection of his nephews would have been important. After all, blood is thicker than water. Harkins asked "*Q. After the killing, did you know of any men invading West Virginia for the purpose of or attempt to kill persons who were "supposed to be connected" with the "different facts of the feud" between the Hatfield and McCoys? A. Yes sir, one raid they come over from Pike County and killed Jim Vance, and next they killed Dempsey.*" The statement, "attempt to kill persons who were supposed to be connected with the different facts of the feud" is very revealing in regard to what feud books want us to believe.

When Harkins asked the above question, it reinforced the fact that the Phillips-McCoy gang was going to kill someone and that wrath had taken over their minds and souls. Hearing that two men were gunned down because they were "**supposed to be connected**" with the "**different facts**", Harkins is finally asking something about Jim Vance with a reference that something was abhorrently wrong. After all, Jim nor Randal McCoy implicated Vance in the New Year's raid when giving their testimony. Was this an attempt of the defense to show the court, that two men were killed at the hands of the Phillips-McCoy gang, with Jim McCoy sitting second chair in the courtroom?

Then, two more questions are asked about the raid into Logan. *Q. When were the men killed that you speak of on the raids and how were they killed if you know? A. I cannot state. Q. Did not Jim McCoy go over there after his brother and sister was killed, to arrest the parties who committed the crime*

---

[41] Logan County Case 024-00037

and upon arrest in a general fight, while <u>an arrest</u> was trying to be made? Mr. Kirk, stating *"an arrest"*. We know McCoy went to Logan looking for Johnse and Cap at Anse's house first, because Randal only knew of three men being at his home when questioned during trial testimony.

Not knowing the answer on why, where, or when Johnse saved Jim McCoy from death is a typical Hatfield and McCoy mystery. Harkins asked Johnse: *Q. You said that you saved Jim's (McCoy) life once, tell how this was?* The Commonwealth objected to this question. The following question then pertained to the two raids that Jim McCoy made into West Virginia. One was the killing of Vance, and the other was the Battle of Grapevine, with the killing of Deputy Wm. Dempsey.

Johnson Hatfield

Q. Mr. Hatfield tell that jury what your age is? A. My age is 35 years, the 6th day of this month. Q. Where is your home? A. In Mingo County West Virginia. Q. What is your fathers name? A. Anderson Hatfield. Q. Have you any brothers? A. Yes sir, Cap, Robert, Anderson, Elliott, Ellis, Joe and Troy. Q. About the year 1888 where did your father live? A. He <u>lived</u> pretty well opposite the mouth of Peter. Q. Where did you live, with them? A. I was living down on Grapevine. I lived most the time with Pa.

Q. Were you at the time acquainted with Randolph McCoy? A. Yes sir, I had seen him several times. Q. Do you remember of the occurrence of his house burned and his daughter Alifair being murdered? A. Yes sir, I remember of it. Q. Where were you at the time you heard of this? A. I was at Pa's at the mouth of Peter. Q. Who brought the news to you? A. Jerry Hatfield told us about it. Q. What time of the day or what time was it you heard it? A. It was the next day about ten o'clock as well as I remember. Q. Where were you on the day the killing was done? A. I was at fathers. Q. Who else was there Mr. Hatfield? A. Pa, Cap, Bob, John Preston Roberts, Jack Roberts, Jack Cline.

Q. What was going on there that night? A. There was a dance there that night. Q. Were you away from the house that night? A. No sir, I stayed there all night. Q. Did you dance any that night? A. No sir. Q. Why did you not dance? A. I was suffering from a shot at that time. Q. How long before that time had you got that shot? A. I think it was on the 20th day of December, as well as I remember. Q. Some days before the party or dance at your father's house? A. I think it was about two weeks before as near as I could state, I was shot before the dance. Q. Tell the jury how you come to be shot and what you were doing? A. We were up the hollow from the house with the boy's rabbit hunting, when Robert let the shotgun go off accidently, and shot me with a shotgun. Q. Will you please take off your coat and show the jury where you were shot? (Deft takes off his coat and shows the jury)

Q. You state to the jury, that that wound was made by the accidental discharge of a gun in the hands of your brother Robert? A. Yes sir. Q. Is he a younger or older brother? A. He is younger. Q. How old is Bob now? A. I do not know he is younger than Cap; I suppose he is about 26 or 27. Q. That was eleven years ago? A. Yes sir. Q. Tell the jury if you were at the house of Randolph McCoy on the night his house was burned, and his daughter was killed? A. No sir, I was never was at his house.

Q. Did you help to burn his house, shoot his daughter, kill Calvin McCoy, and wound his wife Mrs. McCoy or did you advise or encourage anybody else to do it? A. No sir, I did not. Q. You heard the testimony of Mr. James McCoy the other day against you? A. Yes sir. Q. Do you remember when you were brought to Pikeville Kentucky? A. Yes sir, they kidnapped me from West Virginia.

Q. Who brought you there? A. A.P. Ellis and a man named Cunningham. Q. Did they bring you into Kentucky? A. Yes sir, they kidnapped me from West Virginia. Q. Without your knowledge or consent? A. Yes sir. Q. Did they have any extradition papers, if you know? A. No sir, they had no papers.

Q. After you were brought to Pikeville, were you arrested by anyone, if so by whom? A. Mr. Keel read the warrant to me. Q. Who was present besides Mr. Keel? A. Mr. McCoy. Q. Did you say there that you did the killing? A. No sir, I said I was not there.

*Q. **After the killing, did you know of any men invading West Virginia, for the purpose of or attempt to kill persons who were supposed to be connected with the different facts of the feud between the Hatfield and McCoys? A. Yes sir, one raid they come over from Pike County, and killed Jim Vance and next they killed Dempsey.***

Q. What was your information as to what would be done with you, if brought to Kentucky? A. I thought they would kill me that night. Q. Were you under the information and had you heard anything to make you afraid when you [were] put in jail at Pikeville? A. Yes sir.

Q. Tell what you said to James McCoy? A. As well as I remember, "I says, I saved your life once, now you can save mine." He said I need not be uneasy, that I would get nothing but the law. I told him I was willing to take a life sentence in the penitentiary, and that was bad enough. I told him that because I thought they would murder me.

Q. Did you admit to him there or any other time that you participated in the killing of Alifair McCoy? A. No sir, I did not. Q. At that time, did you know you were indicted for the killing of the other McCoy boys? A. Yes sir, I had heard that there was an indictment against me. Q. When Mr. McCoy came to the jail, did he come voluntarily or did you send for him? A. I do not remember now when I seen Mr. McCoy and told him that I would be mistreated; I told him I could rely on what he said. Q. You said that you save Jim's life once, tell how this was? (Pltf objects – (State)

*Q. Was Mr. McCoy among or with the invading parties that went into West Virginia on the occasion mentioned ago? A. Yes sir, they told me he was, I did not see him. **Q. Do you know whether or not Mr. McCoy has visited in that country frequently for the last ten years or at his will? A. No sir, I*** *think not. Q. Do you know whether or not, there is any indictment pending against him there for murder? A. Yes sir, he is indicted for murder.*

Q. Do you know Col. Bill Smith? A. Yes sir, I know him. Q. I ask you before adjournment if you knew Bill Smith? A. Yes sir, I know him. Q. Was he ever at your father's house? A. Yes sir, I have seen him there. Q. I will ask you if you saw him there after the burning of Randolph McCoy's house, and talked to him under a beech tree? A. No sir, I did not; after the burning of the house, on the 18th of March following, I went to the west, and stayed 32 months; that was before my father moved. When I left the family was at the mouth of Peter Creek. On the 12th of the March I started out west to Washington Territory. I was not at home at that time. Q. Why did you go to Washington Territory? A. I went there to keep out of trouble. Q. Was that after they had made the raids over there and killed Vance and Dempsey? A. Yes sir, it was after that. Q. And you remained there 32 months? A. Yes sir, as near as I remember.

Q. So you were not there at the time Bill Smith recollects the conversation under the beech tree? A. No sir, I left on the 12th of March and stayed thirty-two months.

Q. You heard the testimony of C.C. Fannin? A. Yes sir. [C.C. Fannin, never identified before in any feud trial testified that Johnse admitted to being at the raid, and that Jim Vance was said to be present. C.C. Fannin had his own court issues in Floyd Co. for swindling pensioners[42]]

Q. Tell the jury if at Logan Courthouse at Mr. Hatfield's hotel in an upper room, you said or told him that you were shot in the shoulder by Randolph McCoy? A. I never seen him at Logan Courthouse. I seen him at Mingo, at Williamson, and that is the only time I remember of seeing him since he left Blackberry. Q. What business did he have under consideration, when you saw him in Mingo County? A. I think we first employed him to defend Cap Hatfield, we wanted attorneys from that county, and there was some talk about getting the indictments thrown out. He said he could get them thrown out for $500.00. Q. Then you never did see him at Logan? A. I never did. Q. Did you hear the testimony of Frank Hatcher, and Cline? A. Yes sir.

Q. Did you tell them in a conversation mentioned by them, or elsewhere, that you would not have gone up to Randolph McCoy's house that night if you had not been drunk? A. No sir.

---

[42] Big Sandy News 1909 - United States Court – Will Convene on Next Monday – On the next Monday morning the United States District Court for the Eastern district of KY, will convene here and will be presided over by Judge Cochran. The term is like to be a brief one, there being, however, some cases of considerable importance to be tried. The case which will be that of government against C.C. Fannin, which is docketed for trail at an early date during the term. The defendant in the case is charged with having overcharged a couple of applicants for pension with excessive fees, which acting in the capacity of a notary public, in securing their pensions. It is further alleged by the government that he further aided in establishing a couple of claims that are alleged to be fraudulent.......
One of those cases is said to be that of Nancy Finley....another Elizabeth Muncey.

Q. Did you tell them or either of them, that you were there that night, or you was shot by Randolph McCoy? A. No sir, I did not. Q. Do you know Whitt? A. Yes sir, I have seen him; I used to be there, I am well acquainted with him. Q. For two or three days before you heard the house had been burned, was Mr. Whitt with you? A. No sir, the last time I seen Mr. Whitt, I do not know whether it was September or August before this murder you are trying me for was done. I saw Dan Whitt on Moss Creek; it was in September or three weeks after John Wright had made a raid over there and tried to capture us people. I saw Dan Whitt and Henry Mitchell. I cannot state whether I seen him at Pike or not. Q. Then he was not with you, and did not run away to keep from coming over there? A. No sir.

Q. Do you know Williamson who testified here today? A. No sir. Q. Did you ever have a conversation with him at the place he mentioned? A. No sir, I never did. Q. Did you there in the presence of your brother say or complain that Randolph McCoy had shot you in the shoulder? A. No sir, I did not. Q. Do you know Gearheart who testified against you here? A. No sir, I never seen him. Q. Did you ever have a conversation with him? A. No sir, I never did.

Q. Did you tell him while you were logging in West Virginia, for Levi Adkins that Randolph McCoy shot you in the shoulder? A. No sir, I never did tell him that. I did not work one day for Levi Adkins. I worked for a man named Levi Stephenson, and he, I think worked for Levi Adkins.

Q. Did you tell Bill Smith in a braggadocio way, about the fight where that occurred, and that Randolph McCoy run out of the house, and that your gun hung or you would have killed him? A. No sir, I did not. Q. Did you tell Allen Cline that if you had all the McCoy's in one heap that you could burn them? A. No sir, I did not. Q. Did you tell Captain Bill Smith, that it was you that killed Calvin McCoy? A. No sir, I never told him any such thing.

Q. In Speaking of being up the branch with your brother Bob when you got shot, if anybody else was present, tell who it was? A. Troy, Bob, Ellis, Charlie Harris, Marion Porter, and Sam Ferguson. Q. That you say was about two weeks before McCoy's house was burned? A. Yes sir, on the 20th of December.

Q. When was you arrested and brought to Pikeville? A. As well as I remember it was 18 of July.

Q. When did you leave there? A. Sometime in September. Q. Where did you go the first day after leaving there? A. Prestonsburg. Q. How long did you stay there? A. I came here about 8 o'clock that night, stayed until next day and next night, and on that morning, I was taken to Lexington. Q. How long did you stay at Lexington, and when was you brought back here? A. I believe it was the 5th day of January.

Q. When you left Pikeville and after you got here, did you see Jim McCoy here? A. He overtook me on the way some distance above here, and Mr. Leslie. Q. Did you see them or either of them in Prestonsburg? A. Mr. Leslie came along; I do not remember of seeing McCoy. I cannot say whether I did or not. Q. A few days afterward you were took to Lexington? A. Yes sir, the jailor told me they were going to take me to Lexington.

Q. Do you remember who was at your fathers house, the night of the dance spoken of? A. Cap, Bob, John Davis, Preston Roberts, Jake Roberts, Jack Cline, Charles Harris, Malan Prater, Sam Ferguson, John White, Thomas Hardin, Jack Mullins, John Jackson, my sisters Mary, Nancy, Betty, some others, I do not remember, it has been so long ago.

Cross Examined by Kirk

Q. How long had you known Jim and Randolph McCoy, before the burning of the house? A. I cannot tell how long. Q. Are you acquitted with the boys of Randolph McCoy, and how many of them? A. I was acquainted with some. Q. What ones did you know? A. I knew Jim, Tolbert, Farmer, and Calvin.

Q. Was you well acquainted with Calvin, Tolbert and Farmer? A. I was well acquainted with Farmer, better than I was with Tolbert. Q. How old was young Randolph McCoy? Did you know him? A. I have seen him. Q. Where did you see him? A. I saw him once when he was arrested for killing my uncle. Q. Was you in the crowd that helped to arrest him? A. No sir, I saw him on Blackberry in West Virginia.

Q. Where in West Virginia? A. Up at the schoolhouse. Q. Who was with him? A. There was a good many people. Q. Was his brother with him? A. Two of them were. Q. Where did you go? A. Up to the meeting. Q. What time did you leave the schoolhouse? A. Before dark. Q. Did you see the boys anymore that night? A. No sir. Q. What went with them? A. I heard they were killed. Q. Where? A. In Kentucky. Q. How were they killed? (Deft counsel objects. Sustained)

Q. Do you remember when these boys were under arrest, about the year? A. I cannot tell you. Q. How long before the McCoy house was burned? A. I do not know. Q. What night, give the date the boys were killed? A. I cannot. Q. Do you remember the year? A. No sir. Q. Do you remember the month? A. It was in August. Q. Do you know where you stayed that night? A. Yes Sir. Q. Do you know where you stayed the next New Year's night after that? A. No sir. Q. Do you know where you stayed the next after that? A. On Beech Creek. Q. Are you sure? A. To be the best of my knowledge I was. Q. Give an idea how long it was until the time the house was burned from that time? A. I cannot do that Mr. Kirk. Q. Do you know that you stand indicted together with Cap, Anderson, and a number of parties, for the murder of them boys? A. I have heard that we were. Q. Why is it you cannot remember that? A. It was in August, I can not remember the day. Q. Why is it you can remember that and cannot remember the other? A. The reason I remember it was New Year's night, I knew where I was then.

Q. I will ask you if it was not about six [five} years after the first killing until Randolph McCoy's house was burned, and the killing took place there? A. I cannot remember that. Q. Do you know whether or not the parties indicted with you, were arrested before McCoy house was burned? A. I heard of some parties being arrested.

Q. Who was it? A. Wall Hatfield, Sam Mahorn, Sam Massey, and a man by the name of Chambers. Q. How long was that before the house was burned and the woman killed? A. I cannot answer? Q. Was it before the house was burned? A. I think Chambers was arrested before anybody was killed but whether anybody else was, I cannot state. Q. I will ask you if they were not holding an examining trial at Pikeville at the time the house was burned for the killing of the boys in 1882? A. I think as well as I remember Chambers, Massey, were probably arrested for some offense was committed.

Q. You speak of a great many raids being made over there in West Virginia, was any raids made from 1882 until the time of the last killing in 1888, or was it not after the last parties killed, that the raids were made? A. I suppose it was after the last murder was committed. Q. Did a number of parties come over to arrest the parties after the killing of the boy and girl Alifair? A. I suppose so.

Q. Then it was after these three boys were killed, and Jim McCoy sister was killed, that he took part in these raids? A. I never seen Jim McCoy. I guess it was. Q. You speak of Jim McCoy being indicted for murder, what do you know about it? A. I seen the indictment. Q. Who are the witnesses? A. Ellis.

Q. When were the men killed that you speak of on the raids and how were they killed if you know? A. I cannot state. Q. Did not Jim McCoy go over there after his brother and sister was killed? To arrest the parties who committed the crime and upon arrest in a general fight while an arrest was trying to be made? A. I do not know I heard about it.

Q. What was you afraid about you had done nothing to be killed for had you? A. No sir. Q. Where did you go when you left the country? A. To Washington Territory. Q. Did you go anywhere else? A. I was in British Columbia. Q. Anywhere else? Were you in Canada? A. Yes sir. Q. How long did you stay there? A. I took an ocean liner from there, went to West Minster.

Q. I will ask you if you did not have the report sent back to this country that you was dead? (Counsel for the deft objects which is overruled and the deft excepts) A. A friend of mine told me he sent that report. Q. Where was that? A. In Washington Territory. Q. How long was it after that that you came back? A. I cannot tell you. Q. What caused you to go there? A. To keep out of trouble. Q. Did you go to Canada to keep out of trouble? A. No sir, I did not go to Canada to stay. Q. Where have you been since you came back? A. In Mingo County, and Logan. Q. Who have you been with? A. My father. Q. Where have you stayed with or at home? Q. Do you know anything about those forts over there? A. I seen one over there. Q. Where did you see one? A. Above where I was arrested. Q. What kind of building was it? A. A round log building made of pine and oak. Q. What was kept in it? A. Not anything. Q. Who had it built? A. I cannot state, I was not there. Q. Whose land is it on? A. My fathers. Q. Did you stay in there any? A. No sir, I never did in my life.

Q. Where did you live at the time the house was burned and the children killed? A. Down on Grapevine. Q. How far from where your father lived? A. About three and one half miles. Q. How long had you been with your father up to that time before the killing? A. Pretty much all the time. Q. As much as two or three weeks before the house burning occurred? A. Yes sir. Q. Had Cap been with you too? A. We all stayed together. Us three had been staying together. **Q. Did you know Jim Vance? A. Yes sir, he was my great uncle. Q. Where did he live? A. He lived at Thacker. Q. Was he with you? A. Yes sir.**

Q. Was Bob married at that time? A. Yes sir. Q. Where did he live? A. He lived with my Pa. Q. Was Cap married? A. Yes sir. Q. Where did he live? A. His wife lived on Grapevine. Q. You all stayed together? A. Yes sir, pretty much all the time. Q. Did you have any guns? A. Yes sir. Q. What kind? A. 32 Winchester and a double barrel shot gun. Q. Did you have any pistols? A. Yes sir. Q. How many? A. One. Q. Did Cap have any guns? A. Yes sir. Q. How many? A. I do not remember. Q. What kind of guns were they? A. Winchesters and pistol. Q. Did Bob have any guns? A. Yes sir. Q. What did he have? A. 32 Winchester and a shotgun. I do not remember if he had a pistol or not. Q. Did your father have a gun? A. Yes sir. Q. How many? A. I cannot tell several. Q. Did you keep the guns all together at your fathers? A. I kept mine with me wherever I went. Q. Did you have these guns all together at the dance? A. Yes sir, we had several at the dance; I had nothing but a pistol. Q. Who lived nearest neighbor there at your fathers? A. I cannot tell you, he lived across the river.

Q. Who lives just above on the same side? A. Jack Mounts and another man named Williams. Q. Who lived below your father? A. He lived below. Q. How far was if from where Mounts lived down to where Cap lived? A. I never measured the distance. Q. Where did John Banks live at that time? Q. Do you know where he lives, where he come from that night to the dance? A. No sir. Q. Is it not a fact, that John Banks is a man of desperate character that has killed two or three men over there? (Counsel for defendant objects to the manner of cross-examination of the witness – to his arguing with him. Sustained)

Q. Where did Jack Cline live? A. On the river. Q. Where did Malan Prater live, up the river? A. Yes sir. Q. How far up? A. I cannot state; I do not know the distance. Q. Do you know where they had been staying lately? Is he one of the men who boarded the boat you were on in coming here at Whitehouse? A. Yes sir. Q. Did he speak to you when they came in? A. No sir. Q. Did any of them speak to you? A. No sir. Q. Where does Sam Ferguson live? A. I cannot tell you where he lives. Q. What about White? A. He was a stranger to me, I had seen him a time or two. Q. Do you know who come with him to the dance? A. I do not remember. Q. Did you notify him to be present at the dance? A. I did not notify anybody. Q. Was anybody invited to the dance? A. I suppose there was, that my father did not he was with us from the time that I was shot in the shoulder until the night, no neighbors were invited. Q. Do you know who was invited then? A. I think just several gathered in there at the dance. Q. Is it not a fact that White is a stranger and had just come over there?

Q. Do you know about him being arrested and taken back to Virginia for murder? A. I do not if he was. Q. Tom Hardin, was he there? A. On [blank] Branch. Q. How far was it to where he lived? A. I do not know. Q. Did you *notify him to be there that night? A. I did not invite anybody. Q. Is this same Tom Hardin charged with murder in Pike County? A. If he is I do not know anything about it. Q. Whose son was he, who is his father? A. Jack Hardin was his grandfather; I do not know whether he is (W) Rights son or not. Q. What time did he go there that night? A. I cannot tell. Q. How old was Tom Hardin, what kind of looking man was he? A. Very young. Q. Do you know where he is now? A. No sir. Q Charles Harris, was he there that night? A. Yes sir. Q. What time did he come there? A. I do not remember what time. Q. Who come with him? A. I cannot tell. Q. Where did he live? A. In Logan. Q. What part of Logan? A. On Island Creek.*

Q. How far from where Vance was? A. I cannot tell. Charley had been there some little time. I do not know how long. Q. Did he have any guns? A. No sir. Q. Jack Mullins where did he live? A. Jack came with Mr. Roberts. Q. Where did he live? A. I think he lived with Mr. Roberts. I am not sure. Q. How many times did you meet him? A. I do not know. Q. Was he invited to the dance? A. I do not know. Q. Do you know who is his father? A. No sir. Q. Is he a married man? A. I do not know. Q. Ellen Nelson, where did she stay? A. Around in the country. Q. Do you know where she is now? A. She is dead now. Q. Who was her father? A. I cannot tell. Q. Was she married or single? A. Single. Q. What time did she come? A. She was there when I came. Q. Was she staying at your fathers house? A. I do not know. Q. Nancy, how old was she at that time? A. I cannot tell. Q. Mary, your sister how old was she? A. I cannot state. Q. Do you know where these parties you have mentioned, your sisters are? A. They live on Island Creek at Pa's.

Q. Where are these men you have mentioned? A. I cannot state. Q. Where is Cap and Bob? A. Bobs lives at Wharncliffe. Q. Is Bob your brother the same one that went there that night to the dance with you, and who is indicted with you? A. Yes sir. Q. Is your father indicted jointly with you? A. Yes sir. Q. You say you were shot in the shoulder, give the correct date that Bob shot you? A. I think it was on the 20th of December. I am not sure. Q. How is it that you can remember the date of the burning of that house, and cannot remember the date that you was shot? A. .... No answer

Q. Where were you when you got shot? A. Up the hill, up the branch from my fathers house. Q. Was it cleared land? A. It was near some cedar bushes. Q. Tell the jury just how it happened? A. I was before Bob, and he let the gun go off; he was very close to me when the gun went off. Q. Was you going from or to the house? A. From the house. Q. Which was before? A. I was before. Q. Did you kill any rabbits? A. No sir. Q. Who else was with you when that occurred? A. Cap, Bob, Malan, Prater, and Sam Ferguson.

Q. Was White along? A. No sir. Q. Is this Malan Prater the same man you mentioned as being at the dance? A. No sir. Q. Were you then with Cap? A. Yes sir. Q. How long did you stay with Cap after you got wounded? A. Not very long. Q. Where did you go from there? From Caps? A. To my fathers. Q. How long did you stay there? A. Three or Four days. Q. Where did you go from there? A. Back to Caps. Q. How long did you stay at Caps before you went back? A. I do not remember.

Q. How long was it before you went to your fathers again? A. Not until New Years Night. Q. Where were you on Christmas day? A. Up on Whitts Branch. Q. After you was shot? A. Yes sir. Q. Did the shot give you any trouble? A. Yes sir. Q. What time did you go up to the dance? A. About dark. Q. Who came with you? A. Cap, Bob, and father. Q. Had they been with you in any of these rounds? A. Yes sir, we stayed together.

Q. What became of Prater after you got shot? A. He went somewhere else I do not know. Q. Did you see him anymore that night? A. No sir.

Q. **When your father left and went back to Vance's, [from the party] did you go to bed at the dance? A. No sir.**

Q. Give your best impression; do you know what time Christmas come, what day? A. No sir, I do not know. Q. To reference your memory, was not on New Year's night, on Sunday night? A. I do not know.

Q. Did your father have dances on Sunday night? A. If there was enough there we did. Q. Who was the man that told you of this trouble the next day? A. Jerry Hatfield. Q. Where is he now? A. He is dead.

Q. Where were you at when he told you? A. At Pa's. Q. Did he come there the next morning? A. Yes sir, about ten o'clock. Q. Where did you go after he told you that? A. I first went to Pidgeon. Q. Whose house did you stay at? A. I did not stay at anybody's house. Q. Where did you stay at? A. I laid out. Q. Where did you stay before that time? A. We had been laying out for three weeks from the time John Wright came over there until I left the country. Q. Did you lay out all the time? A. Yes sir. Q. Did you stay at your fathers house? A. No sir. Q. Why? A. I was afraid. Q. Did Bob and Cap go with you? A. Yes sir. Q. Did Malan Prater dance any that night? A. I think he did. Q. Did he pick the banjo any? A. I do not remember anyone picking the banjo but Bob. Q. Did Bob take the Banjo with him when he left? A. No sir. Q. Do you know John T. Butler? A. Yes sir. Q. I will ask you if you did not say in his presence and in the presence of James Hatcher and other parties "that you would prove that Cap Hatfield shot you in the shoulder?" A. No sir, I do not think I did; I might have misspoke it. Q. Where was Cap Hatfield at that time? A. I suppose he was in Logan jail. Q. You give it as your best impression that you did not say it was Cap who shot you? A. Yes sir that is my impression. The defendants counsel enters a motion to exclude the testimony in regard to the defendant bearing arms. The motion is overruled and the defendant excepts.

John White

Q. Do you remember of hearing of Randolph McCoy's house being burned? Q. Where were you the night before? A. At Anderson Hatfields. Q. State to the jury how you came to be there, how long you were there, and who you saw there? A. I was there all night. I came very late. I was a stranger, and did not know where I was. They took me in and I stayed until the next morning when I left. Q. What was going on there that night? A. I think there was a dance, somewhere there that night. I went down to where they were dancing. Q. Did you see the defendant there? A. Yes sir, I think I did. Q. How often and how much did you see him there? A. He was there when I went to bed. Q. What time did you go to bed? A. About 10 o'clock. Q. When you woke the next morning, was he there or gone? A. He was there, I think sir. Q. What was his condition there that night if you notice it? A. He appeared to be a little stiff I think; he was not moving around a great deal. Q. How many persons were there that night? A. I cannot tell all, I could tell some. I was introduced to a man named Hardin, another man or two, I do remember their names. I had introduction to another man I think by the name of Prater. Q. Was Mr. Hatfield away long enough to travel 18 or 20 miles, and get back in the condition he was in? A. I think not. Q. You say he appeared to be stiff, did you see anybody dressing any wounds? A. I think I seen his mother working on him a little. Q. Tell what she was doing? A. I cannot tell; he appeared to be very sore about his shoulders, and she was washing him or something of that kind. Q. Did you ask them what they were doing? A. Yes sir, they said they were dressing the shot that he received by his brother. Q. That was on the night, before the house was burned? A. I reckon it was, I heard of it after I left there.

Sam Ferguson

Q. Do you remember of hearing of Randolph McCoy's house being burned? A. Yes sir. Q. Where were you at that time? A. At Anderson Hatfields. Q. Had you been at Anderson Hatfields the night before? A. Yes sir. Q. Who was there? A. Johnson Hatfield, Bob Hatfield, Cap, and the old lady, another lady and a few others; I do not know who they were. Q. During that time was Johnson Hatfield there? A. Yes. Q. From dark then up till you went to bed, Johnse was not away from the house where the dance was going on? A. No sir. Q. Was he away long enough to go nine miles, and participate in the fight and return? A. No sir. Q. If you know tell his condition? A. Yes sir, he was shot in the shoulder. Q. Did you see the wound? A. No sir, I do not think I did. Q. Did you see them doctoring it? A. Yes sir. Q. How long before that if you know did he sustain that injury? A. Two weeks I think. Q. Were you there when he got hurt? A. Yes. Q. Do you know the circumstances under which it was done? A. Yes, we were up the branch hunting, several of the boys along, Cap, Bob, Malan Prater, and several of the boys, when I heard the gun fire, and saw Johns on the ground shot. Q. Upon examination did you find that he was hurt? A. Yes sir.

Malan Prater took the stand, testifying that he attended a dance and that Johnse was present all night at his Pa's. Prater stated that he was present when Johnse was shot by the younger brother of Johnse, Robert Hatfield while hunting rabbits. Beyond who slept where and with whom, and what house, this testimony is about slamming accusations of intent to discredit, which is the prosecution's job. The counsel for the defendant also did his job. The defense attorney asked Prater who he is related to? Prater told Harkins that he is related to the McCoys and that Jim McCoy had threatened his life if he testified for the defendant. Prater testified that Jim McCoy visited his home and made threats. But the offense is on, Mr. Kirk slams back by asking how many pistols did Prater bring with him to court. Prater answers, *none*. In defense, Mr. Harkins asks, *do you know how many [guns] the McCoy brought with them*. Malan worked for Jim Vance in 1886, yet he was a relative of the McCoy's.

Malan Prater

Q. Do you remember of hearing of the burning of McCoys house? A. Yes sir. Q. Where were you the night the house was burned? A. At Anderson Hatfields. Q. How long did you stay there? A. All night. Q. Did you see Johnse anywhere that night? A. Yes sir. Q. Where was he? A. He was there. Q. How much of the night were you there? A. Might near all night, until four o'clock. Q. How much of that time did you see Johnse there? A. All the time.

Q. Since you came here, has anyone made you any threats, about your testimony in this case, tell who it was? A. Jim McCoy said he would have me arrested and put in jail if I testify. Q. How soon after you came here? A. The next day. Q. What day did you come here? A. Sunday. Q. Was it on Monday he said this to you? A. Yes sir. Q. If the defendant Hatfield at the time you were at his father's house the night it is claimed Mr. McCoy's house was burned, was suffering from any wounds tell what you saw? A. Yes sir, he was suffering very much, he was shot. Q. When did he receive the wound? A. It was in December before. Q. How long before? A. I think about two weeks. Q. If you know how he received that would tell how it was? A. Me and Johnse and his brother Bob said the night before the we would go hunting the next day. We went up the hollow. Johnse was walking before and was next to me; the gun fired, and shot him. Q. You say you know Randolph McCoy? A. Yes sir. Q. Did you ever buy a gun from him? A. Yes sir. Q. What kind was it? A. A 32 Winchester. Q. Did you have any conversation with him? A. Yes sir. Q. What did he say? A. He was telling me about shooting Johnse, and I told him Johnse was not there. He said he did not know whether it was Johnse or Hense Chambers. He said he did not know which. Q. Where was this conversation? A. At Pikeville at his home.

Re-examined by Harkins

Q. You say you did not have that talk about killing Calvin? A. No sir. Q. Are you a relative to any of these parties? A. Yes sir, to the McCoys. Q. Since you come to town, has anyone said anything about being at your house since you left? A. Yes sir, Jim McCoy said he had been to my house, if I swore in this case, he would kill me, and I would not leave this house but he would put me in jail.

Re-cross examined by Kirk - *Q. How many pistols did you bring with you? A. None.*

Re-examined by Harkins - *Q. Do you know how many McCoys brought with them? A. No sir.*

At this point in the trial, the defense brings in the interrogatories of Anse, Cap, Troy, Elias, and Robert. All stated that Johnson was shot in the shoulder by Robert (Bob) Hatfield about two weeks before Christmas. They stated that on the night of New Year's Eve, there was a dance at Anse's home, and that Johnse was there all night. All of these testimonies are so close, we will only include Anse as a witness. Bob said he played the banjo the night of the dance. He admitted to shooting Johnse and that the scar was the size of a silver dollar. The interrogatories were taken by Joe Simpkins, a notary of the public. Simpkins signed off on these testimonies on Sept. 19, 1898. The Hatfield interrogatories were then turned over to the Pike County court. The prosecution and Jim McCoy had plenty of time to prepare for this trial before the trial was granted to Floyd County, by Change of Venue.

Interrogatory of Anse Hatfield

Thereupon came the defendant Johnson Hatfield and read as evidence on his behalf the deposition of Anderson Hatfield, Cap Hatfield, Bob Hatfield, Elias Hatfield, Troy Hatfield, and read as evidence upon his behalf, the affidavit of himself as to what he, Nancy Bell Vance, and Mary Simpkins would swear if present as witnesses; and the affidavit to himself showing what the testimony of Sam King would be if he were present in court.

Q. State your age, residence and whether or not you are acquainted with Johnson Hatfield who is charged with the murder of Alifair McCoy? A. My age is sixty years; my residence is in Mingo Co., W.Va. I am.

Q. So you remember about the time Randolph McCoys house burned and Alifair McCoy killed on Blackberry Creek, Pike County, that is, do you remember hearing of the occasion? A. I do, I was told of the occasion by one of the Ferrell's on the 2nd day of January 1886. [The reason 1886 year is used was because when the prosecutor sent the questions to Logan Clerk, he used the year 1886, so throughout the testimony of all the Hatfields, they too use the year 1886].

Q. At the time the killing was said to have been done on New Years night 1886, where was the defendant Johnson Hatfield if you know? A. Johnson Hatfield was at my house at the mouth of Peter Creek, Logan County WV. Now called Delorme, Mingo County WV., on the night that Randolph McCoy's house was said to have been burned and the killing of Alifair McCoy said to have occurred he was at my house the time that Calvin McCoy was said to have been killed as I have always been informed that they were killed on New Years night 1886, Johnson Hatfield was at my house all that night.

Q. How long before and how long after the night mentioned was he at or near your house and how often did you see him during the time? A. He was at or near my house from six to twelve months. I do not remember the exact length of time as it has been so long ago. I saw him every day in at least two months before that time and I think it was four or five months afterwards, I saw him most every day.

Q. How far is the place you then lived and where Johnson Hatfield was from the house of Randolph McCoy there at the time? A. It was nine or ten miles from nearest route.

Q. Before and at the time of said killing of Alifair McCoy was the defendant Johnson Hatfield wounded? A. He was wounded about two weeks before. Q. Where was the wound located and what was the nature of it? A. it was located in the back part of the right shoulder. The wound was considerable size, there being a large hole torn in his shoulder by the explosion or discharge of a shotgun. Q. So you know how he received said wound; if so please state it? A. Bob Hatfield accidentally shot him in the shoulder with a shotgun. I saw and helped dress the wound in few minutes after it was made. Q. How long was this before New Years night 1886? A. It was about two weeks before.

Cross Interrogatory of Anse Hatfield

Q. What is your age, occupation and place of residence? A. My age is sixty, by occupation I am a farmer. My residence is near Devon, Mingo Co. W.Va. Q. Are all your statements in the foregoing answers made from your personal knowledge. If not, which of them are made form information or belief and what is the source your information or the foundation of your belief? A. They are made from personal knowledge. Q. Have you any interest in the action direct or indirect. If any what is it? A. Johnson Hatfield is my son, all the interest I have is that he may have fair trial, that justice be administered to him, and the law vindicated. Q. Have you stated all you know concerning this action. If not, state what you have omitted? A. I have stated all that I know. If there be anything more, I do not remember at this time. And further, the deponent sayeth not. Anse Hatfield.

In the jury instruction number 2, it read; *the mentioned parties* **with Johnson Hatfield are named as Cap Hatfield, Robert Hatfield, Ellison Mounts, French Ellis, Elliot Hatfield, Charles Gillespie, and Thomas Mitchell in killing Alifair McCoy** *and the jury believes from the evidence that either one of the said parties so killed the said Alifair McCoy and the same was not done in the necessary or apparently necessary self-defense of the accused or of those action with him. They will find him guilty of willful murder and fix his punishment at death or by confinement in the penitentiary for life in their discretion.*

Johnse was sentenced to the penitentiary and Jim Vance was not named in the above as a participant.

Observation: The court never writes the name, with ink, that Jim Vance was part of the raid in ANY legal document. There are no good reasons for this exclusion. Dead men can be named in testimony and legal documents. I completely comprehend that Jim wouldn't have had a summons or warrant, you can't serve a dead man. But, when it comes to trial testimony by the men who are testifying, like Jim and Randal McCoy, Jim Vance was never mentioned at this opportune time to cross their T's and dot their I's. Most feud books want to blame the killing of Calvin and Alifair on many things other than drunken men. More than likely, a combination of things caused those killings, such as being hunted by bounty hunters and having to sleep with their Winchesters. These men took action to squash and silence Randal McCoy to stop the torment of being hunted, not to silence Randal for what he could testify to from the 1882 three McCoy killings. He witnessed nothing. They wanted to silence Randal from pushing the *indictments* against them for those killings.

For us, questions arose as to James Vance and his introduction into the feud. Why didn't the defense lawyers bring up in court that Ellison Mounts had been hanged for his confession "of guilt." And, IF Jim Vance were truly guilty, why didn't the defense attorneys place the blame on Vance in their proceedings? For goodness sake they had a confession. Why was Mary Vance, who was summoned[43] two, maybe three times, in Pike Court to testify, dropped from the court listed deponents in the trial of Valentine Hatfield? I suspect, that her testimony was not one that they wanted the public to hear. Mounts confession, was never read in the court, and was not part of the trial. It is part of Governor Buckner's, correspondence files, and was not part of any trial transcripts.

Sam McCoy, a participant in the feud wrote and printed his version of the feud in 1931, and titled his book, *Squirrel Hunting Sam*. On page 34 of his telling, Sam tells how they came upon Jim Vance and Cap Hatfield on Thacker Mountain, and that only **one of them** had a gun. Sam said, *"If Jim would have kept still, he would not have been harmed."* A couple of paragraphs later, on page 35 of this book, he stated that Vance fired on Phillips. Sam said they shot Cap's gun from his hands. Which was it, did Jim have a gun or not? I believe Mary would have answered that question if allowed to testify in Valentine Hatfield's trial. Sam McCoy, who was still alive, and summoned, didn't show for the trial of Johnse in

---

[43] Commonwealths Witnesses - Randolph McCoy, Sarah McCoy, Albert Varney, Thos. Fraley, Sam Simpkins, Dan Whitt, Mary Vance, Nancy Hatfield, David Damron, Ada McCoy, Fannie McCoy, Mont Stafford. - S.G. Kinner, Commonwealths Attorney - Filed in open Court this 24 day of Aug. 1888.

1899. Yet, he wrote about the events thirty two years later and is asking us to believe his version. Remember, Squirrel Hunting Sam McCoy was indicted for murder, not once, but three times in his lifetime, with other misdemeanor charges in Pike Court books. In Logan, he was indicted, then acquitted, for the murder of Bill Staton. Then in Logan, in May of 1888, Sam was indicted for the murders of James M. Vance and William Dempsey, but he never stood trial for the other two murders. We think that Squirrel Hunting Sam loses any shred of credibility because his personal character is in question as to the events given, yet he doesn't bring up his own past in his manuscript. He tells about the night of the New Year's raid, disclosing that he told Calvin of the raid. He said that Calvin ignored his advice and stayed home, instead of leaving. If Calvin knew, why didn't he tell someone. If Randall knew, why didn't he take heed and get help from the constables of Pike County before this event ever happened? Since the Hatfields would have crossed into Kentucky, the constables had legal rights to arrest them under a warrant issued by the Kentucky authorities and Gov. Buckner. Yet, bounty hunters are said to be hunting the Hatfields, and Frank Phillips could have picked them off at Randal's home had Squirrel Hunting Sam McCoy told that to the Pikeville authorities! It's easy to catch the inconsistencies, but proving reality, is so much harder.

We may one day be proven wrong as new documents are found. As we see it, the murder of Jim Vance has been a cover-up to keep the McCoys out of prison. We can't remove Jim Vance from the feud. He has been deeply rooted into the stories and books, that his character, has evolved into the "crazy" Jim Vance written by others. He may or may not be guilty, we can't prove by the documents he is entirely innocent, or entirely guilty. It does not changed the facts; he was killed on his own property in front of witnesses. Jim was dead and easy to blame for all the troubles by many on both sides of the Tug. How does an old man, who, by the records, is never found guilty of a crime in his life time, end up as the instigator, the person blamed for the troubles in these books?

What we do know, is that the McCoys never stood trial for murder. They were afraid to face a Logan court, knowing they would have to prove their innocence. If the McCoy faction could have proven this, they could have given themselves up to the Logan authorities, just as Gov. Buckner wanted the WV feudist to do. Remember, Buckner wanted the Hatfields to face a court of law to prove their innocence. The McCoy faction knew they had warrants against them in West Virginia, for two murders. There were witnesses from the WV raid that said the posse shot old man Jim Vance without provocation. They (KY posse) never asked

Jim and Cap to give themselves up. Reliable witnesses stated that they just started firing until the old man Vance was dead. This is just our opinion, you have the trial testimony, draw your own conclusions.

Since the civil war has been a bone of contention by many regarding the feud, we need to discuss just what that means. Our next chapter is based on Jim Vance, his distant cousins from other parts of Virginia, and his nephew, Anderson Hatfield. You will read of their involvement during the civil war years.

June 23, 1865 - Pike County Page 531 – Commonwealth vs **James Vance***,
Ezekial Counts, King Counts Defendant} Horsestealing – ordered that a bench
warrant issue admitting the defendants to bail in the sum of $750.00 each.
Dec 3, 1865 - Pike County Page 563 – Commonwealth against* **Elijah Vance**
*& others Horsestealing– ordered that the five foregoing causes to continue with
alias warrants.*

In the Pike County Circuit Court Book, the above two entries are
shown for 1865. James Vance and Elijah Vance are mentioned as stealing
a horse during the civil war. Authors use this record to prove old James
Vance was in the war. These entries are cited by all of them. This is NOT
our James M. Vance mentioned in the 1865, Pike County Circuit Court
record. These entries also mention Captain Ezekiel Counts. Zeke was
with the 2nd Virginia State Line, Company B. The 2nd Battalion fell into
Mays 14th Battalion. They disbanded and fell into the 10th, also known as
Mays Company, or Mays-Trembles-Diamonds Yankee Chasers. On the
rolls for the 14th Kentucky Regiment [Appendix H] are Elijah, James H.,
William H., and Abner H. Vance. Per the pension record of James H.
Vance, he fought in the 2nd Virginia Regiment and can be found on a roll
in the Kentucky 10th Regiment on July 1, 1863[44]. This is the same
regiment as Ezekiel Counts. Elihu Jasper Southerland wrote in *Pioneer
Recollections* that Ezekiel Counts signed men mainly from Russell,
Tazewell, and Wise VA. Sutherland states that the 21st Virginia Calvary
had become 2nd Virginia State Line and many of the 2nd Regiment joined
the 10th Kentucky and the 14th had already become the 10th. These same
Vance men joined the 14th, and are moving about within these regiments.
The men are representative of Sutherlands synopsis.

Per Judge William Southerland - Ezekiel K. Counts - Company B, 2nd
Virginia State Line: Zeke (Ezekiel) enlisted at Sand Lick, Buchanan
County on March 28, 1863. Zeke Counts was elected Captain of
Company F on April 1, 1863 and deserted on Nov. 4, 1863. After the war,
he later moved to Jackson County, WV. The Skeen-Counts gang had
been accused of killing Nathaniel Cunningham in 1877, brother to Dan
Cunningham, the bounty hunter. E.K. Counts is found in Commissioners

---

[44] Kentucky Archives Adjunct Generals Report

Book 1[45] of Logan County. E.K. Counts acquired a liquor license for selling spirituous liquor in 1867 right after the war. The establishment name is unknown. It is listed as being Cline land. It looks inevitable that Anse Hatfield and Jacob Cline Jr., after the war, had some knowledge of Ezekiel Counts during the war, as well did the Vance men of Virginia. Aly Hatfield sold land to Counts[46].

To further show the Vance men of the 2nd, 10th, and 14th, we have given a small synopsis of their accounts per court and pension records. James H. Vance is the man with Ezekiel Counts, and Mays Regiment.

James H. Vance, 22nd Co. D, Calvary Regiment and 2nd VSL (per pension) and on July 1, 1863 enlisted in the 14th Calvary (a.k.a. Company I, 10th Kentucky), per the pension of James H. Vance of Tazewell filed on July 3, 1900, and at the age of 67 years of age, was earning $15.00 a month. Then, he filed a second time in 1908, stating that he was earning $30.00 a month in pension. James said he fought in the 2nd Virginia and 22nd Virginia Regiments on both applications. He never mentioned the 10th Kentucky Mays Regiment. Now, following the evolutionary pattern as Elijah, William, and John G. Vance, he did fight in the 10th Kentucky. The 22nd Virginia Calvary shows James H. on its rolls. We know that James H. Vance is the son of William and Nancy Vance. James H. married Eliza Elswick on February 10, 1853 in Tazewell County. During the war, and after the war, James goes by the name of Harvey Vance up until 1910. His official pension paper lists him as James H. Vance. This James is the man who was in Ezekiel Counts Battalion and Mays 10th Kentucky Regiment.

Another interesting item, James Harvey Vance and wife Eliza had a connection to Pike County. Eliza and her husband attended the marriage of her son, Robert Elswick, to Mariah Miller, signed by Robert Elswick

---

[45] Commissioners Book – Logan Co. Dec. Meeting 1867 (Page 53) - Resolved that E.K. Counts be allowed to retail spirituous liquors near the mouth of Pond Creek for three months from this date, said Counts enter into Bond from this date, said Counts enters into Bond $500.00 with John Buchanan security as the law decrees. (Page 65) Feb 1868 Meeting - Resolved that E.K. Counts license for liquor retailing, transferred from mouth of Pond, to Perry Clines opposite the mouth of Peters Creek.

[46] Case 072-00015 WV Archives. Warren Alderson vs Aly Hatfield. In Logan County Aly Hatfield had sold E.K. Counts land on Mate Creek of Tug River. That land was sold to Ellison Hatfield. "also to the said Aly Hatfield and wife conveyed by deed to E.K. Counts the following tract containing 30 acres, situate on the waters of Mates Creek, tributary of Sandy River" "also a tract of said lands containing 100 acres, "situate on Mates Creek" also a tract containing 50 acres, which Counts conveyed to Elias Hatfield.

and M.C.W. Swords on Raccoon Creek, dated June 26, 1865, at the home of Mrs. Cecil, per marriages of Pike County by Clyde Runyun. That bond was witnessed by Eliza Vance, Elisha Bird, and Harvey Vance (James Harvey Vance), in the presence of L.D. Yost, and Thomas Smith. Judge William Cecil of Pike County owned land on Raccoon Creek. William Cecil was in a controversy over that land with a Randolph McCoy in 1850 (Ky Case 1018) and in 1858 (KY Case 1512) This is land that was sold to William Cecil. As a coincidence, the marriage took place on June 25, 1865 and the horse stealing case for Commonwealth vs. James Vance, Ezekiel and King Counts, from the circuit books of Pike was entered June 23, 1865 in Pike County. The court case and the wedding occurred just two days apart, showing that this James H. Vance was in the area of Pike County at this time of the horse stealing warrant to appear.

Abner H. Vance, Co. I, 10th KY dated Jul. 1863; and 34th Virginia and 22 Calvary. Abner H. Vance, son of Elijah and Virginia Jane Matney Vance, was born July 7, 1836 in Tazewell Co., VA. He married Marinda Vance on January 8, 1858, daughter of William Vance and Nancy. Elijah Sr., who married Virginia Jane Matney, has been proven to be the son of Abner and Susannah Vance. Old Elijah Vance had many sons who fought in the civil war. In addition, what we will see is that many Vance men believed in the confederate cause. However, none owned slaves, which is important to state here. Conversely, many of the men mentioned in this book who fought for the union owned slaves. John Dils and Perry Cline both owned slaves, for example.

Elijah Alexander Vance, Company F, 21st Battalion April 5, 1862 mustered out Oct 26, 1862; Enlisted in Co. I of the 14th Kentucky on July 1, 1863; a.k.a. Co. I, 10th KY, Jul. 1863 listed for pension April 15, 1909, in the 10th Kentucky Regiment under Captain John S. Ratliff. He never mentions the 21st or the 34th regiments, but we know him to be in the 21st roll. His pension says he is 67 years of age, born March 28, 1841, and was born in Tazewell Virginia. His disabilities listed is a left arm partially paralyzed. Elijah said he enlisted in Buchanan County, September 2, 1861 and was in the service three years. He enlisted with G.B. Steel of Tazewell and Isaac Boyd of Buchanan Counties with Mathias S. Harman as compatriots in the service with him. Mathias S. Harman married Charlotte Vance. Mathias was in the 34th Regiment.

Chapter 6
PIKE COUNTY IN THE WAR

There are several cases that tell us about the war in Pike County, KY. James Honaker, of Mays 10th KY Regiment D, with others in April 27, 1863, was ordered to confiscate the property of Allan Maynard, at the sum of $646.00 with a dozen other men of the so-called Confederate States. Honaker was under the command of Col. A.J. May, per the testimony of Mays himself. Honaker was a scout and ordered to confiscate horses and other necessities for the purpose of carrying on the war against the north. Honaker took from Maynard a horse, a mule and a pair of boots. Honaker testified that Maynard was engaged as a Pike Home Guard, and that these items were hidden in the woods, in an old shanty. May and Honaker tell of the regimental need for horses and mules, which were turned over to the regiment, and not used for their own good. Col. A.J. May testified [civil case 2092] in March and April, 1863 that he was in the command of four or five companies of mounted men. He stated that James Honaker held the rank of Lieutenant with authority to raise a battalion of men on Feb. 7th, 1863, and was recognized as Company D. George R. Deskins was Captain. They were encamped on Coon Creek in Pike County in complete control of Pike County up to this time. Then in July, the Union Army had moved into Pike County, instituted Camp Brownlow, and caused havoc for the confederacy in the area.

From the book, "Expedition into Southwest Virginia", Chapter XXXV, starting on page 818-820 [Appendix F], is this report of an expedition in which Caudill[47], 10th Kentucky Battalion (Confederate), though May was still shown as being in command on the roll till July 1, 1863 and is mentioned in a battle against several union regiments on July 11th. One Union stronghold was the 39th Kentucky, along with an Ohio

---

[47] July 3-11, 1863 Expedition from Beaver Creek, Ky., into Southwestern Virginia, and skirmished (6th) at Pond Creek, Ky., and (7th) Gladesville, Va. Headquarters District of Eastern Kentucky - Pikeville July 8, 186 3- Dividing my force at this point, I went up to the State line, on Big Sandy River, in pursuit of the enemy, who fled precipitately beyond my reach. Detaching the Second Battalion Tenth Kentucky Calvary (Union), and the First Ohio Squadron (Union), I sent them through the Pound Gap, under Maj. John Mason Brown (Union), who attacked the enemy at Gladesville, killing 14, wounding 20, and capturing 127 prisoners, including the commanding officer (B.E.) Caudill (Confederate) and about 20 officers. In all our operations, thus far our loss had been 1 killed, 13 wounded, and 6 captured while on picket duty. Julius White Brigadier General

and Michigan regiment. Here are two neighboring counties fighting. May commanded the 10th Kentucky, which included the Vance men, as shown by the rolls, until July 1863.

Let us look at Kentucky Case File 2175, Richard Hatfield versus Peter Mullins. James Vance gives his testimony stating that he saw a horse at Peter Mullins and that it was not the same horse he had taken from Richard Hatfield in <u>Feb. of 1862</u>. He stated that he had taken a <u>grey trotting</u> mare, but it was not the same mare as the Mullins mare. He said he had traded that trotting mare off to Captain Levi Collins and that mare remained in the hands of Capt. Collins until March of 1864, when Samuel Bragg had deserted with that horse.

When the plaintiff, Mullins, asked James if the mares are one and the same horse, James said "No". He stated that he had captured a <u>pacing mare</u> in the <u>spring of 1863</u> in the western raids under General Jones. Collins and Vance say the second horse taken by James Vance was a different grey pacing horse captured in the spring of 1863 and sold in the fall of 1863 to Captain Collins.

A <u>grey trotting</u> horse did end up with Spencer Mullins, then to Henderson Mullins, and then finally to Peter Mullins, but this is not the same horse as the Hatfield horse captured in 1862. Two different horses captured at different times. What we can be sure of is that a James Vance captured two different horses at two different times during the war.

We "believe" this to be James M. Vance who says he lived 30 miles from Logan Court House in 1866. We know that our James knew Nancy Simpkins, a witness in this case, (2175) as being his niece through the Hatfields. Elizabeth Hatfield married Joe Simpkins. Nancy Simpkins is the mother of Joseph Simpkins (born 1844) who married Elizabeth "Betty" Hatfield (born 1836). Elizabeth is the daughter of Ephraim Hatfield and Nancy Vance and the sister to Anse Hatfield. We can find Nancy and Joseph in the 1860 Logan Census. A Joseph Simpkins would later place a very large bond for James Vance to assist him to become a WV Magnolia District Justice of the Peace in 1883. As well, a Joseph Simpkins would become an appraiser of James Vance Sr.'s estate in 1888. We can say that Witcher's troops had been in Pike in 1862, because of a court case found in the Kentucky Archives, "Goff versus Blankenship[48]".

---

[48] KY Archives Civil file 2305 Jun. 5, 1866 - Pike Cir. Ct - The pltf John B. Goff states and charges that on the 3rd day of Feb., the deft executed to him, this pltf an obligation here

KY Archives File 2175 - Richard Hatfield vs. Peter Mullins

The Sheriff of Logan County Greetings: <u>*We command you that you summon James Vance & Nancy Simpkins*</u> *to appear before the Judge of our Cir. Ct., of Logan Co., at the Court House of said County, on the first day of Oct., next to testify and the truth to speak of Peter Mullins in a certain matter of controversy before our said Court depending wherein Richard Hatfield is Plaintiff and said Peter Mullins is Defendant; and have then there this writ, and show how you have executed the same. Witness: Crispin L. Stone, Clerk of our Cir. Ct., of Logan Co., at the court house thereof, the 17th day of Sept. 1866, and in the third year of the state.*

The deposition of **James Vance** *taken in the 1st day of Oct. at the county seat of Logan County State of West Virginia in the clerk's office of said County to be read as evidence in an action between Richard Hatfield and Peter Mullins Defendant pending in the Pike Circuit Court, KY.*

The deponent James Vance after being duly sworn deposed and saith that; I took the gray trotting mare from Richard Hatfield in February 1862 and I traded her off in April or May 1862 to Capt. Levi Collins of the thirty-fourth Battalion of the Virginia Calvary, and said mare remained in the said command until March 1864 when Samuel Bragg a regularly enlisted soldier deserted said command and took said mare away with him.

Question by Complainant; at what time was you at the house of the defendant Peter Mullins?

Answer; In January 1865

Question by Complainant; did you see a gray mare at Peter Mullins house that said Mullins claimed and if so, did you or did you not know said mare?

Answer; I saw a gray mare at said Mullins house claimed by said Mullins. I

---

filed marked (A) which in as follows. Due J.B. Goff and J.T. Small one hundred and twenty five bushel of good corn to be paid next fall for a mare, and if Witcher or Deskins Company takes [the mare], they are to lose one half of the amount this the 3rd of Feb. 1862. Signed Wm. H. Blankenship. Pltf further charges that afterwards to wit; on 15 day of 1863. The deft became personally indebted to him J.B. Goff, which evidenced by a note a memorandum have filed marked (B) which is unpaid. The pltf states that on the obligation in this petition mentioned that the deft failed and refused to comply with his agreement filed on this. That he would not and did not pay unto this pltf in pursuance to his agreement of 125 bushels of corn as he bound himself to do. That this pltf alleges that Witcher nor Deskins Co. did not interfere or take the mare in this article mentioned but that deft kept quiet peaceable possession of said animal and converted to his own private uses. He further states that corn in the fall of 186_ was worth and was marketing at one dollar per bushel and citizens glad to purchase at that price. Now pltf alleged that the deft the late William left the county…to the state of Ohio….That when he left he was the owner of a certain tract or parcel of land lying and being in Pike County. On tributary of Big Creek. It being the same land that the deft purchased of James Deskins….John B. Goff June 5, 1866 *knew the mare well, for I had captured said mare in the spring of 1863, in the northwestern raid under Gen. Jones and traded her to Capt. Collins of the said 34th Battalion of the Virginia Calvary during the same spring.*

Question by Complainant; was the mare that you saw in Peter Mullins possession or was she not the same mare that you captured from Richard Hatfield?

Answer: It was not the same.

And further this deponent saith not. James Vance

And Levi Collins being of lawful age after being duly sworn deposed and saith that I traded with James Vance in the Spring of 1862 and got from him a gray mare that was called the Hatfield mare and shortly afterwards I traded said mare to one Samuel Reach a regularly enlisted soldier who shortly afterwards traded the said mare to Samuel Bragg of the 34th Battalion of the VA Calvary, and the said Bragg still owned said mare up to January 1864 at which time I was wounded at Bailey's Bridge near the Cumberland Gap and left the command.

Question by Complainant; Did you ever buy from James Vance any other mares besides the said Hatfield mare and if so what did you do with her.

Answer; In the spring of 1863 I bought from James Vance a pacing gray mare shortly after he captured her, sometime in the fall of 1863. I traded said mare to Spenser A. Mullins, traded her to Henderson Mullins and Henderson Mullins traded her to the said Peter Mullins, which mare is the same that is in controversy between Richard Hatfield and Peter Mullins.

And further the deponent saith not. Levi Collins

State of West Virginia, Logan County - Given under my hand this the 1st day of October 1866.

Crispin L. Stone Commissioner of Chancery

For the taking Deposition two half hours at .75 cents per hour 1.87; Issuing subpoena for witness .20

James Vance witness 1 day at one dollar per day 1.00

Traveling 30 miles going & same returning 60 miles at .5 cents per mile 3.00

Confirming records of the past is no easy task, especially when it comes to the civil war. West Virginia Civil War Rosters are scarce. After the war, part of a civil war soldier's record is a signed document wherein the soldier pledges his allegiance to this country. A James Vance(y) of the 34th Battalion swore allegiance in Charleston in April 1865. Other information per the record; his rank was a private. He was 27 years of age. His eye color was grey. His hair and his skin color were listed as light, and he was 5 foot 11 inches tall. This record says he was a Sergeant and not a Captain. I cannot confirm with any certainty that this is our James M., but there is a high probability that this is, indeed, our James Vance. The other James Harvey Vance can be found in Mays Regiment in 1863, while Elijah was in Witcher's Battalion and was listed in the

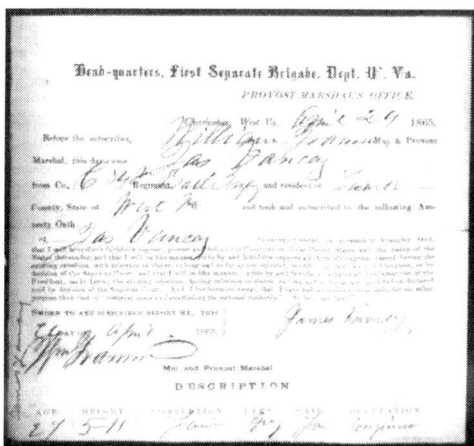

newspaper as one of the men who had deserted Witcher's Battalion, the 34th. So, it is possible that James H went from Witcher into May's Battalion at this time. James H. Vance was never listed in the 34th per his pension. That leaves only one other James Vance, who was at this time a younger lad in the Logan census.

If in fact it is our James M., then we can confirm that he never fought with Anse Hatfield in the 45th. James M. Vance was living in the Paynesville area for 10 years. We know from the tax records that James was paying taxes in McDowell, at this time, up until 1866. According to Tazewell Chancery Records, Mr. Peery is suing James Vance. In this 1866 case, our James was not to be located in McDowell. By this time, his brother, Richard had died in 1863, and his mother had disappeared after 1865/6. But, we don't find James M. Vance as owning any land in Pikeville, KY., or Logan, WV., at this time of 1866 to 1868. The first purchase of land is on Thacker Creek in Feb. 1869[49], when Mary acquired land from the heirs of David Mounts.

One significant piece of information was found in the amnesty papers of James Vance(y). The James Vance who is shown in 1865, said he was a resident of Tazewell, State of "West Virginia". When James M., received his land patent and deed in 1856, the land was then known as "Tazewell,

---

[49] Mounts to Vance} Deed – This deed made on the 27th day of Feb. in the year of 1869 by and between Alexander Mounts and Michael Mounts Sr. as administrators of David Mounts deceased of the first part and Mary Vance and her heirs of the second part all of the Co. of Logan and State of WV. Witnessed that the said parties of the first part for and in consideration of the sum of $100.00 to them in hand paid by the party of the second part.....On what is called Thacker Branch of the Tug Fork of Sandy River to wit. Beginning on the top of the ridge at what is called the Tobacco Fork of said branch. Running with the conditional line between John Ferrell and the said Mounts heirs so as to include the entire Mounts claims on said Thacker Branch to have and to hold the said tract of land with its appurtenances unto her the said Mary Vance and her heirs forever. The said Alexander Mounts & Michael Mounts will warrant the title to said land specially to the said Mary Vance and her heirs forever in witness whereof the parties of the first part have hereunto set their hands and seals the day and year first above written. Alexander Mounts & Michael Mounts

Virginia". Within a very short time, it is shown in the land books as Logan County, and within a few more years, the land is shown as McDowell County, West Virginia. In April of 1865, when the 34th disbanded at Lynchburg, his home would have been McDowell County, West Virginia. Was he confused and stated Tazewell County, VA? I am not sure why in April of 1865, in Charleston, a James Vance(y) would state the city as Tazewell and state as WV., when it never existed in 1865, but in fact did exist, per James' land patent in 1856. Now in this observation, James H. Vance did live in Tazewell, Virginia, but never mentioned Captain William Stratton in his pension papers. Therefore, as you can see, nothing should be taken for granted when it comes to the records. Stratton, of the 34th Battalion, said in 1863, WV Chancery records, he took his family to Tazewell where he stayed until after the war.

Private James Vance of the 34th Battalion Calvary, Virginia - Enlisted with William Stratton and appears on Muster Roll January 18 to June 30, 1862 – Dated: July 28, 1862. Enlisted: May 4 1862 – Where: Logan County, VA. - By Whom: Wm. Stratton - Period 3 years - Present

Private James Vance Company B 1st Battalion Virginia Mounted Rifles - Muster Roll: July 1 to Nov 30, 1862 – Dated: Dec 1, 1862 – Enlisted: May 4, 1862 – Where: Tazewell County, Virginia - By Whom: Capt. Stratton – Period; 3 Years - Last Paid: June 30, 1862 - Present

2nd Sergeant James Vance 34th Battalion Calvary Virginia - Company B, 1st Battalion Virginia Mounted Rifles - Muster Roll: Dec 1, 1862 to Feb 1, 1863 – Dated: Feb 1, 1863 – Enlisted: May 4, 1862 - Where: Tazewell - By Whom Capt. Stratton – Period: 2 years

Chapter 7
SOME HATFIELDS IN THE CIVIL WAR

Let us look at Anse's service in the Civil War in comparison to that of James Vance. Of all the civil war records found, not once is James and Anse mentioned together, in the same unit or otherwise. In the June Term of 1865, in Pike County, there is an entry for a murder charge;

Commonwealth vs. Rufus Baley [Bailey], Valentine Hatfield, Elias Hatfield, and Anderson Hatfield.

Thomas and Rufus Bailey can be found in Witcher's Battalion with a status of "deserted" according to a newspaper article printed in Abingdon VA., with the heading, Company C in 1st Battalion Virginia Mounted Rifles on Feb. 20, 1863[50]. This shows that the regiment was formed in Jan of 1862., along with E.V. Harman's Company. Rufus Bailey's records show that he joined Maj. Witcher on two different dates, June 18, 1862 [present] and Oct 1862 [absent dated June 1863]. Anse is NOT shown as deserted from Witcher's, just to be clear. Rufus Bailey owned land on Harts Creek in Logan County in 1855, with patent warrants 21514 [Wyoming] and 15330 [Huffs Creek Logan]. On the military rolls, Rufus shows up in Witcher's Company C, and a Thomas Bailey, who was later killed in action, was present. Witcher's Battalion Company C was never a company that Anse, Elias, or Elixious Hatfield fought under, according to their records. Bailey also shows up in the Mays 10th. Anse was listed with Company B of

---

[50] The article here from Abingdon in March 20, 1863 listed Company C; named its deserters. Regiment is found in Tazewell, per the news articles as its military encampment, the date of January 19, 1862, may be when the company had formed. Elias V. Harman, son of Nancy Vance Harmon was Company C., the Partisan Rangers. James Vance land warrants are recorded by Harman and can be found in Tazewell and McDowell. If James Vance were in the war, it would have been Company C.

the 45th Reg. Virginia, signed up by Capt. John Buchanan. Anse again is found in Company D, but absent, in 1864, when signed with B.H. Justice. When men changed companies it wasn't always tracked, so they could very well be seen as deserters of one company while possibly fighting within another company. We do not know who Bailey, Anse, Elias, and Valentine were thought to have killed, but we do know that they were indicted together.

In the KY Archives Criminal and Civil Case File 2049 Bazel Hatfield vs. Anderson Runyon - Pike Circuit Court, there is a person by the name of Capt. John Buchanan listed. This is the same John Buchanan that Anse enlisted under in the 45th Regiment of Virginia. It is possible that this company was assigned under Mays KY 10th, which is why Bailey and Anse are listed in the same Pike Co., indictment above. The KY 10th, Mays Battalion, was, according to the records, camped on Johns Creek and Coons Creek during 1863, and Col. A.J. May claimed this was his territory to protect. (He said Pike and below were part of his territory.) Not being a civil war expert, it's all conjecture, but we can place Capt. John Buchanan with the 10th Kentucky Calvary. So it's possible that Anse, even though not recorded on the rolls, may well have fought with Bailey and Buchanan in the 10th, as well as the Vance cousins.

Case 2049 - Bazel Hatfield Pltf vs. Anderson Runyon, Montaville Farler, John Gooslin, Joseph Smith, John Buchanan, William Ferris, Andrew McCoy, Moses Chafin Defts] Amended Petition - The Plaintiff Bazel Hatfield states by way of amendment to his original petition herein states that <u>John Murphy aided and abetted the defendants John Gooslin, Montaville Farler, Anderson Runyon, John Buchanan</u>, Wm. Ferrell, Andrew McCoy, Joseph Smith, Moses Chafin in <u>taking & carrying away the six head of fat hogs</u> as stated in his original petition wherefore he prays this be taken as an amendment to his original petition. The Plaintiff prays Judgment as in his original petition & other proper relief. B. Hatfield. Sworn before me May 21, 1866 Damron Clk.
Pike Cir. Ct - Bazel Hatfield Plaintiff against Anderson Runyon & others Defendant] Answer
The Defts Anderson Runyon & Montaville Farler & John Gooslin for answer to the Pltfs petition says that they were confederate soldiers under the command of John Buchanan in the <u>10th Rebel KY Calvary</u> and whilst in said service the said <u>Capt. Buchanan</u> did take a small lot of hogs, the property of the plaintiff, the number and value they do not know, they say that said hogs was taken for the said confederate service and used by them, that the same was necessary – they say that they invoke of their own accord –Sworn to before me this 6th day of Dec 1863.

Case File 2589, Asa McCoy vs. Henry Davis in Pike Circuit Court. In

1863, Asa P. McCoy and his brother John were working the field, when the plaintiffs **Henry Davis Jr., Ellison Hatfield, John New, and Moses Chafin stole four fatten hogs**, weighing 800 pounds and worth $10.00 a pound. This suit came into court the April Term of Pike County, in 1872. This wartime raid also happened in April of 1863, when May was in the area of Pike. One of the interesting facts in this case came from Moses Chafin, stating that they took "six hogs worth $40.00" up to Mate Creek, in Logan. Henry Davis said they took the hogs back to camp, to John Murphys on Mate Creek, then killed and divided them. I think this is a great record, as it tells us that Mate Creek in Logan was an enacted military camp.

Case File 2074: Morgan, Lewis, and Thomas Sowords vs Robert Jackson. This file named quite a few men who had robbed the Sowords from Lawrence County. The Hatfields mentioned are **Patterson, Anderson, Robert, Elias, Ellison, and William Hatfield**. This file names them as an armed body of men of the so-called Confederate States. This suit was brought Oct. of 1864, prior to the end of the war, for $3000.00. Even though this case was against Jackson and others, this case was in defense of William A. Taylor, a Union man who returned home to Pike, then was accused of coming up with the plan to rob the storehouse with confederate men.

Sowards & Co Plaintiff against Robert L. Jackson & others} Affidavit
The pltf Morgan Sowards, Lewis Sowords & Thomas Sowords state that the claim in the action against the defts Robert Jackson & others is for money due for goods, wars, taken, and that it is a just claim and that they ought to, as they believe, recover three thousand dollars and that the said Robert Jackson, Thos. Collingsworth, Julius Williamson, Hammond Williamson, George Lawson, Melvin Lawson, Harrison Deskins, Robert Hatfield, William A. Taylor. Anderson Hatfield, Elias Hatfield, Ellison Hatfield, Patterson Hatfield, John Livingston, Wm. Hatfield and Elijah Tackett are in a military body of men co-operating with the army of the so-called Confederate States of America, and that they have left the county of their residence for the purpose of _. A military body of men co-operating with the army of the so-called confederate states of America and have been absent from there thirty days and that the ordering process of law cannot be served upon them. Sworn Oct. 12, 1864

In Oct. of 1864, these men were absent from home and could not be served with an alias warrant. They were a body of men who were co-operating with the confederate states. The storehouse was said to be robbed in Oct. 1864 by the testimony of Trout[51].

Case 2155, James Hatfield vs. Peter Cline: This war lawsuit will end up being the start of a series of cases where Anderson and Vicey Hatfield are in court over land. Peter Cline, along with others, raided the farm of his neighbor James Hatfield. James Hatfield sued Peter Cline for damages. Anse will be fighting for his Kentucky property in 1920. Anse testified on behalf of Jacob Cline Jr., in KY Case 2180[52]. Cline was part of a robbery on the storehouse of Sowards in Lawrence, but took no goods of Sowords. Anse being part of this raid, testified that Jacob only stood guard with him, and that he was made to go by men who killed. The reason I used Jacob Cline Jr., is that he was about 17 years old, his father is said to have died in 1858. Anse is shown on the muster roll of Company B, of the 45th Battalion, and did sign Amnesty in 1865. Anse was at Saltville in 1863 under Captain Buchanan. John Buchanan, the same man Anse had once enlisted under in the 45th can be shown in the KY 10th with Counts in case 2049, Pike Civil [2373 & 2541]. William (Bill) France was a Union Captain. His estate was in controversy in records after the war. His son James M. France was in civil cases #2386[53] and

[51] The deponent Stephen Trout being of lawful age and are duly sworn deposes & sayeth; I lived at the house of William A. Taylor home for in the county of Pike in the year 1864. When the store of Sowards and company was said to be robbed, by a Company of rebel soldiers in the month of Oct in that year.

[52] KY Archives Civil File 2180 - Pike Cir. Court - M.C.W. Soward, Lewis Soward, Thos. J. Soward vs. Jacob Cline & Ralph Steel Deft} Petition...State if you know where deft Cline was at the time, Sowards goods were taken? A. He was on the point this side of the store of Sowards, something near half a mile distant he was placed there as a piquet. Q. By same; did Jacob Cline get any of the goods taken? A. If he did I do not know it, he did not take any from the store, I was with him and come out with him from there and if he had any goods I did not see them. If he had any goods, I think I would have certainly seen them. Q. Would he not have endangered his life by refusing to go taking anything into consideration that is all the surrounding circumstances of the case? A. He was threatened that if he did not join the company by men who did kill sometimes. Q. State as near as you can the amount of goods taken from Soward. Also how much they had in store at the time of the robbery? A. I don't think there was exceeding $500.00 worth of goods in Sowards store at the time and I think $300.00 would be the greatest possible amount of the goods taken. And further this deponent saith not. Anderson Hatfield

[53] KY Archives File 2386 - Jacob Phillips Pltfs against Frederick Wolford, Daniel Wolford, Peter Cline & James M. France Defts} Petition to transfer to US D. Court - The defts....state that on the _ day of 1862 they entered into the military service of the US in Co of _ Regt._, Ky., Vol. as privates and continued in said service until the _ day of _ 18__ where they were discharged. They say it may be true they were present when the several articles were taken as charged as the pltfs petitions. It very also be true that they or some of them had some of said articles in their posession after they were taken. But they state at the time the property was taken and at the time the same was in their posession, they were in the military service of the US and that said property was taken under claims of military claims from the President of the US and the military officers of said Government. The pltf there being, are every of the same, and in armes and in the service and interest of the so called confederate

#2355[54], involved with Peter Cline and others in the robbery of Jacob Phillips and Richard Ferrell in Logan during the war.

Joseph Hatfield is shown in case File 2039[55] vs. John Goff: Joseph says that in 1862, John Goff, J.B. Williamson, Wallace Williamson, and Lorenzo Deskins took from him a bay horse, and a mule. Williamson claims he was not part of the confederate force who trespassed and asked that the case be dismissed.

Thomas Hatfield [case file 2038[56]] said in 1864, that he was robbed

---

states, they state, and charge that two years had elapsed after the alledged taking of the property & the bringing of the pltf suit. They plead and rely on the statute of limitations in are of the pltfs action. They pray that this suit be transferred to the US Cir. Ct. for the District of Ky., for judgment for their costs and all proper relief. May 6, 1868

[54] KY Archives Case File 2355 - Richard Ferrell vs. Frederick Wolford, Peter Cline, Daniel Wolford, James M. Frances} Petition - The pltf Richard Ferrell states that in 1862, the deft Frederick Wolford, Peter Cline, Daniel Wolford, and James M. Frances come to the house of the pltf in Logan Co. WV., and with force and arms unlawfully took from the possession of the pltf...1 mare $125.00, 1 horse $125.00, 9 coverlets $90.99, 9 blankets $50.00, 7 pair sheets $20.00, 1 razor and box $3.00, 1 side of leather $3.50, 1 ladies shawl $ 8.00, 3 mens coats & hat $35.00 total $467.50 The pltf states that the deft maliciously and forcibly took the above property from this pltf and carried the same away and converted the same to their own use. Wherefore the pltf prays judgment for $500.00 Sept 6, 1866

[55] KY Archives Civil Case File 2039 - Joseph Hatfield vs. John B. Goff - Pike Circuit Court - Joseph Hatfield Pltf against John B. Goff, J.B. Williamson, Wallace Williamson, Lorenzo Deskins} Petition - The pltf Joseph Hatfield states that on the day of 1862 in the county aforesaid with force and arms unlawfully entered the pltf and took there from one sorrel horse of the value of $150 one bay horse of the value of $100 & one mule of the value of $100 the property of the pltf and taken from his possession to the damage of the pltf of $500.00 & all appropriate relief. June 24 1865

Pike Cir. Ct - Joseph Hatfield Pltf vs. John B. Goff} Answer of J.B. Williamson - The deft John B. Williamson for answer to pltf petition says it is not true that he with force and arms unlawfully entered the pltf and took therefrom one sorrel mare of the value of $150 on bay horse of the value of $100 & one mule of the value of $100 the property of the pltf. He says that it is not true that he in connection with is confederates, or alone committed any of the trespasses charged in pltf petition, wherefore having fully answered he prays to be dismissed with his cost & all proper relief. John B. Williamson June 1, 1866.

[56] KY Archives File 2038 - Thomas Hatfield Pltf vs. Joseph Smith, Joseph Rutherford, Moses Chapman, Thomas Chapman, Franklin Hunt, Gilbert Blackburn, Apperson Romines, and Daniel McCoy Deft's} Petition - The pltf Tho. Hatfield states that the defts Jos. Smith, Jos. Rutherford, Moses Chapman, Tho. Chapman, Franklin Hunt, Gilbert Blackburn, Apperson Romines, and Daniel McCoy on or about the day of 1864 unlawfully entered the house of this pltf, they being armed with deadly weapons went up into the loft of this pltf house and without the consent....took and carried away from this pltf 8 sides of leather....taking and carrying away of said....The pltf states that said 8 sides of leather were in tan in a large troupe, pltf loft and that deft in unlawfully taking said 8 sides of this pltf leather spilled and scattered the tanage over the house of pltf and over the bed and bed clothes of the pltf. The pltf states that at the same time the above named deft's unlawfully destroyed one bee gum, of the value of $600 whereby the same was entirely lost to this plaintiff...He prays judgment per $150 and for all proper relief. The Pltf states that the wrongs and injuries

by Franklin Hunt, William Romaine, and Daniel McCoy, confederate soldiers, and sued for $600.00.

John Dils didn't escape the courts during the war. Dils, along with William Damron and William Ford, is sued by Thomas May Sr. in May of 1866. Dils regiment, under his command, took 2 horses, 4 head of cattle, and 18 gallons of brandy with force and arms. John Dils along with the widow, Melinda Ford, wife of Wm. Ford, first denied the charges, but then accepted that it was his troops who was doing the pillaging. Col. Johns Dils says this about the taking of property with arms:

Thomas May Sr. Pltf against John Dils Jr., Wm. Damron, Malinda Ford executrix of Wm. Ford deceased defts} Amended Answer & Petition of Dils

The deft Jno. Dils amends his answer & states in Sept. 1862 he entered the military service of the US in the capacity of Colonel of the 39th KY Vol., Infantry & continued in said service until Dec. 1863. The deft Malinda Ford executrix of Wm. Ford states in Sept 1862 her testator Wm. Ford entered the military service of the US in the capacity of Captain of the 39th KY Reg. Mounted Infantry Volunteers. Continued in the military service of the US until in Nov 1864, when he died in the line of his duty. The deft Dils & M. Ford states that it may be true the property of pltf May has been taken by soldiers, of where they the deft Dils and Wm. Ford had the command. That the property when taken was necessary for the public service & was turned over to the property officer to recover property impressed for the public service, and was turned over, and said by & per said Government, except the brandy. Deft says what the deft Dils & Wm. Ford did, what was done in their capacity of officers in the military service of the US, and under call of military authority derived from & for use under the President of the US. And, their superior officers who they was in duty bound to obey, they deny defts Dils or Wm. Ford converted any part of pltf property to their own use. The defts further state that the taking of pltf property had occurred more than two years before the bringing of pltf action. They rely after & plead in for of pltf action the statute of limitations in said case made provided & pray that this cause be transferred to the Circuit Court of the US to be holden for the District of KY they pray Judgment and other proper relief. Jno. Dils May 31, 1867. The deft Dils & Malinda Ford deny any brandy of pltf was taken by deft's Dils or Wm. Ford.

Col. John Dils Jr. was a complex, well connected man. During the recording of the 41st Kentucky Congress in Dec. 1869, John Zeigler

---

above complained of and committed by the deft s above named they at the time acting or professing to act in the interest of the so called Confederate States of America and not acting under any authority from the Gov. of the US of America. Wherefore pltf prays Judgment for $150 and for all proper relief. R.J. Burns Attorney Dec 3, 1865.

contested John M. Rice as the representative for the Ninth District. The forty-eight year old John Dils Jr., gave testimony about Rice, and what he believed Rice had done during the war. This was March 15, 1869 at the storehouse of Dils and Thornsbury in Piketon, KY. Thornsbury was said by all who testified to be a man of dishonest character. John M. Rice was accused of supporting the confederacy, therefore, Ziegler contested his seat as a Representative, telling that Rice fought with the south. The case said that Kentucky held a disdain for anyone of the confederacy holding office at this time, and that confederate supporters were not to be trusted. In this deposition, Rice was in town in Oct. of 1861, in Pikeville, when Col. John Stuart Williams of the confederate force 5th Kentucky Infantry occupied the town. Dils was arrested and taken prisoner. Hibbard Williamson said, *"John Dils was then lying out in the woods when Williams was in this place, and stayed out till Williams sent after him."* Dils said as to why he was arrested, *"Col. Williams wrote to Judge Braxton, that I was a dangerous union man, the most dangerous and influential he found in the mountains of Kentucky."* He tells of Rice purchasing a gun from his storehouse, and Rice naming his gun the "Yankee Killer". John Dils Jr., was escorted to Libby Prison, and delivered before Judge Braxton. Rice wrote a letter on behalf of Dils, in support of Dils freedom. Anne Dils, his wife, may have carried that letter from John M. Rice. Dils was vague when asked who brought the letter to Richmond. Dils was set free, and there was not enough evidence against Rice to prove that he had joined the confederacy. He kept his seat in the Legislature, and Dils considered Rice a very good friend, even if Dils testified to his buying a gun and telling of Rice as a possible confederate soldier.[57] Judge J.M. Rice was the presiding judge in the trials for the Hatfield members. Rice also, asked Buckner to take Cline and Kinner, at their word, when it came to giving the rewards for the Hatfields.

Logan in the War

Logan County, VA, (later WV), is known as a burned county during the civil war. I found no war history for Vance or Hatfield in these records, however, we thought it important to tell of the Logan court house burning during the war. Finding records that tell us some remnant of life during the war can be slim, unless we find a case such as these. Joseph A. Dempsey and Rebecca Deskins are married in the summer of 1862. It was said in the depositions of Wm. Straton and John Brewster,

---

[57] 41st Congress 2nd Session} House of Representatives Misc. Doc No. 9 Ziegler vs Rice. Contest of a seat in the 41sr Congress as a representative from the Ninth Congressional District of Kentucky.

that the Yankees were in Logan, and that many of the court books were taken to Ralph Steele's to be in safe hands. John Brewster, son of Comfort Brewster, had gone to Logan for a marriage license where the Federals were camped at Elijah Cartwright's. Capt. William Straton of the 34th Battalion VA Infantry, Company B, also known as Witcher's Battalion, is the man testifying below. Straton/Stratton was also the county clerk during this period, which, he turned over the books to his deputy clerk, as Straton left during the war to Tazewell, Virginia.

[58]*Then came William Straton another witness introduced by the plaintiff being of lawful age, and being by me first duly sworn deposed and said in answer to the following questions. Q. State your age, residence and occupation? A. I am 69 years old and live at Logan Court house W.V. and am a lawyer. Q. State if you know who was clerk of the county court of this county 1861 to 1865? A. I was the clerk during that time. Q. Did you have any deputy in said office during that time, if so who? A. I had a deputy George E. Bryan. I might have had some other deputy, but if I did, I have forgot all about it. Q. Which stayed in the office and attended to the business during that time, and especially in 1862? You or your said deputy, George E. Bryan. A. I was about the office myself very little during the year 1862 or any other time during the war. My deputy stayed about here, and about home, more than I did and during all of that time, there was but little business done in the office anyway. It appears to me that it was in the winter of 1862 and 1863 that they burned the courthouse and clerk's office. What become of the records of marriages kept in said office in 1862? A. There were some books such as deed books and order books carried to Ralph Steels on Island creek, in the summer of 1861, and put there for safe keeping. But, I don't think the record of marriages was taken there, but was left in the clerk's office with most of the books and papers belonging to said office. I was not here at the time but the common understanding afterwards was that all the books and papers were burned.*
Cross Examined
Q. Where did you live during the latter part of 1862 and the year 1863? A. I lived at Logan Courthouse. Q. Where did your family live during that time? A. Here. Q. When was it you speak of taking your family from here to Tazewell Co. Virginia? A. I took my family, I think, it was in November of 1862 as refugees to the county of Tazewell. Q. How long did your family remain there? A. Until the fall of 1865.

The case of Anthony Lawson, his sons Richard Lawson, and James Lawson, purchased cattle acquired at confederate prices of $100.00 a head, for the war effort, in order to feed the troops camped at Burkes Garden, in Nov. 1863. This case was contesting land of Cook in

---

[58] WV Archives 014-00031 Stuart Wood vs Joseph Dempsey

Wyoming County, and a note of $725.00 for the price of the cattle, case 071-00001. Tazewell became into a refugee camp, and headquarters for the confederate army during the civil war.

In case 073-00003, in 1870, Jane E. Mead versus Lewis Dempsey, administrator of William Mead, who passed away Oct. 17, 1854 in the case file. Here, Straton, of Witcher's Battalion, will testify as to the records of Logan County during the war. Straton said *"many of and most of the records and papers of said office was destroyed by the burning of the courthouse and clerk's office and particularly the records of Wills, and Settlements, and all matters relating to administration, inventory, sales, bills, and are not now remaining in said office."*

John E. Peck, Commissioner, made mention the court house was burned in 1862. William Meads heirs consist of James Mead, John Mead, Reuben Mead, Lewis Mead, John Fields and Mary (Poly) his wife, Hiram Rose and Priscilla his wife, Silas Damron and Lydia his wife, Thomas Mead, and Paris/Pyrrus Mead infant heirs of William Mead deceased who sue by their next friend John Mead. Jane Ellen Mead married to George R.C. Floyd. The object of this suit is to require a settlement of the account of the estate of William B. Mead deceased.

Chapter 8
DEATH OF ASA H. MCCOY

Did Jim Vance shoot Asa Harman McCoy, a Union civil war soldier who died near the end of the war? It is the question of all questions regarding the feud folklore. This accusation has defined three men for eternity, Asa H. McCoy, Anse Hatfield, and James Vance. The subject of the civil war and the killing of Asa McCoy was introduced into the feud by Randal McCoy, during a visit by Sam E. Hill [Appendix C], to his home, just days after Jim Vance was killed on his own property. This histrionic bit of folklore was invented by none other than Randal McCoy, who by that time was living in Pikeville. Buckner sent Sam Hill down into Pikeville to get the story from the Pike crowd. Randolph didn't convince Hill, nor prove that it had any effect on the situation that Randal had found himself in. Sam Hill wrote that the feud was personal and not political. Randolph and Anse had fought for the same confederate states, per Hill. Looking at the previous chapters, we find that Randal and Jim McCoy both said that the feud started in 1882 and ended in 1888. We will see evidence that the son of Asa Harman McCoy, Jacob, married Elizabeth Vance, Jim and Mary Vance's daughter. They had business dealings and sold land between Mary Daniels and Jim Vance. Even Perry Cline hired Jim Vance as his deputy, and Jim went the bond of Perry Cline when he was elected as the Pike County Sheriff.

Martha (Patty) McCoy, widow of Asa Harmon McCoy, gave us revealing evidence in her pension application. Martha says, "*He was killed by rebels in route back to his regiment*", in Dec. 1864. Asa enlisted with the union army even when Pike was called a confederate county by Col. A.J. May. By mid-1863, Pike was full of union soldiers. If the Asa McCoy family needed protection from confederate men in 1864/5, there would have been many union soldiers to assist them, including their own home guard. Camp Brownlow, mentioned by Col. Dils, himself, in pension papers for Johnson, said the camp was in the town of Pikeville. Mays testified that Pike was under confederate control up to April of 1863, when union troops moved there in July of 1863. Pike was then under union occupation.

What the actual records show is that Asa H. McCoy was sent home, and that the men were suffering from frost bite. The records show that their stint in the union service had expired. The records show that Asa had enlisted and was on his way back to rejoin his regiment on Dec. 1864, per Martha, when he was killed by "**rebels**". Mary Hunt says that

Asa died Jan. 7, 1865 and that she had seen him buried. Martha, Mary Daniels, and Mary Hunt disagree about the date of Asa's death[59].

When reading about the 45th KY Volunteer Mounted Infantry, Asa H. McCoy was in Company E, where it says that many men died, less of bullets, but mustered out of this company because of FROST BITE.

States; *From its constant duty in most inclement weather the Regiment suffered even more seriously than from the bullets of the enemy, and a large proportion of the men were mustered out injured by frost-bites. This Regiment was mustered out by Battalions at Catlettsburg, Kentucky — Companies A, B, C, D, E, and F on the 24th December 1864. Companies G, H, I, and K, on the 14th day of February, 1865.*[60]

Martha filed for a civil war pension in Nov. 1888, shortly before an 1890 Pike County Special Poll was taken, where-in, she states that her husband died of FROST BITE [Appendix K]. This is at the same time John R. Spears of the NY Sun is writing his article in current literature. Spears quoted Randal McCoy as saying that Jim Vance owned no land and that Jim fought with Anse during the war. Yet, as previously shown, the two are never shown being under the same company, nor are they mentioned in any war lawsuits together in the Pike or Logan records. With Camp Brownlow in Pike just miles away, and under union control, there was no reason for Asa to hide out from trouble in the cave, especially if he had frost-bite, and risk dying of gangrene. Asa could have obtained help from his union neighbors, and many others of the 39th Kentucky Regiment, or the Pike Home Guard, which existed according to the records of Col. A.J. May, and others. I believe that "even if" Jim had lived in Pike in 1865, that he would at least have been summoned for murder charges and there would have been a record, especially since Asa McCoy was technically a civilian, not a soldier, when he was suspected of being killed. Asa left his family, like most

---

[59] General Affidavit - State of KY, Co. of Pike. In the matter of Martha McCoy widow of Asa H. McCoy Co. E 45 Regt. KY, Vol. W381.608; on this 9th day of Dec. A.D. 1891. Personally appeared before me a Justice of the Peace in and for the aforesaid county. Duly authorized to administer oaths. Mary Hunt, aged 52 years, a resident of Edgarton, KY. in the Co. of Pike, and State of Ky. Whose post office address is Edgarton, Ky. Mary Daniels, aged 45 years, a resident of Edgarton, in the Co. of Pike and state of Ky., whose Post office address is Edgarton, Ky., well known to be reputable and entitled to credit and who, being duly sworn, declared in relation to aforesaid case, as follows: We have been acquainted with Asa H. McCoy & Martha McCoy all our life until the death of Asa H. McCoy, which was on the 7th day of Jan. 1865. We seen him buried. Mary Hunt & Mary Daniels Attest Wm Daniels & Jacob McCoy
[60] Kentucky Adjutant Generals Office Report Vol. 2. 1861-66, page 459

after a death, in a world of hurt, Asa left them in debt.[61]

Let's explore this, the soldiers were mustered out Dec. 24, 1864. If Asa were on his way back to join his troop, which now didn't exist, he would still have been a citizen until he signed papers, and murder charges would have been applicable. Many men were summoned for horse stealing, assault, and murder in Pike in 1865. Asa could have died of frost bite, and Martha may have written this in her pension in order to collect a soldiers pension. No one can blame her for that, she had a family to feed. In her statement below, she swore Asa never served "subsequent", to his discharge of Dec 24, 1864.

State of KY, County of Pike. In the matter of Martha McCoy widow of Asa H. McCoy Co. E 45 Regt. KY, Vol. W381.608; on this 89th day of Dec. A.D. 1891 personally appeared before me a Justice of the Peace in and for the aforesaid county, duly authorized to administer oaths Martha McCoy, aged 61 years, a resident of Edgarton, Ky. P.O., in the County of Pike, and State of KY., well known to be reputable and entitled to credit and who, being duly sworn, declared in relation to aforesaid case, as follows: That her late husband Asa H. McCoy deceased never served in the military or naval service subsequent to Dec 24, 1864 and Martha McCoy further states that she has no means nor no income to support on and is not able to work, and that her property was assessed at three hundred and eighty five dollars.

In the end, it is all conjecture and what people want to believe. *What you see and what you hear depends a great deal on where you are standing.* There is not a shred of evidence in the court records that anyone killed Asa Harman McCoy. And furthermore, if he died after being released, he was a civilian, which would have been classified as murder! Where are the court records? Just because Randal said it to Hill in 1888 doesn't make it absolute. Where was he standing! On a murder charge.

---

[61] May 27, 1870 KY Archives Civil File 2922 - Richard Daniels vs. Martha McCoy & others The Commonwealth of Pike County, Greetings: We command you that of the Estate of Martha McCoy widow, Mary Daniels. William Daniels, Jacob McCoy, Larkin McCoy, Lewis McCoy, and Asa H. McCoy heirs at law of Asa H. McCoy deceased. [Nancy L. McCoy Hatfield Phillips is not mentioned as a child]. Late of your bailiwick. You cause to be made the sum of sixty two dollars, to be levied of Estate of the assets to them. Demand which Richard Daniels late in out Pike Circuit Court, hath recovered against him for debt. Witness, R.M. Ferrell Clerk of said Court, this 9th day of May 1870. (written on side) Levied the within upon fifty acres of land lying on the Robert Branch of Peter Creek, May the 27th 1870. J.M. Ferguson dstor. and J.E. Ratliff - Oct 15, 1871 – Mr. J. Ratliff sheriff, Sir please to make M.G.B. Davis a deed to the land I sold belonging to Martha McCoy the estate of Asa H. McCoy. I now authorize you to make deed to M.G.B. Davis and the said Davis is to pay you your cost the 15th day of October 1871. William Daniels Richard Daniels

Chapter 9
FAMILY RECORDS

James and Mary Vance have children, John, Jane, Elizabeth, James, and Amy. The records, our sources, bring to the table signatures, and relevant information, thus giving us the timing of events such as marriages, land transactions, divorces, and other life events. These records give us insight as to how the family interacted with the community around them. In the mountains, many of those transactions involved neighbors, or family members. Elizabeth Vance, on April 8, 1875[62] married Jacob McCoy in Pike County, KY. Jacob is the son of Asa Harman and Martha Cline McCoy. He was 21 years old. She was 18 years old. Pike county records reveal that Jacob McCoy and Elizabeth were married in the home of her father, James Vance. Jacob McCoy and Perry Cline attested to the rites of matrimony.

In sharing the marriage of Elizabeth Vance to Jacob McCoy, son of Asa, we show that the families knew one another intimately. Family folklore says that Asa Harman McCoy's family hated James Vance, telling that he had murdered their father. No records of proof exist, nor does that folk tale have any relevance, as is already shown by Martha's statements in the records. The question arises, wouldn't Jacob's mother have been alarmed, if not disappointed, that her son would marry into the family of Jim Vance, much less enter into nuptials in the very home of the man who Randal McCoy claimed killed her husband? What absurdity. With Perry A. Cline attesting to the marriage, the story becomes even more doubtful. This was the same year that Jim Vance was given the job as deputy sheriff of Pikeville under Perry A. Cline. This is also the same year Jim Vance purchased land from Mary and Bill Daniels. Mary is the daughter of Asa McCoy. Mary McCoy Daniels sold Jim Vance land on a rather large note in June 1875. James Vance paid Daniels nearly $1050.00 up front for that land.

Dan Cunningham, the bounty hunter, stated in his telling of the feud, that Jim Vance was part of the raid with Anse in killing Asa McCoy. Cunningham was listening to the stories that were told by the Pike crowd, in the months AFTER Jim was killed. The stories that were told, in fact, by the very same people who were under indictment in Logan County, WV. If we buy into the stories that some want us to believe, that the civil war left the McCoys with hatred toward others, then I have to

---

[62] Pike County Marriages page 308 and 309.

wonder why it was that Jacob McCoy married Jim's daughter, and sold land to Jim Vance. Folklore says Lark McCoy, who was 8 when his father died, swore to kill Jim Vance. The records prove otherwise. The interactions of these families show that there was no animosity. They sold property on a substantial note of $1500.00 to the man who they suspected of killing their father? Plus, Lark was not the man who killed Jim Vance.

William Daniels[63] deed to James Vance} This indenture made this 29th day of June 1875 between William Daniels and Mary Daniels his wife who joins in this deed. Relinquishing her right of dower of the first part and James Vance of the second part witnessed that the parties of the first part in consideration of the sum of $1500.00 dollars all in hand paid but $447.50 have bargained and sold and by these present. Do convey and confirm unto the said party of the second part his heirs and assignees forever a certain tract or parcel of land lying in Pike Co., KY. Described as follows. Beginning at the mouth of the branch above said Daniels house thence running up the said branch to the fork point. Thence up the said point to the back line. Thence with the back line to Ephraim Hatfield's line. Thence with said Hatfield's line to the river. Thence running with John Ferrell's line to the mouth of the fish trap branch. Thence running up the River to the beginning. The piece of land that belong to Madison Hatfield is to be conveyed as said to James Vance by the parties of the first part containing 1000 acres more or less. To have and to hold, said protect with its obligation, comes thereunto belonging unto the said granted. His heirs and assignees. The said party of the second part that they will warrant generally the title to the property hereby conveyed a lien is hereby retained upon the property hereby conveyed as surety for the payment of said note for unpaid purchase money in testimony upon of the parties of the first part have hereunto subscribed. Signed by Wm. & Mary Daniels; Admitted to record Jul 2, 1875.

Perry A. Cline stated that Jim Vance purchased some kind of property from him in May of 1872, for $1200.00, and Jim had not paid the entire note. Cline takes Jim Vance and William Daniels to court for money he believes is owed on the property [Case file 3631]. Cline wants Daniels to pay him, because Jim had sold the above land "back" to Daniels. So Cline wanted Daniels' money, instead of paying Vance for this property. Cline is accusing Wm. Daniels of backing Jim Vance. Cline even states that William and Mary (McCoy) Daniels had not purchased this land back from Vance and that Daniels had waived the debt of Vance in order to keep the money and land. Cline accused Daniels of making payments to James Jr. in order not to pay Perry. A William Daniels is named in records as an employee of James Vance and was shown to be working with him in 1885, in his timbering business. On August 31, 1880, we show that even Wm. Daniels and Anse Hatfield had a working relationship, since Daniels is holding rafts on his property that belong to Anse. Anse stated that he has two oak rafts at Wm. Daniels, and Dr. Rutherford can have that as a payment for a debt paid by Rutherford to Isom Romans[64]. Logan holds a court case[65] of L.P. Smith against Anderson Hatfield, for 1888, where L.P., is suing Anse, and his business partners, Wm. Daniels, and Andy Varney, an established partnership that started in 1882. In this case, its mentions Daniels had purchased of Jim Vance a team of oxen, rigs, and other $300.00. We know that Anse and William Daniels, had a business relationship.

Therefore, here we have Cline suing Vance and Daniels, with Cline being the Uncle of Mary McCoy Daniels. As part of the bond, the court says that Perry Cline shall pay Jim Vance no more than $1616.00 if the suit is found to be a false claim. The very fact that Perry Cline is an uncle to Mary Daniels makes it even more illogical that the families of Asa McCoy stood behind Jim Vance Sr., when they didn't support Uncle Perry Cline in the dispute. Even crazier, Perry Cline, himself, was selling land, timber, or animals to the man who supposedly killed his brother-in-law. No deed has been found to tell us what he purchased for this $1600.00. Yes, Randal McCoy was the first person to assert that James Vance killed Asa Harmon McCoy. Since Cline was stating that Jim owed him in arrears less than $400.00 of the already $1200.00 paid, certainly there would be hard feelings for both Cline and Vance, and more so for Daniels. The debt that Cline said Vance owed him is a different amount than that of the land between Daniels and Vance, therefore the property of Daniels is NOT the property Perry sold Jim.

Yet, Perry hired Vance as his deputy just prior to these events. Court records indicate that this was, perhaps, still being paid in Aug. of 1876. Spring Term of court for 1874[66] shows a court entry in Pike County

---

64 Logan County Deed Book G - Anderson Hatfield to Dr. Rutherford} Bond
I owe Dr. Rutherford seventy five dollars money he paid Isom Romans for me and for which I have turned over 2 oak rafts, now rafted in the Tug River at the house of Wm. Daniels in pledge for said loan Aug 11, 1880. Anderson Hatfield
65 WV Archives Case 047-00026 - L.P. Smith vs Anderson Hatfield
66 Spring Term 1874 Pike Circuit Court 6th day [Referring to case 3341] - Cr. by James Vance one hundred & fifty dollars August 29, 1876 (this is written on side of the following entry). James M. Lawson vs. P.A. Cline} Ordinary - The deft having duly served, with process and failing to answer the statement of the petition is taken as true. It is therefore ordered judgment by the court that the pltf recovers of the judgment the sum of one hundred & fifty-nine dollars & eighty-three cents with interest at the rate of 8 per cent annum May 21st 1872 until paid also his cost herein expended.

records; James Lawson vs Perry Cline, and written on the side of that court book entry, is a credit of $150.00 paid by Jim Vance, written in August of 1876. In 1874 James Lawson sued Perry A. Cline on a note of 159.83 cents for a debt unpaid [Case file 3341] by Perry. It is possible that James Vance, who owed Perry Cline $400.00 in case 3631, paid this lawsuit for Perry, for money owed to Lawson by Perry, in case 3341, since this $150.00 was listed as paid by James Vance, next to the Lawson case. Jim was not involved with the Cline and Lawson case 3341. These court cases don't always give us an exact ending. We find that case 3631 was never extended in the court records, showing that the Cline debt was either paid or dropped. With the many lawsuits of Cline, if it had not been worked out, Perry would have kept suing.

Perry A. and Martha Cline had generated nearly 26 civil cases, starting in 1873 and lasting until Perry died testate, he did have an estate shown in 026-00044, where Martha claims to be left destitute. Martha was sued over Perry's estate, and the commissioner put his Johns Creek land for sale [KY Archives Case 6638].

One of the more fascinating cases of Perry and Martha was case 3417. Perry and Martha sued men over a brawl at the neighbor's home. With Martha pregnant and having to witness a brawl, Martha claims she was made ill and that it endangered her health. Perry filed a suit in court for $5,000.00, and ended up with $100.00, of which Brewer and Adkins would get $50.00.

Civil case file 3441, shows Perry Cline and Martha are suing John Smith. Cline stated that Smith had told someone he was *well acquainted with Cline's wife*. In this suit, Cline brings a civil suit of $10,000 against John Smith. Smith denied that he said anything like that about Martha. Smith said that Martha was a virtuous lady, and believed himself to be a friend of Perry Cline's.

Chapter 10
THE CONSTABLE, DEPUTY AND
JUSTICE OF THE PEACE

Proven in county court records, James Monroe Vance Sr. was elected as a Logan County WV constable in 1870 for Magnolia Township. In 1875, he was a deputy sheriff in Pike County, KY, and in 1883 was asked to take the position of Justice of the Peace in Logan County, WV until the new term of 1884. Jim was elected by his peers and his neighbors. When I mention a man's character, what do the records reflect? These records are seemingly left out of ALL the Hatfield and McCoy books. It would be rather hard to sell Jim Vance as the ruthless, vindictive, desperate man that the feud writers portray, when records like this can be found in the court books, showing him to be a well-respected community member.

When we talk about men who drink, use weapons, fight, or commit any kind of crime; those infractions will usually show up in the court books. At some point, if James Vance were this type of man, he would have been arrested for a crime. Jim Vance was never charged with a single crime. Jim was elected constable only five years after the death of Asa McCoy, in 1870 in Logan County, WV. His associates and neighbors trusted this man who was hired to keep peace.

Logan County Commissioners Book page 242
1870 - Results of election <u>*Magnolia Township*</u> *Valentine Hatfield elected of the office of Justice, William Tiller to the office of supervisor, Moses Mounts to the office of township clerk,* <u>*James Vance to the office of Constable,*</u> *and Wm. Alderson and F.S. Varney to the office of school commissioner.*

In 1871[67], Logan County, Margaret (Taylor) McCoy divorced her long time husband Daniel McCoy. Daniel is the father of feuding Randolph McCoy. We know this because Margaret mentions her children in this suit. She also mentions that during her marriage, that Daniel hardly supported the family. She stated that she made all the children's clothes when they were growing up, and that she raised a horse and pigs to sell in order to raise her children and buy land. Daniel had let the pigs loose. She gathered and raised them. She stated that Daniel made her leave his home, among other events. Daniel told her to take her mule and go. *"You're an old love"* he said.

Jim Vance, as Special Constable, served the court summons for Daniel McCoy to appear in court to give his deposition. Margaret was given $2.00 a month in maintenance during the suit, and $100.00 total was paid in nine months. The first picture is Jim Vance's signature from the case noted of Daniel McCoy. The second photo is his signature in a later case of James Vance against John B. Bromley. They are every bit alike, ensuring that James Vance was the constable in 1871.

By January of 1875, while living in Pike County on land acquired of Wm. Daniels, Jim was working as a deputy sheriff. During the time period that some had asserted that Jim Vance was a poor man, Jim signed a bond for Perry Cline to serve as sheriff[68]. By signing this bond, it's stating that Perry will complete his job in a respectful manner and the men posting his bond will ensure that all requirements are met. The men who posted that bond are O.C. Bowles, James Vance, and John Dils Jr. Our James M. Vance was a trusted, upstanding citizen, it seems. Colonel John Dils Jr., Civil War Union Officer, wouldn't have thought that Jim

---

[67] File 072-00072 Logan Co. Records, WV Archives – Daniel McCoy vs Margaret McCoy

[68] Page 246 Pike Ct Order Bk G - January Term 1875 - This day Perry A. Cline sheriff of Pike County this day appeared in open court and took the oaths according to law. This day Perry A. Cline sheriff of Pike County made motion to court to give bond for the collateral of the _ of the county of Pike for the state of Kentucky and entered into covenant with the commonwealth of Kentucky with O.C. Bowles, John Dils Jr., and James Vance as his sureties who acknowledged covenant according to law.

killed Asa Harman McCoy, and allowed Jim to post bond for his protégé for office in 1886. Perry had his eyes on a political career. Dils had the connections. How would that look for Dils or Cline if Jim Vance had a reputation as the murderer of a union soldier in Pike County? In Pike County, June of 1875, Jim is found in court records for delivering court enacted road orders as deputy. Logan Minute Book Page 52, June Term 1881 James Vance Sr., Valentine Hatfield, and Moses Chafin declare a highway; James Vance Jr. is appointed the surveyor in Logan County.

In Dec. of 1875, one year after Sheriff Perry Cline appointed Jim Vance and James Thornsbury as deputies, both men are dismissed of their duties under Cline[69]. Not once, in this 1875 Pike court term, did anyone complain of Jim Vance as a deputy, and those kinds of records are numerous in the court books. Jim served as a respected deputy sheriff. Jim moved back to Logan, WV in 1876, so he could not fulfill that job in Pike County, KY. In 1883, James Vance is asked to take the position as **Justice of the Peace** in the Magnolia District of Logan County, WV. As you can see, in the Commissioners Book (also in the Logan Law Order Book), due to the resignation of Joseph Simpkins, and at the request of the county leaders, Jim Vance was appointed. They must have thought Jim was a reasonable and fair man, who was honest, qualified, and educated sufficiently to hold this office. During this same term of July 1883, John Chafin made Jim Vance Jr., son of James M. Vance Sr., his deputy. A year later in Oct. of 1884, the elections were held once again. In Magnolia District, Valentine Hatfield was elected Justice of the Peace; John Francisco, son-in-law of Jim Vance, lost to F.M. Kennedy as Constable. Valentine's term would not have ended until Dec. 31, 1888. Frank Phillips arrested Valentine before his term was up. L.D. Chambers, and J.B. Buskirk were his sureties for J.P.

July 1883 Logan Law Order Book Page 394 - James Vance Sr. is hereby appointed to Justice of the Peace in Magnolia District in this County to fill vacancy of said office occasioned by the resignation of Joseph Simpkins which was tendered to this court at the last term of court which said resignation was accepted by the Court to take effect until this day whereupon the said James Vance was appointed in court and together with Hugh Toney, Floyd Hatfield, J.R. Browning and P.H. Dingess his sureties entered with and acknowledged a

---

[69] Page 450 Pike Ct Order Bk G - December Term 1875 - This day Perry A. Cline sheriff of Pike County made motion to have James M. Thornsbury his deputy dismissed, ordered by the court that he be dismissed as deputy sheriff of Pike County. Upon motion of Perry A. Cline sheriff of Pike County to have James Vance dismissed as his deputy, ordered by the court that James Vance deputy sheriff for P.A. Cline is dismissed as said deputy sheriff.

bond in the penalty of $2500.00 conditioned said to law for the faithful discharge of the duties of said office which bond was approved by the amount said theretofore that the James Vance appeared in Court and took the several oath required by law as Justice as aforesaid.

Other offices held to note before the feud, James Jr was appointed as deputy sheriff, while a year later, John Francisco, the son in law of James Vance, lost his bid to become constable.

Logan Law Order Book B page 401 - July Term 1883 - On motion of John Chafin Clerk of the Court and with the consent of the court James M. Vance Jr. is admitted as his deputy in said office during and therefore the said James M. Vance Jr., appeared in this court and took the several oaths required by law as deputy clerk aforesaid.

Law Order Book B page 471 - October 1884 (1st day) October 10th - That at the election held in the district of Magnolia in said county, for the office of Justice of the Peace Valentine Hatfield received one hundred and one votes; M.A. Ferrell received sixty-four votes; and Thomas Murry received two votes. For the office Constable F.M. Kennedy received ninety-four votes, John Francisco received fifty-seven votes and Kirk McCoy received eighteen votes.

Minute Book page 276 - December Term 1880 (1st day) - Elias Hatfield who was at a general election held for Logan County on the 12th day of October duly elected by the qualified voters of Magnolia District to the office of Constable thereof for the term of four years commencing on the first day of January this day appeared in court and together with Moses Ferrell, Valentine Hatfield, Henry Ragland, and John Chafin his sureties entered into and acknowledged a bond in the penal of three thousand dollars, conditioned according to law for the faithful discharge of the duties of said office. Which bond was approved by the court and thereon the said Elias Hatfield took the several oaths required by law.

Chapter 11
JAMES VANCE LAWSUITS

1876 Civil Case of D.C. Adkins vs. James Vance

This case speaks for itself, and may well be the worst crime we can pin on old Jim Vance, or should I say, his criminal cow, which stomped a field of corn. So the case goes, while in the fall of 1875, James was still living on the Kentucky side of the Tug. Well, his mischievous cow, we will call her Belle, had gained access and stomped a field of corn. Doc Adkins sued James Vance one very long year later, for the sum of $150.00. Now whether Adkins knew about the cow in his field, or if Jim knew about the cow, doesn't matter. Since the cow belongs to Jim, it's his damage. Adkins waited a full year to sue in court. During this same term of court, Adkins and Cline were being sued by Martin Smith for ruining a young fruit orchard, by allowing their oxen to roam free. Jim Vance testified in Martin's case that started in 1875. Jim and Anse are later deposed in 1879, KY. Case File 2831.

KY Archives Case 3639 - Pike Circuit Court D.C. Adkins (Pltf) against James Vance (Deft) - The plaintiff D.C. Adkins states that sometime in the fall of 1875 he was the owner and in the possession of one lot of corn, containing about 120 bushels worth $125.00, of corn fodder worth about $30.00 and the defendant without right as the knowledge or consent of this plaintiff turned and kept his stock and the same until the whole thereof destroyed and became a total loss to him. Plaintiff says that the same was destroyed by defendant or caused to be done by him unlawfully and without right and that no part of same has been accounted for by him by that the defendant owes him the value thereof with due damages for the wrongful destroying of the same. He says that by reason of the acts of the defendant he has been greatly damaged in the sum of $150.00. Whereof, the plaintiff prays Judgment for the sum of $150.00 in damages, and for a general attachment against due property of the defendant – James Vance for costs and all other proper relief. Connelly & Ratliff, Attorney; State of Kentucky Co. of Pike} Sworn to before me by D.C. Adkins this 6th day of June 1876. W.M. Connelly Notary Public Pike Co., Pike Cir. Court

From the Adkins case, we can determine that the ex-deputy sheriff, Jim Vance, was a non-resident of Pike, and again living on the West Virginia side of the Tug River in October of 1876, as previously seen. Jim had kept the land acquired by his wife Mary, from 1869. They moved back to this property in 1876. Mary had a real attachment to this property that was purchased from the Mounts family. It was one of the last pieces of property sold by her, prior to leaving Logan. Jim also acquired land in the name of Jim Vance Jr., on the Logan side of the river in December 1877[70], 1500 acres from Anse Hatfield. This land belonged to James Sr. We know this fact because of a lawsuit from 1908, "Darnell versus Flynn", in Logan county. Amy Flynn is the daughter of James Sr. Amy testified that the land belonged to her father and not her brother Jim Jr. Even then, it was under some dispute. Because Jim Sr., did in fact put his land in his son's name, proving Amy correct, and the court correct. He did move the ownership. This is not uncommon to put the ownership of property into the names of your children. L.M. Hall would later acquire portions of this land and sell it to Thacker Coal and Coke. Those portions included the 1869 Mounts property, and the Thacker land sold to the children by their father, Jim Vance Sr. Amy says the following in her testimony, when talking about her fathers estate:

Q. Did the money come out of the same land situate on Thacker Creek that had been owned by your father James Vance. Is that right? A. Yes sir. Q. Do you not remember that your father conveyed that land to your brother, James M. Vance? A. No sir, he did not. I know that much. I know he didn't do that.
The records show otherwise Mrs. Flynn.
Q. Do you mean to state that you know your brother, James M. Vance, never

---

[70] Anderson Hatfield to James Vance Jr.} This deed made this 24th day of Dec. 1877 by and between Anderson Hatfield and his wife Louisa Hatfield of the first part and James Vance Jr. of the second part. All of the Co, of Logan, State of WV. Witnessed in consideration of sum of $1400.00 to them in hand paid by the party of the second part. The receipt whereof is hereby acknowledged. Do hereby bargain and sell unto him the said James Vance Jr parcel of land situated lying, Co. of Logan on Grapevine Creek of Sandy River. Beginning on three beeches near the mouth of Wolf Pen Fork. Then running a straight line across the creek to the top of the mountain between Grapevine and the river. Thence running with the top of the said mountain to the dividing ridge between Grapevine and Beech Creek. Thence with said ridge to a large rock, on a knob at the head of Thacker Creek. Thence down the dividing ridge between Thacker and Mates Creek to a large black walnut near the top of said ridge. Then crossing the head of Thacker with said Hatfield's line to the top of the Grapevine ridge. Thence up said ridge to a large rock on the top of the ridge. Thence down the top of the ridge between the Wolf Pen and the mill seat fork to the three beeches to the beginning corner. Supposed to contain 1500 acres...land with its appurtenances unto him the said James Vance Jr. and his heirs forever.

had a deed to or claimed the Vance lands on Thacker Creek either by conveyance from your father, James M. Vance, or from your mother Mary Vance? A. Not to my knowledge. Q. Who paid you the money you received out of the Vance lands on Thacker Creek? A. Mr. L.M. Hall.

Kentucky Archives Criminal and Civil File 3821

The case of Martin (Mart) Smith vs. Perry A. Cline was brought on Jan. 30, 1875. Martin was suing Perry Cline over a farm, which included an orchard, a home place, a farmhouse, and at the time of sale, a fence that kept the animals away from the orchard in order to prevent the destruction of the young trees that were planted. This land was on the Tug River, near the branch of Peter Creek, in Kentucky. Smith claims the orchard consisted of 500 apple and 300 peach trees. Smith sued because he said that when he purchased the home place, the orchard was in good shape. When Mart finally took possession, the fencing was down, and the oxen had destroyed those trees. He sued Perry for $925.00 for the loss of 500 apple trees and 300 peach trees, $100.00 for the broken fencing, and $250.00 for the stomped ground about the home. At the time of sale, Cline and Adkins stayed upon the place, which Cline refused to give possession of the dwelling houses and farm upon the contract. Being that Cline allowed Adkins and one Thomas Chatman to move into the farmhouse, Smith could not take possession until the spring of 1876.

Perry Cline answered back to plaintiff Smith, denying that he agreed to give the farm in good condition. Cline said there was only 300 apple trees and 100 peach trees, and denied turning the oxen loose on the property. He also denied that he said he would give possession to Smith in March of 1875. Cline denied that he refused to move Adkins from the main dwelling house. Cline said he could not remove himself off the property at the time of contract, due to the illness of his wife. Cline lived in the home place. When Adkins did leave, Cline said Smith could have worked the farm, and said Smith agreed for him to remain on the farm. Though, Smith disagreed under testimony he stated that Perry's wife, Martha, wanted to keep the land, and had threatened to destroy it. Jim Vance and Anderson Hatfield, among others, were asked for depositions in 1879 to testify as to the condition of the land, testifying for the Plaintiff, Mart Smith.

Deposition of James Vance and Anderson Hatfield

Q. Mr. Vance state if you was acquainted with the farm purchase of Martin Smith and P.A. Cline on the 30th of January 1875, if so, do you know of a young orchard having been set out before that time if so, of what kind of trees did it consist of, and how many trees of each kind. What was the value of each tree at that time? A. I was acquainted with the farm about that time and I know of the young orchard being set out on the farm before that time, consisting of, I think, from about three to four hundred northern apple trees and I can't know how many peach trees. I think these trees were worth one dollar and twenty-five cents each at that time.

Q. Do you know of said orchard and trees having been destroyed after the trade and before the plaintiff got possession of the farm, if so, how many trees was destroyed. A. I know of a part of the orchard and a part of the trees destroyed after the trade and before the plaintiff got in possession of the farm after January 30 day 1875. My impression is that the greatest part of the trees was destroyed on said orchard by reason of the fencing being down in diverse places all around the farm and around the orchard. Also by cattle and other possessions from the property had free access to said orchard. Q. State how much the plaintiff has been damaged by the destruction of said trees? A. I think the plaintiff was damaged by the destruction of said orchard about $325.00 dollars.

Q. What condition was the fencing in around the farm and orchard at the time of trade? A. I think the fencing around the farm, around the orchards, was totally good at the time of the trade and sufficient to have protected said orchard and farm by the fencing that had been put up. Q. What amount was the plaintiff Smith damaged by the fence having been thrown down around the farm after the trade and before he got possession? A. I think the plaintiff was damaged by the destruction of the fencing and by his having to repair the same, about $50.00 dollars. I saw some of P.A. Cline's heads tearing the fencing down by hauling wood through the fence and railings. Q. Do you know of his lands being tromped by property after the trade and before plaintiff got possession, if so, how much was the plaintiff damaged by the same? A. I do know of said land being trampled by property after the trade and before plaintiff got the possession of said lands. I think under the condition plaintiff was placed in, I think he was damaged one hundred dollars by the tramping of the land.

Q. State if you know when plaintiff Smith got possession of said farm? A. I think he got possession of the lower end of the farm between the 15th and 20th of March 1875. I think he got possession of the upper end of the farm between the fifth and tenth days of May 1875. Q. How much was the plaintiff Smith damaged by not getting possession of the farm on the first day of March 1875? A. I think the plaintiff was damaged two hundred and seventy-five dollars by not getting possession on the first day of March 1875 of said farm. Q. State if you had a conversation with the defendant P.A. Cline in regards to the time he was to give possession of said farm to the plaintiff Smith to when was it and what did he say? A. I had a conversation with defendant Cline on the ninth day of April 1875 and he said to me that he was to give possession to plaintiff Smith the first day of March 1875, and he asked me to let Doctor C. Adkins have land to tend so he, Cline, could get Doctor C. Adkins to give Plaintiff Smith *possession of the land, and that he, Cline, had sold to plaintiff Smith. That is, the upper end of the farm that plaintiff had bought of him that Doctor Adkins was then living on. James Vance April 3, 1879*

Deposition of Anderson Hatfield

Q. Mr. Hatfield state if you are acquainted with the plaintiff Martin Smith and the defendant P.A. Cline if so, how long have acquainted them? A. I have been acquainted with Martin Smith about six or seven years. I have been acquainted with P.A. Cline since he was a boy. Q. State if you were present when the plaintiff Martin Smith purchased a farm of the defendant P.A. Cline, if so, when was it and where does the farm lay? A. I was present when the plaintiff Smith purchased a farm of defendant Cline. I think it was about the 30th day of January 1875. The trade was made in the store house. It lies on Tug River above the mouth of Peter Creek, Pike County, Kentucky. The farm on which Martin Smith now lives. Q. Did you hear a contract agreement between the parties at the time when the plaintiff was to take possession of the farm land dwelling house, if so, tell the contract between them in regards to the condition that the farm was to be delivered to the plaintiff in, tell all the contract that you heard? A. I heard the contract and was called a witness to the contract. The plaintiff was to have possession of the farm and buildings in so to work on farm the time the trade was made and defendant Cline was to have possession of the dwelling houses to the first day of March 1875. And then defendant Cline was to give plaintiff Smith possession of dwelling houses on the first day of March 1875 that is of all the dwelling on the farm at the first day of March 1875, at the time of trade the plaintiff Smith said to Cline that he Smith was afraid to close the trade. For the defendant Cline's wife was mad over the trade and she would destroy the fruit trees. The defendant P.A. Cline said there is not damage in that if anything was destroyed with place that he the defendant Cline would tend to that.

Q. So you know how many young apple and peach trees there was set out on the farm at the time of the trade? A. I think there was about four or five hundred northern apple trees set out on the farm at the time of the trade. I can't know how many peach trees, though there was a good many of them. Q. Do you know of any of said apples and peach trees having been destroyed after the trade of plaintiff got possession of the farm? How many of each kind and what was they worth each? A. I know of some of the trees being destroyed after the trade and before plaintiff got possession of the house. I was at a peach chopping at the defendant Clines and I saw the hands hauling with a team of cattle and they was hauling the wood over the fruit trees. I saw property among the trees and the trees was cut off and smashed of the ground. I think the trees was worth one dollar each. Q. What do you think the plaintiff was damaged by the destruction of said trees? A. I think the plaintiff was damaged two hundred and fifty dollars from what I saw myself? Q. Do you know of the enclosed land having been tromped by property after the trade and before plaintiff got possession of the farm and dwelling house? A. I know of the land being trompled a good deal after the trade and before the plaintiff got possession of the farm. Q. How much was the plaintiff damaged by the tromping of the land? A. I think the plaintiff was damaged about one hundred dollars by the land being tromped so hard.

Q. Do you know of the fencing having been turned down around the farm after the trade and before plaintiff got possession of the land, if so, what was the plaintiff damage by the same? A. I can't know but little about that. Q. Do you know of the plaintiff Smith demanding possession of the dwelling house, if so when was it, and where did he make the demand? A. I know of plaintiff making demand of Doc. Adkins for the possession of the dwelling house. I think this was after the first day of March 1875, & Doctor C. Adkins stated that he would not give Smith possession for he stated that P.A. Cline had rented him the house and land. That is the upper end of the farm. Anderson Hatfield

Civil Case 4829 - 1886, John C. France vs James Vance Sr. et al.

KY Civil court file 4829, the case of John C. France and Jacob Mounts versus James Vance and William Daniels, Feb. 1886. This case provided for a legal suit in Pikeville, KY which stirred up a hornet's nest for Vance and Daniels, against Perry Cline and John France. Jim Vance, as shown, was named in the lawsuits of Louvicy Hatfield vs. J.H. Charles[71], as someone who purchased timber from Anse. What we see in the lawsuits is that Daniels bought from Perry Cline a *note* of Anse's originally owing Green Taylor, now owing Perry Cline. Daniels sues Perry and Anse for non-payment. Perry says....whoa there, nephew Bill, I no longer own that "*note*" and the problem is yours. The below case is not about land, but about timber sold to Jim Vance from Wm. Daniels (via Anse) on that land. Here is how this civil suit worked.

William Daniels sold to Jim Vance 154 trees. The trees were sold to Daniels by Anse Hatfield, who owned the 800 acres of Peter Creek property in 1875. Then, John France and David Mounts said that the property belonged to them, and that they owe them $231.00 for the cut trees. However, Daniels, in his testimony said neither France nor Mounts owned the land. The land was once owned by Peter Cline and was acquired by James Hatfield in a civil suit against Peter Cline in 1865. Then it was sold to Anderson Hatfield. This is categorically true; and can be found in civil suit file 2155, where James Hatfield sued Peter Cline. France and Mounts said that they acquired the land through a grant. That grant was illegal since the land was already owned, replied Daniels. France denied Daniels' claims. Jim Vance cut the trees in 1875, though,

---

[71] KY Archives Criminal and Civil Case File 16678 February 3, 1920

the primary suit did not begin until 1886, more than 10 years after the timber was cut. This case was not settled until 1889, after Jim was dead.

In response to this suit, Jim Vance gave money earned from the timber to H.S. Carter to hold until the land survey, ordered by the court, was decided in Pike County, KY. France denied again, however France was wrong. France found out after a court ordered summons for Henry Carter, in the April Term 1889, that Carter was holding the funds, provided by Jim Vance. In another suit Henry S. Carter, himself was sued by Jacob Hatfield over timber civil case 4562 in the year 1884.

There was a summons for James Vance to appear in court in Pike County, KY, in December of 1887, which was two weeks before James Vance was murdered in Jan. of 1888. Jim did appear, traveling back from Wayne County, WV, in Dec., 1887. Soon after Jim Vance appearance in court, proving that Carter held the money, Jim Vance Sr., was murdered. James Vance Jr. was the administrator of his father's estate and was part of the civil suit in 1889. In the April 8, 1889 term of court, William Daniels and H.S. Carter were held in judgment of $150.00 with $30.00 going to P.A. Cline. Neither Jim Vance Sr. nor Jr. were held responsible in this suit. Jim's estate says France owed the estate $100.00 on the note. When a civil case is bonded, then filed falsely, the plaintiff pays the defendant that bond.

Oct 1886 - Pike Circuit Court - John C. France, Jacob Mounts (Pltf) vs. James Vance Sr. & James Vance Jr., Wm. Daniels (Deft)} Petition - <u>The Plaintiffs John C. France and Jacob Mounts state that some years ago the Defendants James Vance Sen. and James Vance Jr. bought of one Wm. Daniels who then claimed to be the owner one hundred and fifty four poplar trees. Sometime thereafter Defendants sold timber to Plaintiff for agreed price of $1.50 per tree amounting to the sum of Two (231) hundred and thirty one dollars and they paid Defendants therefore. Plaintiffs more state that Defendants had not then nor has not yet paid the said Wm. Daniels for the timber neither is he entitled to pay for it. ....Connolly & Cline, Attorney – Sworn John C. France this 14th day of</u> October 1886.

Pike Circuit Court - John C. France vs. James Vance et al., James M. Vance Deft} Answer of Daniels - <u>The Deft Daniels for answer. Herein, as for the timber described in Plaintiffs petition. Denies that it was agreed between all the parties or with this Defendant that the money was to be held and paid over to the proper parties. Either Plaintiffs or Daniels deny that there was an agreement to hold the money until the timber title was settled – deny that the Plaintiffs are the rightful owners of the land for which the timber grew or that such has been</u>

established by actual survey – or that the Plaintiffs are the owners of the timber. ....Deft Daniels says that about the day of 1875 or 76 he bought this timber from one Anse Hatfield and paid him for the timber. Hatfield at the time was the owner of the land and the timber and he had a right to buy and Hatfield a right to sell it. That after this the money was paid over to Smith Carter. He was told the same. They say that in 1865 one Peter Cline entered surveyed and obtained a patent for the land on which the timber in contest. At a sheriff sale was bought by James Hatfield. He held the same to Anderson Hatfield and Anderson Hatfield sold the timber on its land to the Defendant Wm. Daniels. Said Daniels sold the said timber to his co-defendant James Vance and James Vance Jr. They sold to the plaintiffs. They now chose that after the defendant, Vance sold said timber to the Plaintiffs and after they cut and removed the great part thereof, they, the Plaintiffs made an entry survey and obtained a patent for said land. That land on which its timber stood and for which they obtained the patent had already been patented to said Peter Cline. And was not vacant or unpatented land, and was not suspect to entry survey a patent and is therefore null and void they further say that after the Pltf bought its timber of their Deft they were exempt from setting up claims to it by them after entry and survey wherefore they pray to be dismissed with cost and for all other relief. James Vance, James Vance Jr., William Daniels says he believes its foregoing statements are true. Wm Daniels for to before me by them Daniels this 15 Oct 1886.

Henry S. Carter against James Vance 1885

What happened in this case, and was there a judgment against James Vance? There are many questions to this case, and for good reason. If you go back to the lawsuit of John France versus James Vance in 1886, France brought a civil case against Jim over timber that was cut in 1875, but not heard in court until 1886. This was timber that Wm. Daniels said he owned, previously sold by Anse Hatfield to Wm. Daniels, and then sold to Jim Vance. H.S. Carter was the man who had held that money from Jim Vance on the timber in that lawsuit., meaning that Carter was holding money on a case. Jim had him hold the money until a survey was done to determine the rightful owner. Carter had to be forced into the suit to make him pay the funds given to him by Jim. Now, Henry S. Carter brings a civil suit against Jim Vance in the below civil case one year before, in 1885.

In this case 4804, Jim Vance Sr., and Jim Jr., had appropriated two push boats by putting them into the hands of John Cisco [Francisco], son in law of Vance. John Cisco and James Vance held Carter's goods for 5 days. Carter said that a pretense "attachment" was given from a Justice of Logan, his goods were held, stating that his goods were to be levied. Valentine Hatfield was elected Justice of the Peace in 1885. The argument that Carter used is that the attachment of the Justice of Peace was only in his name (Carter) and not in the name of his firm or the business partner's name, making the attachment of the Justice of the Peace ineffective, and that the justice had released the store goods within 5 days. Carter still prays for relief in the suit for $500.00 in damages for lost revenue and property that he considered ruined.

1885 Dec 22 - H.S. Carter & Co Plaintiff vs. James Vance & c Defendant} Petition - The plaintiffs Henry S. Carter and W.W. Campbell make that they are partners doing business as general merchants on Peter Ck., in Pike County, KY and as such merchants they had in transit on two push boats coming up the Tug River a large lot of goods consisting of dry goods, groceries, notions, hardware, saddlery, and leather, time ware, drugs, furniture, books, and shoes in fact various other articles such as general merchants keep said stock of goods was of lot, value of other three thousand five hundred dollars and were being conveyed by flat boat men to the wharf of Peter thence to be hauled to the store of the plaintiffs. Plaintiffs now said that while said goods were in transit the defendants James Vance and James M. Vance unlawfully took possession of said goods and caused them to be put in the hands of one John Sisco and caused him to take possession of such goods while they were within the mile of the mouth of Peter and detained them for five days and prevented the flat boatmen from delivering the said goods for a period of five days this they did under a pretense attachment from a Justice in Logan County West Virginia when attachment was levied by the said Sisco a son in law of the defendant James Vance, and said goods on Sunday said levy was made under the mandate discretion of the defendants and bail bond authority the said Sisco not being any officer – the said damage seizure and detention of their plaintiffs goods caused one of their plaintiffs to come to the town of Pikeville and employ an attorney to go to West Virginia to relate said goods which was at great expense to the plaintiffs – plaintiffs charge that after which trouble and expense the said attachment said which was against H.S. Carter alone and was not for any claim against these plaintiffs as a firm, was devised from by the said Justice, and the goods said finally released, plaintiffs say that by reason of the detention of plaintiffs goods, they were delayed in getting there to the store and by reason of keeping the goods to detained until bad weather set in some of such goods are still at the mouth of Peter a distance of seven miles from plaintiffs store which could have been taken to the store in good weather had it not been for the delay caused by the deft – such delay also caused their plaintiffs great damage by the loss of trade and greatly impressed their credit by reason of _ and _ of fullen goods and put them to great expense in lawyers expense and other expenses in procuring the release of such goods to be damaged of their plaintiffs in the sum of five hundred dollars.

Plaintiffs make that their claim is this, a claim against the defendants Jam. Vance and James M. Vance as for money due them for seizing and detaining their goods, that it is a just claim, that they ought to recover the sum of five hundred dollars and the defendants named are non-residents of Kentucky and are about to remove a material part of their property out of their state not leaving enough therein to satisfy the plaintiffs claim or the claims of defendants creditors wherefore plaintiffs pray judgment against its defendants for five hundred dollars in damages and an attachment against their property and for all proper relief.

With this case, we only know the outcome as Henry Carter receiving his goods. We are not sure if James Sr. and John Cisco is held responsible for the sum of $500.00. None of these suits against Jim Vance ever showed up in his estate as money owed.

Henry S. Carter was a soldier in the war, shown in cases 2177[72] wherein he was charged with looting the home of George Hatfield. He was also charged with looting in case 2154 but this time, he was acting with the Hatfields. Case 5562, Carter, along with Bud McCoy, was held responsible for shooting the horse of Frank Phillips. Case 4169[73] is a suit against Wm. Daniels over a broken contract. Carter sold out his half of a timber business to Daniels. In this suit, Daniels received the ox, rigging,

---

[72] Kentucky Archives File 2177 – Geo. Hatfield plaintiff Vs. Peter Cline, Isaac Smith (son of Martin) Elijah Mounts Sr., H.S. Carter and John Charles and Jas M. Francis admin of the Wm. Francis estate} The pltf states that on or above the day of 1862 the deft Peter Cline, Isaac Smith. Elijah Mounts Sr., H.S. Carter unlawfully took from the possession of the pltf the following belonging to this pltf (Viz) 15 head of beef, 1 yoke of ox, 1 mule, 25 head of hogs, 1 ox cart, Blacksmith tools, Mill irons, Spun yarn, 37lb of wool, bed clothing, wearing apparel, farming tools, 15 yards, cupboard ware, castings, 15 head of sheep, value of $901.00. Pltf states that the deft took unlawfully the above property from pltf reasonably worth the above amount. Carried the same away and appropriate it to their own use and benefit. Whereby the same property was entirely lost to this pltf to his great hurt and damage. Whereon he prays judgment for $901.00 in damages. Feb 7, 1866

[73] KY Archives Civil File 4169 - H.S. Carter Pltf against Wm. Daniels Deft - Wm. Daniels testified as follows; I am deft in this action. Pltf and myself are partners in timbering & in team of cattle & c. the pltf became dissatisfied and wanted to sell out to me & I bought the cattle and timber & c., charged in plaintiffs account at the price charged & paid him in the assignment of an execution in my favor & against Martin Smith & Anderson Hatfield, which execution was assigned by me in writing & I fell in debt to pltf $4.50 on that settlement & gave him my note for same. This was 2nd Jan. 1880. John M. Ferguson who was deputy sheriff has the execution with him & wrote the assignment on it & wrote the note counted up the execution & all the matters between us. I never agreed to said contract with the deft . I only made one trade & none other & that was 2 Jan. 1880. Pltf came to me & wanted to rescend & I refused to do so & told him that I had sold one of the oxen. I am positive that I never made on against to rescend the contract with pltf & I had those articles in my posession all the time.

and other goods. Daniels, then gave Carter the note of Anse Hatfield's (1st note in a case of Perry Cline which we will discuss later on), Anse was held for that $500.00 note in Pike County court to owe Wm. Daniels. Carter first took the Hatfield assignment from Daniels, but then realized he couldn't get blood from a turnip. Therefore, Carter then goes back to Daniels, revokes the contract and wins his case against Daniels in court for $435.25. Later, it is said in case 16678[74] that Smith Carter sold the Anderson Hatfield's 800 acres to U.K. Williams and Fred Mounts, who would eventually sell to J.H. Charles. Anderson and Levicy will end up in court with J.H. Charles in 1920 over the 800-acre tract on Peter Creek. We will discuss those cases further on.

Q. What land does that deed describe, go ahead and read the description of it. A. "A certain tract or parcel of land, lying and being in Pike County, KY, on Peter Creek, beginning at a spruce and beech near a cliff at upper end of narrows, a short distance above Point Rock Branch, thence straight up said ridge to a spruce pine and white oak standing on top of the point, thence up the center of said ridge, around the head of the Point Rock branch to where a line of an eight hundred acre survey made in the name of Peter Cline crosses said ridge, thence with said ridge around until it comes to Peter Creek, thence up the said creek with the center thereof to the beginning, containing seven hundred acres, more or less. The above described lines is to run so as to include all of the land owned by the said parties of the first part on and about the mouth of said point Rock branch." Q. Do you know U.K. Williams got title to this land from? A. He got it through Smith Carter and Fred Mounts heirs. Q. Since the date of your deed from U.K. Williams, who has had the possession of this property? A. I have had it. Q. Tell how you have had it, what possession and what acts of ownership you exercised over it since that time? A. Well, my father had it in possession for a while, and it adjoins on to my home place where I live myself, and some of the family and renters have lived on it all the time, or most all the time, up until now.

These court cases are a web of owed *notes* being passed about. Then there are the court ordered *assignments* against Anse Hatfield, over one note that started with Green Taylor, Perry Cline, and Anse. That is our next court case, then you can start to see just how many cases involved these two pieces of land; the 800-acre Peter Creek tract and the 5000-acre Grapevine tracts.

---

[74] KY Archives Civil Case File 16678 February 3, 1920 Levisa Hatfield vs J.H. Charles

Chapter 12
ANSE HATFIELD LAWSUITS

This was a pivotal lawsuit for Anse Hatfield and Perry Cline, and it set the tone of discord for many years to come. This 800-acre plot of Peter Creek land would cost Anse dearly, for many years, especially after the fire setting and murders at the McCoy homestead. Anse Hatfield never crossed the Tug again into Kentucky because of a warrant looming over his head, for the events of the feud. Knowing that Anse would never cross the Tug again, families believed that the property should be theirs. Various lawsuits were filed against Anse, or others holding notes, in the 1870's and 1880's.

Jan. 14, 1903, Anse put the deed to this 800-acre Peter Creek land into his wife's name. In 1912 and 1920, they were back in court fighting for the right of ownership. But, not before the 1902 case of Martin Smith against Anderson Hatfield. I believe this early lawsuit of James Hatfield versus Peter Cline, over Peter Creek, along with the Grapevine land, led to some considerable contention. Control of some rich coal and timberland would be argued in court, and everyone claimed to own a piece. In Logan County, WV is case 079-00044, Martha Cline vs. Richard Torpin. The Grapevine land had a value of $16,800.00 at the time Perry sold it to Anse in 1877, per J.B. Ellison, Martha's Lawyer. By 1893, the value was said to be $80,000.00. That explains the reason for these lawsuits.

The lawsuit over these Peter Creek 800 acres went on until 1920, involving a series of lawsuits. The lawsuits started with land acquired in Pike County that was lost by Peter Cline. Peter was accused of looting during the war.

Case 2155, was between James Hatfield versus Peter Cline, wherein Peter Cline stole a horse, some hogs, and personal property was destroyed. James Hatfield sued the defendants named; Peter Cline, Andrew France, and William J. Hagerman. Peter Cline, who owned 800 acres on the Pike side of the river would pay the price for those union civil war raids. A raid was made by the men of Pike County, the 39th Kentucky at this time. The looting was in Nov. of 1862. Peter was sued on Dec. 27, 1865. James Hatfield heard Peter Cline giving orders, as well as William J. Hagerman and Andrew France, as those recognized.

Witnesses for James Hatfield included; Fred Wolford, Henry Daniels, and Elijah Mounts who testified that Peter was there and giving orders. Peter Cline lost this lawsuit, then having the housekeeper of the county, Colonel John Dils Jr., appraise the property and arrange for its sale. Peter Clines 800-acre plot of land went up for sale at the courthouse doors. James Hatfield bid and took possession, only to sell to Anse Hatfield.

Civil Case 2155 - 1865, James Hatfield vs. Peter Cline et al.
December 27, 1865 Pike Circuit Court
James Hatfield vs. Peter Cline, William J. Hagerman, and Andrew France Defendant. - The Plaintiff James Hatfield states that he was the owner of one Iron Gray Horse of the value of one hundred & twenty-five dollars of one colt near two years old of the value of sixty dollars of the seven hogs of the value of one hundred dollars also of a considerable amount of household & kitchen furniture. The Plaintiff further states that the defendants Peter Cline, Wm. J. Hagerman & Andrew France & others, in the month of Nov. 1862 with force & arms unlawfully entered on the premises of this Plaintiff. Took from him this Iron Gray Horse, his colt, seven hogs, and household & kitchen furniture of the value of twenty-five dollars. At the time, said property was taken from him, the defendants Peter Cline, William Hagerman & Andrew France was present ordering, acting & approving of the unlawful taking of his property & afterwards the same to their own use. To Plaintiffs great damage wherefore Plaintiff prays Judgment for five hundred dollars damages a Judgment for costs & other proper relief. James Hatfield

KY Archives Criminal and Civil File 8421

Let us skip ahead to the year 1902, case file 8421 Martin Smith vs. Anderson Hatfield. In this file, we get a description of what Martin Smith says happened[75]. This suit didn't involve Jim Vance accept to say that he and Wolford cut the timber on the property purchased by Jim.

---

[75] The deposition of Martin Smith on the 1st day April 1903 to be used as evidence on behalf of Plaintiff wherein Martin Smith is Plaintiff and Anderson Hatfield is Defendant pending in Pike Circuit Court. Q. Did you become surety for Anse Hatfield on a note to P.A. Cline? A. Yes, sir. Q. Do you remember the amount of the note? A. I don't exactly remember the amount of the note, but the amount of the Judgment taken against me was something over $500.00. Q. Was there a bond executed to you by Anderson Hatfield before you signed the note as surety on a tract of land of 800 acres on Peter Creek & being the same land described in this action? A. Yes, sir. Q. What was the purpose of the bond? A. It was executed to me as a matter of identity so that if I had to pay the note I should have the land. Q. Was a Judgment taken against you for this amount of the note with interest and cost? A. Yes, sir. Q. Who satisfied the Judgment you or Hatfield? A. Me in full. Q. Has he ever paid you any part of it? A. No sir. Q. So you know where the bond is? A. No sir. Q. Have you made search for it? A. Yes, sir. Q. State where you last saw the bond. A. I last saw it, when it was filed in the suit between P.A. Cline, William Daniels, A. Hatfield and myself.

Anse Hatfield was indebted to Perry Cline for a debt of over $500.00 in 1876 to 1877. He states that Smith signed a bond for Anse Hatfield and Perry Cline on the debt. In return, if Anse did not pay the note to Cline, he would sign over 800 acres on Peter Creek., to Smith.

He stated that Perry sold that $500.00 note of Anse to William Daniels. Daniels executed on the note and won in Pike County Court. Smith said Anse never paid the note to Daniels. Smith believed the land to be his. The bond Daniels and Smith executed on went missing from the files in the courthouse per the plaintiffs. However, the deed was never executed to Smith. This will lead to who settled on the 800 acres.

Anse replied with the following answer in court; that he and Vicey admit that they lived in Pike County, years ago; that Smith did sign a note as defendant's (Anse) surety, to Perry A. Cline for $500.00. Anse admitted that he executed the Bond on the Peter Creek land. Anse admitted that Cline sold the note to Wm. Daniels. Finally, he admitted that the title bond was never admitted to court because Smith never paid Wm. Daniels. The court ruled that Smith never paid the note to Daniels, and asked why he waited so long to bring the suit, from 1875. Anse proved he had settled the note with William Daniels and had Mary Daniels signature on the note as paid. Mary Daniels declined ever signing. She couldn't remember how her name was on the paid note. She stated that she never heard her husband telling the note was paid. In testimony, Mary Daniels and Martin Smith are asked if they had conspired to get the land in their name by claiming that the note was unpaid. They both denied that charge. This land was valuable coal land and would be mined and timbered by J.H. Charles.

This journey for Anse and Vicey was far from done in the courts. The Peter Creek land was still in jeopardy, with Anse never stepping foot back into Kentucky territory. June 1, 1912, Vicey sued Turkey Gap Coal and Coke Company, in KY Civil Case File 48. D.J. Wolford testified that Jim Vance had, in fact, checked with Wolford for the right to cut the timber on this land, in the company of Anse, and that the timber was legally cut. Wolford testified, "Vance didn't want to buy it (timber) until he knew my grandfather was willing for him to take the timber off." Jim Vance was a businessperson, which we will show in a following chapter on Vance, Bromley and Vance, where Jim employed many Tug residents. In this case, Wolford shows Jim Vance's interaction of a business deal, where Jim makes sure the property this wood is cut from was agreed to by all parties, which is what any reasonable businessman would negotiate. Now, for Anse and Vicy, it was just one hurdle to overcome to the next case.

Testimony of D.J. Wolford [portion of testimony]

Q. Where is Freeburn? A. That is the Turkey Gap Coal & Coke Company, where the mine is located, on the property that I owned and that I sold out to them when I moved away. I sold them the surface and kept the coal and minerals. Q. In what county and state is that located? A. Pike County, Kentucky. Q. And what creek? A. Well, the farm is on Tug River partly and part of it lies over on Peter Creek. Not all that farm, you might say, lays on the watershed of the Tug River side, just above the mouth of Peter Creek. Q. Are you acquainted with Anderson Hatfield, known as "Devil Anse?" A. Well, I have been acquainted with him ever since about the year 1865. Q. Are you acquainted with the land that is in controversy in this section, known as the Peter Cline 400-acre survey, on Rockhouse Branch of Peter Creek? A. Yes, Sir. Q. I will ask you if you ever cut and removed any timber from this tract of land? A. No, sir, not that tract. Q. The Rockhouse? A. Not the Rockhouse. I removed some off the Peter Cline survey, but not off the Rockhouse. Q. Which tract was that, the Point Rock tract? A. Yes sir. Q. From whom did you purchase the timber? A. James Vance. Q. Who did he get it from? A. Anderson Hatfield. Q. When did you cut and remove that timber, Mr. Wolford? A. I don't know the year, but it was the year 1882 or 1883 is my recollection. Q. You say Vance bought the timber from Anderson Hatfield? A. Yes, sir. Q. Did anyone make any objection to you removing the timber from the Point Rock? A. From when? Q. Well, from 1883? A. Well, Anderson Hatfield had been in possession of it until sometime along about 1880 or 1881, as I remember it, or right about that time, until he sold it to my grandfather for this timber, and my grandfather was in possession of it until he deeded it to his son Asbury, or willed it. I don't know which, and Asbury Mounts was in possession his lifetime and his heirs since.

Cross Examination - By Mr. Harmon

Q. Now you say that Anderson Hatfield was the recognized owner of that land up there on Rockhouse for; how did he get title to it? A. My recollection is that Anse Hatfield bought it either from Jim Hatfield or by a public sale; I wouldn't state which; I have heard it discussed quite often. Q. And you say that Anderson Hatfield sold it to Elijah Mounts? A. Yes, sir, he sold it to Elijah Mounts for the timber I got. He give him the land for the timber taken off of the Point Rock. Q. What did Anse Hatfield do with the timber on Point Rock? A. Sold it to Jim Vance. Q. When Anse Hatfield sold this land to Elijah Mounts did he execute a deed to him for it? A. That I couldn't say, as to that part of it. Q. You don't know whether or not there was any writing at all executed? A. No, I couldn't say. Jim Vance and Anse Hatfield came to my grandfather's house, and Jim Vance was buying the timber, and they dismissed the matter. Vance didn't want to buy it until he knew my grandfather was willing for him to take the timber off. Q. Now the timber which you have spoken of above, that Jim Vance bought, stood on what is known as the Point Rock of Peter Creek? A. Yes sir.

KY Archives Criminal and Civil Case File 16678 February 3, 1920

This next lawsuit, case file 16678, will be the end lawsuit for Anse and Vicey involving the land on Peter Creek. This lawsuit now involves J.H. Charles, from Mason Coal and Coke. In this lawsuit, Anse testified that he traded James Hatfield for land he owned in Virginia, a nice home, and James gave Anse a nice boot in this trade (the lawsuit of James Hatfield vs Peter Cline). There is over 50 pages of testimony in this case, which will not be included here. The important thing to take away from this case is that Anse and others knew the value of the land was in its minerals. Anse was then 72 years old, going on 73, he said. The case shows how he acquired the property and the paper trail that led to Anse through all of these suits. I have not researched the result. In this suit, there is a deed from Anse to J.H. Charles. This is the deposition of Anse Hatfield in this case, then we will explain more in the next case.

Kentucky Archives file 16678 - Levisa Hatfield vs. J.H. Charles

The deposition of J.H. Charles and Alex Bishop, taken at the office of Bert Shumate, in the Court of Williamson, Mingo County, West Virginia, on the 30th day of January 1914, ...of Levisa Hatfield & c., against J.H. Charles, and Levisa Hatfield &c., against Mason Coal & Coke Company etc., pending in the Pike Circuit Court.

The witness Anderson Hatfield being first duly sworn, deposes and says;
Q. I will read you the Judgment rendered in the Pike Circuit Court, at this Jun. Term 1866, the 8th day of Jun., in favor of Jam. Hatfield and against Peter Cline for the sum of $177.50 and will ask you to file that judgment as part of your deposition? A. I do file and same and mark it Anderson Hatfield exhibit No. 2. Q. I will read you a Fifa issued from the office of the clerk of the Pike Circuit Court, of date Jan. 24th, 1871 in favor of James Hatfield, against Peter Cline, defendant, and the levy endorsed thereon by the sheriff and will ask you if the property described is that levy endorsed on said Fifa is the same land in controversy and the land described in this patent just filed as part of your deposition. A. Yes Sir. Q. I will read you the appraisement of John Dils Jr., and Richard Robinson of some property in the suit of James Hatfield against Peter Cline, on Feb. 27, 1871 and will ask you if the property described in the appraisement is the land in controversy and patent and your deposition? A. Yes sir, that is the same property. Q. I will now read you the sheriff's report of sale of property in the action of James Hatfield against Peter Cline of date Feb. 27th,

1871 and will ask you if the property described in that report of sale as being tract No. 2 is the same property in controversy and that that is described in the patent filed in your deposition. A. Yes sir, same land. Q. I now hand you a writing purporting to be an assignment from James Hatfield to Anderson Hatfield, recorded on the margin of book of Record of land sales, at page 383 of date Mar. 12, 1874 signed by James Hatfield and attested by O.C. Bowles, and will ask you if the land described in the assignment is the same land described now in controversy. A. Yes sir, the same land.

Q. Was it recorded before you got it, before it was delivered to you? A. Yes sir, that is what was claimed, he passed the papers, handed them to me when I bought it. Q. Where were you when you purchased the land from James Hatfield, this land in controversy, I mean? A. On Peter Creek. Q. On Peter Creek? A. Yes Sir, I wouldn't be positive which side of the river I was on, but it seems to me that we was upon this property when we closed the deal. Q. What did you pay him for it? A. I traded him other real estate and took that as a payment, and he paid me the balance to boot between the property I sold him and this. Q. Do you mean you conveyed him another tract of land? A. Yes Sir, a nice home. Q. And in addition to giving you the land in controversy he was to give you something more? A. Yes Sir, I couldn't state exactly what it was, but was a good boot. Q. You mean by that, that the land that you let him have was valued at more than the land you got from him? A. Yes Sir. Q. What is the chief value? A. Why the coal and minerals on it would be the chief value. Q. You may say whether or not you have information that the defendants are threatening to enter on this land and cut timber and remove the timber and coal? A. I heard that, I don't know. Q. You have information? A. I have good information that they are opening a coal plant and have cut timber off of it, but I don't tell you that they have done it. I haven't been there. Q. Are you acquainted with the boundary lines of this land? A. Yes Sir, I took a surveyor and run it out. Q. The Point Rock tract? A. Yes Sir, run it from the three beeches, every call around and back. Q. When did you do that? A. A short while after I bought it. Q. Have you executed a deed of conveyance to anyone for this land except to your co-plaintiffs, Elliott R. Hatfield, and Louvisa Hatfield? A. No, nobody at all. Q. How long have you been away from the State of Kentucky? A. Twenty some odd years. Q. Have you any reason for not going back there? A. Yes Sir. Q. Good reasons? A. Good reasons, do you want what them reasons is? Q. None, I believe you go by the name of "Devil Anse" Hatfield? A. Yes Sir. Q. No I believe you, and none of your land was ever sold for taxes? A. None in that state that I know of, that I owned.

These suits over the 800 acres on Peter Creek, in Pike County, Kentucky, and the 5000 acres of land in Logan, WV, both had originally belonged to a Cline. Coincidence, I think not. These two suits do cross, starting with the Logan land.

KY Archives Criminal and Civil File 3442 3632 and 8421

Unfortunately, the 1870's gave way to many lawsuits, with even more detail than can be presented here. Let's look at the big picture. Brothers, Perry and Jacob Cline Jr., grew up next to the Hatfield's. Jacob Cline Sr., purchased land after a lawsuit with the Green heirs in 1827. When Jacob Cline, father of Perry died, Perry was raised by his negroes until he became a young man. In Pike County KY, August Term 1868, John Dils Jr. was appointed as Perry Cline's guardian. Perry moved to Pike County and became a sheriff, lawyer, and was elected to the legislature for one term. In 1878, Perry initiated a chancery case over the land of his ancestor, Jacob Cline, in Scott County against E.F. Tiller, the person appointed administrator of old Jacob Cline's estate in 1858. By this time, Perry had already sold that land to Anse Hatfield, in 1877.

Anse, a farmer and timber man, can be seen in this case 2180, as a man who protected his neighbors from the union pillaging, and went on confederate raids as well. Above all, Anse stood with the neighbors. Anse had gone into court for Jacob Cline Jr., and told that Jacob had been forced to go on that raid to Sowords Storehouse with the confederate forces. There is no doubt that Perry and Anse respected one another, and had problems with business deals. The question being…was there any plot on Perry Cline's part, to take back lands in order to become wealthy from its minerals? Let's face it, when a case goes on for over 45 years, as this 800-acre tract did, with people constantly in court, being summoned, and paying court costs, at some point the joie de vivre leaves and resentment begins in any friendship. Perry Cline died in 1891, but Anse stayed in court until 1920. In the 1870's Perry and Anse conducted business together. There were other cases involving the 800-acre tract; cases 3442, 3632 and 3748.

In Pike, case 3442 Jacob Cline (Jr) versus Green Taylor, is the issue we see in many lawsuits, which is the right to timber. Green Taylor sold to Jacob Cline Jr., timber rights believed to be on Alexander Mounts (deceased) land, sold to Taylor by Nancy Steel, and heirs. In so, Jacob Jr and Perry cut only part of the trees, and built a road in which to haul their trees. Boundary issues arose; were the trees being cut from the property of Mounts, or Anse? Later in 1875, Anderson Hatfield says he owned the land on which the trees were now being cut, and stopped all cutting. Jacob Cline Jr sued Green Taylor. Green said in 1875, that he could not help that the Clines waited too long to cut the rest of the trees. Though, Green wouldn't commit as to whose land the timber was on.

119

After all, Green was the defendant, and Jacob Cline Jr., said he paid Green for the timber. Anse was then named in the suit, as another defendant. With many other accusations, this led to more lawsuits in Kentucky and in Logan, WV.

Case 3632, what we have is TWO personal notes over land as shown earlier. The first note discussed was for $500.00 from Anse Hatfield to Green Taylor for land in Kentucky. The note of Anse was then sold from Green Taylor to Perry Cline.

Then we have a later, second note from Anse to Martin Smith. The second note says if Anse defaults on the first note, Martin Smith would get the 800 acres of land on Peter Creek, if Martin pays the note. It sounds complicated, and it is. So, first we have Green Taylor selling the first note to Perry Cline. Perry previously owed Daniels money and sells the first note to Wm. Daniels. Daniels tries to collect on the first note from Anse, as he learns of a second note to Smith. Daniels who owned the first note wants clarity. He takes Anse to court in case 3632, William Daniels versus Anderson Hatfield.

Later, case 8421 is the case brought by Martin Smith and Mary Daniels, in 1902, over the 800 acres, where its clarified what happened earlier in 1875/7. In the final judgment of case 3632, Anse owes Wm. Daniels. They agree on the sum of $573.56 with interest. The causes were dismissed for everyone else who sued over these lands. We know by case 8421 that Anse paid Daniels long before Wm. Daniels died, clearing the note for the Peter Creek land, causing Perry to make the deed to Grapevine to Anse in 1877. With both notes paid, Anse received his deed.

It is adjudged that the evidence fails to show that the mortgage made by Defendant Martin Smith to John Smith was made in contemplation of insolvency the petition as to John Smith is dismissed. The cross petition of Martin Smith excepts to this Judgment upon the suit consolidated. Where, with, of Wm. Daniels aforesaid Anderson Hatfield, Martin Smith. It is adjudged by the Court that Wm. Daniels recover against the Defendant Anderson Hatfield and Martin Smith the sum of $573.56 with interest thereon at the rate of 6% per annum from the first day of May 1876 until paid. And his cost herein expended and may have execution therefore the cost occasioned by the attempt to enforce the lien upon land shall be taxed against said Defendant as it is adjudged on lien except in favor of Wm. Daniels the cross petition of Smith in this suit is dismissed. Defendant Smith excepts of this Judgment.

The Torpin case is discussed in many of the feud books. By this time in 1894, Anse didn't own what was left of the Grapevine property, it went to back taxes, but not before Anse sold the mineral rights to part of the land. Richard Torpin Jr and others owned it. A northern investor had acquired the property through J.D. Sergeant. Martha in case 070-00044 said she didn't sign the conveyance to Hatfield in 1877, she has rights through dower of her husband Perry, she thought. In this case, exhibited is the 1877 deed from Perry and Martha to Anderson Hatfield, and the Will of Perry Cline, which makes no mention of the Grapevine land. Anderson first purchased the Grapevine land for $1900.00, per this case. Martha said that Anse traded to Cline, the land on the Kentucky side purchased of Green Taylor for the Grapevine land.

On Jan. 1, 1894, Martha is shown as a resident of West Virginia, living in Logan County, posting a bond in court for $200.00. Martha says Old Jacob filed his Will in Logan in 1858, and that during the civil war, with the burning of the courthouse, the Will no longer existed. Torpin says that Perry sold out his interest in the land 25 years prior, and since had no interest in this property. Torpin claimed Martha had no dower rights to this land, and Perry never claimed the land in taxes. As already stated, this was one piece of expensive real estate. The 800 acres and the 5000 acres, both properties, were a gold mine of resources.

If one wants to explore Ellison versus Torpin, and cases of Martha Cline, here are a list of other cases in Logan Chancery one should acquire from the West Virginia Archives. All of these cases mention the Hatfield land on Grapevine. 014-029-00059, 00A-00067, 00B-00067, 00C-00067, 051-00052, 014-029-00059, 079-00044, 037-00044, and 026-00044.

This Deed of conveyance, made and entered into this 23rd day of March, 1877, between P. A. Cline and Martha Cline, wife of P. A. Cline, parties of the first part, and Anderson Hatfield, party of the second part, witnesseth; that said parties of the first part, for and in consideration of the sum of one tract of land, lying on Tug River, in Pike County, Kentucky, it being the land that Anderson Hatfield purchased of Green R. Taylor, valued at $900.00, do hereby sell and convey to the party of the second part, his heirs and assigns the following property to wit, all the lands that was willed to P. A. Cline by Jacob Cline, Sr, his father. Said land being lying on Tug River, in Logan County, West Virginia, containing 5 acres, more or less, To have and to hold the same, together with all the appurtenances thereon, to the party of the first part, his heirs and assigns forever. And the said parties of the first part hereby covenant with the said party of the second part—that they will warrant the title to be the property hereby conveyed, unto the said party of the second part, and his heirs and assigns forever. A lien is retained upon the property conveyed, as security for the title to the aforesaid lands, that is the Deed for the land from Anderson Hatfield.

In testimony whereof they hath hereunto subscribed their names, the day and year aforesaid

P. A. Cline
Martha × Cline

Chapter 13
VANCE LAND DEEDS

Sometimes we can't explain the reasons why things are done. We can't explain if a lawsuit had a favorable ending. We can't be in the heads of our ancestors to know their motives, unless it's documented. As already seen by the previous cases, we can't always tell who won or lost a case. What we can see by these cases, is that these men didn't always deal with banks this early on, and that bartering was a way of life. Your "word" had to be worth as much as the X you placed upon the *note*, and signed for services.

By 1884, Jim Vance was selling bits of acreage to his children. [Appendix J] The children were planting roots of their own. The families are being married, and having children. Many times, the father, would help to supply land to his daughters, as a kind of dowry. By Feb. 1886, James and Mary were making big land deals with James and Pherabe Hull. The new land purchased is at Round Bottom, Wayne County, directly on the Sandy River. James and Mary Vance are the parents of Elizabeth Nichols, Jane Ferrell, Amy Francisco Flynn, John, and James Vance Jr. The first pieces of land were sold in 1884 to Elizabeth Vance Nichols, and to Jane Vance Ferrell. By 1886, Jim and Mary had sold land to their daughter, Amy Vance Francisco.

From this point, Jim has made a rather large move into Wayne County, West Virginia, directly on the Sandy River, on Feb. 20, 1886. The land is noted to be on Round Bottom, now the city of Pritchard. This land is located with Smith, Johnson, and Deans land and connecting on the Sandy River and crossing the main county road, containing "only" 50 acres of land for the large sum of $6500.00

James Hull and Wife to James M. Vance and others} Deed – This deed made this the 20th day of February 1886 between James Hull and Phoebe Hull his wife of Round Bottom, Wayne County, State of West Virginia of the first part. And James M. Vance and Mary Vance of Logan County and State of West Virginia of the second part. Witnessed that for and in consideration of the sum of ($6500) six thousand five hundred dollars. And one thousand dollars of which is in hand paid and residue secured to be paid by bills or notes of same date herewith which is to be paid as follows. ($2000) two thousand dollars on or before the first day of June 1887 and ($1500) one thousand five hundred dollars on or before the first *day of June 1889. With legal interest on the deferred payments from the 1st day of March 1886 paid by the parties of the second part. The parties of the first part hath this day sold and by these present hath bargained sold and conveyed a certain tract or parcel of land lying and being in Round Bottom Wayne County West Virginia and bounded as follows. ...[description] James Hull Phoebe Hull*

This is an immense amount of money for 50 acres of land. When we look at what Jim sold to Jane and Elizabeth at $2.00 per acre, this Round Bottom land is much more expensive at $130.00 per acre, or there about. For a man in 1886 to afford that land, Jim had to be making some serious cash. From Feb. 1886 to Dec 1887, Jim and Mary lived outside of Logan County, WV and nowhere near the feudists. Which is important to realize. James M. Vance is clearly debased in the Hatfield and McCoy books as a man without much intellect, or provenance. Which we will show in the next lawsuit, that Jim Vance, was not just another Tug resident. He employed many men, and helped to give people of the Tug a work life. People needed employment to help pay taxes, and buy goods to survive.

The deeds made from Jim Vance Sr. and Mary can be found in Appendix J., showing the sale of lands to Clay and Headley, Thacker Coal and Coke, and to his children.

Yes, we trace Jim Vance Sr. through the lawsuits, and deeds, and court related cases. You will be trace this way too, in 200 years from now. It's important to know, that Jim Vance had minor lawsuits up until his death, when the family lost everything. Prior to his death, he brings a suit against John B. Bromley.

Chapter 14
VANCE, BROMLEY, AND VANCE - TIMBER BARON

The firm of James Vance Sr., John B. Bromley, and James Vance Jr., was a timbering business that existed from July 1885, and employed many of the Tug Valley residents within the two years of the business records provided in this case. This case, found in Logan County Court records, was initiated by Jim Vance Sr., as Plaintiff, against John B. Bromley, as Defendant. The suit was for non-payment of funds. They were partners, and were accountable for wages and provisions in March 1887. Bromley, in counter language, asked the court to take into account that Vance had not included some timber into the business, which Vance had bought from John Sansom. Jim claimed this timber was purchased before he went into a partnership with Jim Vance Jr., and John Bromley. When this partnership began, it was James Vance Jr., J.G. Gauge/Gauze, and John B. Bromley. John B. Bromley can be found in the 1880 census in Wayne County, WV., as a timber merchant, which makes a great deal of logic, this is also where Jim Vance Sr. lived. Gauge/Gauze withdrew from the business. Jim Vance Sr. acquired his part of the business, financially keeping the business alive. James Vance Sr., claimed Bromley had not supported the firm financially. The case was sent to District Court in Charleston in 1887, and from there the outcome is not found.

One thing that tells me that Jim was in good standing in this case is the fact, that Bromley asked that it be moved into district court for appeal, at Bromley's expense, meaning Bromley was contesting the lower court's ruling. The important part of this case is not the suit itself, but the fact that this suit exhibits that Jim Vance Jr and Sr., were well connected, industrious, and well educated. Jim Vance Sr., as can be seen in this suit, was the person who kept the records, which were well written and well-kept for that period of time, when many men and women had no proper education. As well, the company hired many hands from both sides of the Tug River, from West Virginia and Kentucky alike, from July 1885 to July 1887. Of those listed are the men paid to raft, cut, and haul logs, and names of business men with whom Vance conducted business. [See Appendix L for two of those images]

Logan County Chancery Book B page 596 April 6, 1887 - James Vance, James Vance Jr. vs. John B. Bromley - On motion of the plaintiffs by their attorneys for reasons appearing to the court, and it appearing that they had failed to file their bill herein at rules they have cease to file the same in open court which is accordingly done and the cause is remanded to rules to be there proceeded with.

Logan County Chancery Book C page 53 July 16, 1887
James M. Vance and James Vance vs. John B. Bromley} In Chancery
This day the defendant John B. Bromley tendered this petition herein praying that this court proceeds no further herein except to make an order removing this cause to the District Court of the United States sitting at Charleston West Virginia exercising Circuit Court powers for the District of West Virginia, which said petition being duly verified and accompanied by the necessary bond. Conditioned according to law which said petition and bond are ordered to be filed among the papers in this cause and the court being satisfied of the truth of the facts stated in said petition and demurring said bond sufficient is of opinion that the said defendant is entitled to have this cause removed to the said District Court. It is therefore ordered that this cause be removed to the said District Court to be therein further proceeded with according to law.

Albert McCoy	Eph Hatfield
Albert Williams	Evan Ferrell
Alex Mitchell	Evermont Staton
Alex Varney	F. Lane
Anthony Sansom	F.K. Sansom
A. Coleman	Ferrell Maynard
Bob Stone	Floyd Hatfield
Brooks Williams	Frank Maynard
Buck Sipples	French Ellis
Bud Endicott	G. Atwell
Bud Hurley	George Hatfield
Bud Norman	George Prater
C or G. New	H. Maynard
Comp Harden	Harrison Prater
Dan Mounts	Harrison Steel
Dick Mahon	Harry Harden
E. Chapman	Harve Lewis
E. Sullivan	Henry Chapman
Ed Chapman	Henry Stepp
Elbert Hurley	Henry Toler
Eli Baker	Ira Coleman
Eli Kennedy	Isaac Fletcher
Elizabeth Nichols	Isaac Wallace
Elliott Hatfield	J.J. Jordan
Ellison Prater	J.D. Nichols

Jack Harden
Jacob Blankenship
Jacob Francisco
James Ferrell
James Mahon
James Mullins
James Wallace
Joe Norman
John Allen
John Chapman
John Francisco
John Harden
John Kennedy
John Mounts
John Vance
Johnse Hatfield
Joseph Sipples
L.D. McCoy
Lafayette Vinson
Lawyer Hatfield
Leland Smith
Lewis Acord
Lewis Harden
Mahan Prater
Marshall Mullins
Matthew Hatfield
Mel Romans

Mike Lockhart
Miles Diamond
N.B. Nichols
Oscar Clark
P. Bartram
Rich. Blankenship
Richard Prater
Rich. Shortridge
Riley Harden
Robert Davis
Sam Francisco
Sampson Hatfield
Thomas Harden
Thomas Sansom
Thomas Wallace
W.J. Hatfield
Wash Stone
Wesley Romans
William Daniels
William Kennedy
William Lane
William Maynard
William Mead
William Mounts
William Ratliff
Sam Bromley

On June 27, 1885, Jim Vance is under a contract with Lewis S. Steel for trees. This contract was written like a deed and hard to read. It seems to be for 800 feet of walnut and some poplar trees for which Vance will float down the river for Steel. Steel is mentioned as owing Vance $551.00 for a wagon, tools, yoke and a rig. The timber is part of that payment. The rest would be sold, and then given back to Steel. Jim is actually working in order for Steel to pay him back for a loan, logging the Steel trees to do it. Only Steele would have to get the trees to the river and floated after being cut by Jim Vance and crew. It just goes to show how industrious and accommodating this man was, and how egregiously he was defamed by journalists, feud writers, and the McCoy faction. Desperate? I say not!

Chapter 15
THE ESTATE OF JAMES M. VANCE

James M. Vance Sr. died on Jan. 8, 1888, in Logan Co., WV., according to the Gov. Buckner papers collection in the KY Archives. His estate was probated in Logan County, WV. Although, one newspaper credits his death to the 7th of January, it is a moot point. James Monroe Vance Sr. was murdered on his own property by men who invaded West Virginia without warrants. Jim reveals a very small estate, mainly logging essentials. Jim went to his grave leaving a loving wife, Mary, who when Jim was fired upon and killed, never left Jim's side. Mary had grit, which comes from being an early resident of the Appalachian Mountains. He left five children, and numerous grandchildren.

James Vance Jr. filed the paperwork to become the administrator of his father's estate on February 18, 1888, with John F. Vance and Elias Hatfield as his sureties. John F. Vance is not James Sr.'s son, he is the son of Richard and Matilda Brown Vance. At this time, John F. and Elias were both constables in Logan. On March 5th, 1888, the Bond was recorded and Jim Jr. was sworn to disperse the assets. Jim Vance's son, John, seemed to be absent from much of what was happening on the Logan County side of the Tug for some time, even long before his father's death. John as the elder son, would usually have assumed many of the duties as the oldest son of the family. He did work for his father and younger brother in the business. I've wondered why Jim and Mary had never allocated land to John or his children, as he had Elizabeth, Jane, Amy, and Jim Jr. during 1884 to 1887. If he did, I've not located that deed.

1888 - James M. Vance to State of West Virginia} Bond
Know all men by these present, that we James M. Vance, John F. Vance and Elias Hatfield are held and firmly bound unto the State of West Virginia in the sum of Five Hundred Dollars, for the true payment of which well and truly to be made, we bind ourselves our heirs, executors and administrators, jointly and severally, firmly by these present, seal with our seals and stated this 18th day of February 1888.
The condition of the above obligation is such that whereas the above bond, James M. Vance has this day been appointed administrator of the personal estate of the said James Vance deceased.

Now therefore if the said James M. Vance admin as aforesaid, shall account for and pay over to the parties thereto entitled all money and other effects which shall come into his hands, by virtue of his said office then the above obligation to be void, else to remain in full force and virtue. James M. Vance, John F. Vance, and Elias Hatfield in Logan County Court Clerk office this March 5th, 1888. The foregoing Bond was this day duly admitted to record.

By June 11, 1888, James Vance Jr. filed his father's estate. The appraisers were Joseph Simpkins and W.S. Ferrell (Shang Ferrell). James and Mary sold off some of the land in Logan to their children years before. We see farm animals, some furniture, tools and one Winchester rifle. Frank Phillips and his Phillips-McCoy posse had taken what money and guns from Jim's trunk, when they ransacked his home on the day he was killed, according to Shepards report to WV., Governor Wilson. That same report said that Phillips' men had tossed the family possessions from the house, after stealing his money, guns and bullets from his chest. Jim's estate registered one Winchester. There was no side arms or bullets. This was hardly the repeating rifle and the 2 pistols Buckner claimed he owned in the Jan 30th letter to Gov. Wilson.

I recently acquired a copy of Squirrel Hunting Sam, a book with the memoirs of Sam McCoy, produced by his heirs, and Leonard Roberts. In this book, Sam said as they approached the house of Vance, a woman (Mary) came down the slope of the hill, and yelled to her husband. When Sam viewed Vance and Cap approaching, Sam wrote that only one of them had a gun. In a later paragraph, Sam said that Vance and Cap fired on them, and that they shot Cap's gun from his hand, and then Cap made a run for it. In the testimony of Allen Cline, he said this, when speaking of Cap, "He was talking about the Thacker fight; he said that Bud McCoy said he shot him in the hand, but that he snagged it." Sheppard claimed Vance's gun and his bullets were stolen from Jim's trunk, from inside his home, along with his money. So did Vance even have a gun in the woods? Did he "ever" fire upon the gang from Kentucky, as they claimed? Ferrell, one of two hostages taken by Phillips, said no, that Jim was fired upon without provocation. Ferrell witnessed the event as a hostage of Phillips. Sam said if Vance had held still and not moved, that he wouldn't have been killed. The question is and will always be, did they shoot and kill an unarmed man because he was a friend of the Hatfields? That is what Sheppard said in his letter to Gov. Wilson. Was he guilty by association or was there something more sinister involved?! Who in the blazers is telling the truth, the witnesses or the murderers? However, the facts are this: Jim Vance was NOT under any warrants for arrest, and NOT associated with any of the perceived events. He was on his own property, and at the time of his murder, no one, not even Phillips or the McCoys, would have known IF Vance participated in the New Year's tragedy. Jim had every right to protect himself on his own property from this gang of thugs, intruding into WV., without the clear and proper rights to be there. That is the feuding truth!

The total worth of Jim's estate was $313.00. A one-acre lot in Wayne was in the name of Amy and John Francisco, and was not included in the estate. Amy's home was in Logan, WV, where she lived. No household goods in Wayne were accounted for.

Also mentioned here, is a note of $100.00 from the lawsuit of France. When in court, if a man is accused of filing a civil suit falsely, it works against the accuser. France filed a bond to initiate the earlier case. Since France lost that case, he would owe Vance the amount of the bond. Jim's estate looks to be that of a farmer, and hardly that of a well off man at this point, and the creditors were coming out of the woodwork. Jim Sr., and Jim Jr., owed some serious money, enough so that the property of the family, as his heirs, had to be sold, and was put up for auction.

Logan County James Vance Jr. Administrator
To Appraisement Bill
James M. Vance Sr. deceased

1 Yoke Oxen.......................50.00
1 Cow.............................20.00
20 sheep..........................30.00
1 calf.............................5.00
5 Hogs @4.........................20.00
Francis Note 100.00
1 Winchester.....................10.00
Notes..............................3.00
House Hold and Kitchen Furniture 75.00

Given under our hand____313.00
This 11th day of June 1888
Joseph Simpkins} Appraiser, W.S. Ferrell} Appraiser - In Logan Co. Court June 11th 1888, The foregoing Appraisement of the former property of James M. Vance deceased was this day duly admitted to record.

Devoted Mary, Deceased

Mary died of the flux near Milton, Cabell Co. WV, on Sept. 19, 1894.

Her death was reported by her now son in law, Charles Stephen Flynn, husband of Amy. Mary is known as "Aunt Mary" per the Logan Banner. Charles Stephen Flynn and Napoleon Bonaparte Nichols, both of whom were sons-in-law, probated her estate on Sept. 26, 1894, when a bond was executed in Logan County, WV and probated in Cabell County, WV. Both men are her sons-in-law, and one is the widowed husband of Elizabeth Vance McCoy Nichols. Mary was known for her great shot with a rifle, able to knock a squirrel out of the tree as well as any man, per the Logan Banner. Before Mary died, she watched four of her five children perish. Mary died leaving the following estate in Cabell County. The estate lawsuits in Logan had taken just about everything of real value, the 1500 acres on Grapevine and Thacker, which included the land and its resources. What was once a prosperous family, employing many men of the area, her estate had dwindled to just one cow, two horses, and $922.68 cents owed from a land sale to Thacker Coal?

Logan County Bond Book B. - BOND Know All Men By These Present that we C.S. Flynn and N.B. Nickels are held and firmly bound unto the State of West Virginia, in the just and full sum of Three Thousand Dollars, to the payment whereof, well and truly be made, we bind ourselves, our heirs, executors and administrators, jointly and severally, firmly by these presents. Sealed with our seals, and dated this 26th day of September 1894. THE CONDITION OF THE ABOVE OBLIGATION IS SUCH that whereas the above bound C.S. Flynn has been this day being by the Clerk of Logan Court of said County appointed administrator of the personal estate of Mary Vance deceased. Therefore, if the said Flynn shall faithfully discharge all the duties as such administrator and account for and pay over to the parties thereto entitled all money and other effects which may come to his hand by virtue of his said office.
Cabell County Appraisement Book page 374
Appraisement Bill of Mary Vance deceased - Cabell Co. WV Feb 18, 1985
We the undersigned appraisers appointed by the county court of Cabell County do appraise the personal estate of Mary Vance deceased, and being duly sworn do appraise the following property to wit:
One milk cow 5 years old $16.50
One black 5 year old horse $100.00
One bay 5 year old horse $75.00
S.G. Carter, G.W. Ball, J.M. Barcus
At a county court held for Cabell Court at the courthouse thereof on the 23 day of July 1895.
The appraisement bill of the personal estate of Mary Vance deceased was this day presented in court which being seen and inspected by the court is approved and ordered to be resolved. F.F. McCullough Ck.

Estates and Property Settlements

Before Jim Vance died, he had sold Pherabe Hull back the property at Round Bottom, though it wasn't recorded in the clerk's office until after his death. There could be lots of speculation as to why Jim Vance Sr., came back to Logan County, WV in late Dec. 1887, no more than two weeks before his death. Jim was summoned to appear in Pike County, KY in the case of France vs Vance in Pike County, and he became the plaintiff in Logan County, along with his son Jim, against John B. Bromley. That court date was for Dec. of 1887 in Logan County, WV.

The lawsuits after Jim Sr., died piled up against the family estate, leaving them no choice but to sell the Vance property to pay for these debts. These were lawsuits filed by Krish, Hurst & Miller, who were merchants, and one by the estate of Lawson. There is mentioned in this suit with Krish, the company of "James Vance and Son", which we know this is a timber business. In the joint answer, from both James Sr. and James Jr., both being defendants, they said; the bill is not true and that Krish recovered a judgment against him in Wayne Court for $322. That one H. Krish, agent, recovered such judgment against James Vance and Son. The defendants are not aware who H. Krish is agent for, and deny the right of H. Krish to carry on this suit. Krish, and Hurst and Miller both sued in Oct. 1887. [Appendix I] Logan court demands that a newspaper article to be issued in Logan and Wayne Counties. Wayne is where James Sr. lived at the time. Jim was moving the deeds in Wayne into Jim Jr's name. Back and forth from Hull etc., to keep the creditors from securing the land, I suspect, a practice he and many others often did. This was not an unusual practice. Jim Sr. and Jr. finally sold back to Hull, except for a one-acre lot, which was then in the name of Amy Francisco.

The first initial bills added up over $1,347.00 from Krish and Hurst/Miller. [principal and interest]. Then after Jim died, two more creditors joined what becomes the estate suits, Joseph Brigal and Company, and Jennie Lawson suing as administrator of the Lawson estate. Some of the money owed had to be for goods, since Hurst and Miller were wholesalers out of Catlettsburg. The Lawson debtors were heirs recovering what was owed the Lawson estate. These lawsuits were paid. The court ordered the sale of the Vance land, Jim Vance Jr. complied, and sold to J.D. Sergeant (and James O'Keefe) for a whopping $5025.00. It wasn't until Oct. of 1890, that the estate debts were paid by the court.

In May of 1888, Jim Vance Jr. sold to Clay and Headley the mineral rights (timber) (Deeds Appendix J) off the Vance land. Around this same time, Jim Jr. acquired a house and store in Nolan, WV (then called Duncan, WV.). Jim Jr. was not the only person to sell resources to Clay and Headley of Kentucky, or R.S. Lowry of Virginia, and J. Dickenson Sergeant of Pennsylvania. Here is a surprising fact. Gov. Buckner, of Kentucky, offered rewards against the 1882 Logan men that killed the McCoys at the paw paw bush incident. The month of Sept. 1887, Plyant Mahon, Doctor Mahon, Sam Mahon, and Valentine Hatfield sold the mineral rights to their properties for fifty cents an acre to R.S. Lowry. Floyd Hatfield, Harrison Hatfield, Andy Varney, and Moses Christian joined them in September and October of 1887. These sales were shortly after the rewards were placed on the West Virginia men. Elias Hatfield sold his in Feb. 1888 to Sergeant. Anse Hatfield waited until May of 1888, also selling to J. Dickenson Sergeant.

Later, many of the people who sold or lost their lands, ended up in Chancery Court. Jane Ferrell, Elizabeth Nickles, and Amy Flynn will end up in court against Sergeant. Jim Sr. and Mary had sold land to his daughters, and the county made claim that taxes were not paid, and tried to sell the land to Sergeant and O'Keefe. Both stayed in the court house buying up what they called "School Property." That was property that was taken for "back taxes", then sold to middlemen like O'Keefe and Sergeant, who would buy the property for far less than the real value. Only paying mere dollars for land, when the value of the Grapevine/Thacker land was worth much more. They only had to pay the court costs, and back taxes. The counties claimed to sell that land to add to the school fund. Jane won her case against the county and Sergeant, proving that she and Mary, her mother, had paid their taxes[76]. None the less, it shows that men who claimed to be there in order to help the counties flourish, were there to make money, selling land to men like Torpin.

Tragedy for a Son

On January 24th, 1884 in civil file 4684, we find James M. McCoy and wife Mary selling land to John Vance. This James M. McCoy is the son of Daniel and Margaret Taylor McCoy, and brother of Asa and Randolph

---

[76] WV Archives 019-00047

McCoy. Though, it didn't take long before John, about the age of 34, didn't make the final payment. Jasper McCoy son of James M. McCoy purchased that land from the court ordered sale in Oct. of 1885. James McCoy had given John Vance a note on the land. John Vance paid him $490.00 up front, in hand at the time of the sale, with a note of $310.00. With a later payment of $70.00 of an ox and a cow. When a final payment wasn't paid, John Vance lost his land. John moved over to Logan County, WV.

For Mary, who lost her husband, Jim Vance, in the feud, she now watched her children perish one at a time. James Jr. died in May 1892 of unknown circumstances. Daughters, Elizabeth Vance Francisco and Jane Vance Ferrell both died in 1894. Sons in-law John Francisco died on April 2, 1889, while Evans Ferrell died sometime in 1894, both of unknown circumstances. Amy (also called Anna) was the only surviving child of the Vance family. None of the deaths were recorded in the county books, except to say, if an estate was administered, as it was with Jane Ferrell. We found testimony relating to their deaths in the Supreme Court of Appeals of WV., Viola Darnell versus E.E. Music, over the John Francisco land case 1299, which can be located in the WV. Archives. These deaths must have been catastrophic for Mary.

Son, John Vance died a hero in my book, under tragic circumstances for all involved. John stepped in front of his mother who had a gun pointed at her by an angry young man, Melvin Lee Runyon. This tragedy occurred after the death of Jane Vance Ferrell in 1894. Jane gave birth to a baby, Grover in 1892. The Logan court appointed an administrator of Jane's estate. As well, a person was appointed guardianship of all of Jane's and Evan's children. Her children were placed among family members to be raised. M.A. Ferrell was given guardianship of the older children.

It just so happens, one of her children, Mary Etta Ferrell Runyon, was old enough to be married. She wanted guardianship of her younger sibling, Grover. The court appointed Napoleon Nichols as administrator of Jane's estate, as well as guardian of Grover. Word had reached Mary, that the child was not being raised with proper care in the Runyon household. Mary had Napoleon bring the child to her. Melvin Runyun went to the Justice of Peace, and nothing was done to his satisfaction for the return of the child. Napoleon was the child's guardian. Melvin then departs to Mary's home, and there makes a demand for the baby. Melvin was pointing a gun at Mary. John was in the room. John stepped up and told Melvin, "You don't point a gun at a woman." Melvin shot John in the stomach. He lived only a couple of days. Melvin then escaped to Kentucky to avoid arrest. Stephen Flynn, (Amy's husband), offered up a reward for the arrest, to be paid upon Runyon's return to Logan. Melvin Runyon was arrested when he came back to Logan by Sheriff Elias Hatfield. The deaths of James, Mary, and their children left very few to tell the story of James Monroe Vance Sr. from the Vance perspective.

Logan Banner July 12, 1894 - Shooting at Thacker - Death of John Vance son of Jim and Mary Vance **** There was a serious shooting affray in which John Vance has probably lost his life at the hands of Melvin Runyon. Some two or three months ago Mrs. Jane Ferrell, a relative of Mr. Vance died, leaving an infant child less than a year of age. At the last term of the County Court an order was made appointing Reece T. Ferrell guardian of the child but by a subsequent order left the child in the custody of Mrs. Melvin Runyon a sister of the child until the next term of the court. We understand that one day last week someone took the child from Mrs. Runyon and left it with Mr. Vance. Runyon at once went to Joseph Simpkins, a notary public, for a warrant for the child but was refused. He then went to Mr. Vances, and Vance attempted to put him out of the house, when Runyun drew his pistol and shot Vance. The ball entering the bowels. Runyon at once crossed the river into Kentucky, but was followed, and we suppose caught before this time. Vance's wound is said to be fatal.

Logan County Banner July 19, 1894 - The facts about the killing of John Vance are as follows; Jennie Ferrell as sister of John Vance, died a short time ago, leaving a baby less than a year old. Mel Runyon a son in law of Jennie Ferrell, took charge of the child, and Mrs. Mary Vance, the grandmother of the child, hearing that the child was not well treated, had the child brought to the house of Boney Nichols, a brother in law of Jennie Ferrell, where Mrs. Vance was staying. Runyon followed, and drew his pistol on Mrs. Vance, the mother of John Vance, when Vance stepped between them and told Runyon not to draw a pistol on a woman, Runyon then fired on Vance, inflicting wounds from which he died the next day. Runyon made his escape into Kentucky and has not been heard of since.

Logan Co. Banner July 26, 1894 – July 26, 1894 - Mel Runyon who killed John Vance about two weeks ago at Thacker was captured on Trace Fork of Pigeon Creek on Tuesday by Allen J. Shepard and others, and lodged in jail. The reward of three hundred dollars, which was offered for his capture, was promptly paid by Charles Flynn. Runyon had his examination before Squire Stowers yesterday and was sent on to the grand jury. Deputy Sheriff Elias Hatfield and J.W. Chambers took Runyon to Huntington this morning for safekeeping.

Logan Banner Apr. 17, 1895 – In some way our watchful jailor Elias Hatfield learned that some week or two days ago the wife of Melvin Runyun, who is confined in jail here for the murder of John Vance at Thacker, had been trying to get a pistol in the jail to him. On Monday, Mrs. Runyun with a brother of Runyun, and Mr. A.J. Shepherd came over to see him. Mr. Hatfield thought it was his duty to search Mrs. Runyun before she was allowed to go into the jail, which he did at once. And found a hatchet under her dress. The hatchet was taken from her and she was not allowed to go in. Mr. Shepherd and Mr. Runyun were however, allowed to go in and talk with the prisoner. The jailor is commended by all for his action.

Viola and Maggie Francisco

In Logan, the last lawsuit brought by Amy's daughters, Viola and Maggie Francisco, over their fathers land in Logan, against Little Kanawha Lumber Company, in 1894. The girls, believed that the land owned by them, was being used by this timber company, and abused. They won this lawsuit against Kanawha Lumber. Shortly after, Amy and her girls move to Cabell County, WV, and then into NC, where they lived, and are buried. [Appendix J]

Case 079_00054 Viola Francisco vs Little Kanawha Lumber Company - Viola Francisco and Maggie Francisco infants under the age of 21 years, who sue by their next friend C.S. Flynn, plaintiffs against the Little Kanawha Lumber Company, a corporation Charley Stephens, Levi Stephens, Jacob Spaulding and Amy Flynn defendants filed in the circuit court of Logan County, WV.

Stores in West Virginia owned by Jim Vance Jr.

Jim Vance Jr. married Vicey Stepp, daughter of Aaron and Parlee Jane Stepp. After the administration of the estate of James Vance Sr., and the sale of the Vance land, Jim and Vicey set up housekeeping in Nolan, WV. They give birth to a son named James ((third in the line born 1892) see picture in front of book)). This youngster would later marry Elizabeth Barbour. Jim Vance Jr. died in May of 1892, and Vicey remarried to Charles Tipton. The baby, James, of 1892, will state on his WWII papers, that he was born in Nolan in April of 1892. He was just one month old when his father died. He will inherit one of the three lots purchased by Jim and Vicey in Nolan, WV. One such lot was a house and store. One had a gas well on the land. The families of son James Jr. would inherit royalties from the gas well land for many years.

James Jr. and Mike Young owned a store in White House, Ky., according to a lawsuit found in the Kentucky Archives, case 5615. This would have been owned prior to the store in Nolan, WV. In this suit, Jim Jr., once again gets in over his head. He was sued for money owed to a Louisville firm for merchandise acquired for a store in White House, KY. Sister, Amy Flynn, paid the debts after her brother died. Later, Amy would bring a suit against Vicey Vance[77], wife of Jim Jr., never to recover this debt in Logan, WV. The WV lawsuit tells us that James Jr., died in Kentucky, but there is no such document to date, that tells us how Jim Vance Jr. died. The picture presented on the next page is a grandson of James Vance Jr. and Vicey, who married Katheryn Massey. The picture in the front of the book, is Jim Vance I, and his bride Elizabeth Barbour.

---

[77] WV Archives Logan County, 028-00055

James M. Vance and Katheryn Massey, son of James Vance and Elizabeth Barbour.
James is the great grandson of James and Mary Collin Vance.

Permission of James Vance

Julius Vance York, son of John
Vance and Sarah Johnson
(Mounts) Vance and grandson of
James and Mary Collins Vance

John B. Vance, son of John Vance
and Jane Chapman, and grandson
of James and Mary Collins Vance

Permission of John Vance

L to R: Allen Ferrell and Henrietta Ferrell Lyons about 1938.
Allen is the son of Jane Vance and Evans Ferrell
Grandson of James and Mary Collins Vance

Permission of Connie Lyons Chancellor

James Ferrell, son of Jane Vance and Evans Ferrell
Grandson of James and Mary Collins Vance
Owner is Jeff and Hazel Diane (Ferrell) Golomb

Permission of Connie Lyons Chancellor

Above: L to R - Barney Cisco, Woodrow Cisco, Isabelle Ferrell Cisco holding Allie Cisco and Doc Lee Cisco.
Permission of Donna Blankenship

Below: Allen Ferrell, James Ferrell (son of Evans and Jane Vance Ferrell), John Ferrell (boy with James), Elsivay Ferrell (girl standing), Richard Ferrell, Isabelle Ferrell, George Ferrell (sitting on ground), Cora Ferrell, Amy Ferrell (sitting on ground), Elizabeth Francisco Ferrell and William Thomas Ferrell.
Permission of Brenda Ferrell Sampsel

Above: Richard Ferrell
Son of Evans and Jane Vance Ferrell
Grandson of James and Mary Collins Vance

Below: Anderson Ferrell and Nancy Workman Ferrell
son of Evans and Jane Ferrell

Permission of Connie Chancellor. Owner: Ruby Wingo

Above: sons of Allen and Jessie Compton Ferrell
L to R. Oscar Clifford Lyons, Robert W. Ferrell, Elmer Ferrell and James Ferrell.
Taken in Columbus, Ohio about 1939.

Below: Oscar Clifford and Henrietta Ferrell Lyons with children, Columbus, OH,
1943, with Constance (Connie) LeVerne Lyons Chancellor, Judith Ann (Judy)
Lyons Hodge, Barbara Jean Lyons Drake

Permission of Connie Chancellor

143

Henrietta Ferrell Lyons
Daughter of Allen Ferrell
Permission of Connie

Chapter 16
THE KNOWN DESCENDANTS OF JAMES AND MARY VANCE

These are the known descendants of Jim and Mary Collins Vance, through their children Jane, John, Elizabeth, James and Amy. We have not included all descendants in our lineages below, nor all the dates. Some descendants played a role in many of the court related cases, and therefore, we could trace them. Some dates may be approximate, due to the early census records having incorrect data. When possible, we were able to add exact dates when found, from courthouses, archives, other documents, or family members. In some cases, even the heirs of the children, who helped with information, might not know the details, as most of these grandchildren of James Sr., were raised by other family members, or family friends, due to the early deaths of Jim's children. We expect that anyone who uses this data, will do further research to substantiate, prior to their own use.

Descendants of Jane Vance

Generation 1

1. JANE VANCE was born in 1848 in Logan Co, VA. She died between 18 May-Jun 1894 in Logan Co., W.V. (Will presented in court July 25, 1894). She married Evans Ferrell, son of William Ferrell and Mahala Tiller, about 1868. He was born about 1843. He died after 1894 in Logan County, WV[78].

Evans Ferrell and Jane Vance had the following children:

2. i. James Ferrell was born in Apr 1867 in Logan Co, WV. He married Elizabeth Francisco (Cisco), daughter of Franklin Francisco and Mourning D Mahon, on 17 Jan 1892 in Logan Co, VA. She was born on 11 Apr 1870 in Devon, Logan Co, WV. She died on 28 Jul 1953 in Williamson, Mingo Co, WV.

3. ii. Mary Etta Ferrell was born on 16 Nov 1871 in Logan Co, WV. She

---

[78] Notes for Jane Vance: Appraisement Bill presented in court. Taken Sept 5, 1894. Signed Nov 5, 1894 by R.T. Ferrell and N.B. Nichols. Will was made May 18, 1894 and presented in court July 25, 1894. Jane left six of her children all her estate until they were able to earn enough to support themselves. They were Amy, George W, Jane, Anderson, Allen and Grover Cleveland Ferrell. She named children James, Mary Runyon, Richard, John and Elliott as being more mature in years and that they were satisfied with the division of her property. The youngest child, Grover Cleveland was born May 1894, a few days before she made her will. At least that is what the 1900 census has when he was living with M.A. Ferrell and Lelitia.

died on 22 Aug 1965 in Logan Co, WV. She married (1) Melvin Lee Runyun, son of John Tyler Runyon Sr., and Lucinda Staten, on 14 Feb 1891 in Logan Co, WV. He was born on 18 Apr 1868 in Logan Co, WV. He died in May 1900 in Logan Co, WV. She married (2) George W. Bentley in 1897. He was born in 1868 in Logan Co, WV. He died in 1940.

4. iii. Richard Ferrell was born on 03 May 1874 in Logan Co, WV. He died on 14 Jul 1959 in Glen Alum, Mingo, WV. He married Lucinda Miller 21 Jul 1896 in Mingo Co, WV. She was born on 30 Jun 1873 in Pike Co, KY. She died on 08 Jul 1955 in Gen Alum, Mingo Co, WV.

5. iv. John A Ferrell was born 18 Nov 1876 in Logan Co, WV. He died 03 May 1962 in Mingo Co, WV. He married Nancy Spence, daughter of James J. Spence and Nellie, on 24 Apr 1900 in Logan Co, WV. She was born 1880 in Mingo Co, WV.

6. v. Elliott "Ell/Greenville" Ferrell was born in 1879 in Logan Co, WV. He died on 07 Mar 1932 in Welch, McDowell Co, WV (Browns Creek District). He married (1) Manda J "Amanda" Miller in 1897 in Mingo Co, WV. She was born in May 1879. He married (2) Florence Mahan on 31 Oct 1906 in Pike Co, KY. She was born in 1882.

vi. Lucy Ferrell was born in 1879 (Logan Co, WV).

7. vii. George Washington Ferrell was born on 20 Feb 1880 in Logan Co, WV. He died on 25 Sep 1951 in Huntington, Cabell, WV. He married Lily Hagerman in 1906 in Pushmataha, OK. She was born in Dec 1888 in Indian Territory, Choctaw Pushmataha, OK. She died on 06 Jul 1961 in Mingo Co, WV.

8. viii. Amy "Anna" Ferrell was born in 1884 in Logan Co, WV. She died on 24 Aug 1942 in Mingo Co, WV. She married Boon Miller in 1904. He was born on 01 Apr 1884 in Logan Co, WV. He died on 13 Jul 1927 in Mingo Co, WV.

9. ix. Jane Ferrell was born on 08 Dec 1884 in Logan Co, WV. She died on 28 Dec 1976 in Boone Co, WV. She married Millard Oliver Thompson on 17 May 1904 in Thacker, Mingo Co, WV28. He was born on 09 Mar 1873 in Boyd Co, KY. He died on 13 Mar 1960 in Boone Co, WV.

10. x. Anderson "Anse" Ferrell was born on 05 Sep 1886 in Thacker, Logan Co, WV. He died on 04 Nov 1964 in Man, Logan Co, WV. He married Nancy Alice Harmon in 1907 in Logan Co, WV. She was born on 05 May 1890 in WV., died on 22 Dec 1961 in Gilbert, Mingo Co, WV.

11. xi. Allen Ferrell was born on 17 Mar 1889 in Thacker, Mingo Co, WV. He died on 23 Aug 1946 in Mingo Co, Magnolia, WV (Buried Claypool Cemetery, Logan Co, WV). He married (1) Jessie Compton on 31 Aug 1910 in Logan Co, WV. She died in Nov 1918 in Hellier, Pike Co, KY. He married (2) Katherine "Cathie" Miller, daughter of Hosea S Miller, on 25 Sep 1922 in Pike Co, KY. She was born 28 Oct 1898 in Lawrence Co, KY.,

died on 06 Dec 1976.

12. xii. Grover Cleveland Ferrell was born between 28 Jun 1892-18 May 1894 in Thacker, Mingo Co, WV (Not sure of date). He died on 23 Aug 1926 in Wayne Co, WV. He married Amanda Ferrell in 1912.

Generation 2

2. JAMES FERRELL (Jane1 Vance) was born in Apr 1867 in Logan Co, WV. He married Elizabeth Francisco (Cisco), daughter of Franklin Francisco and Mourning D Mahon, on 17 Jan 1892 in Logan Co, VA. She was born on 11 Apr 1870 in Devon, Logan Co, WV. She died on 28 Jul 1953 in Williamson, Mingo Co, WV.

James Ferrell and Elizabeth Francisco (Cisco) had the following children:

13. i. Isabelle Ferrell was born in Sep 1893 in Mingo Co, Magnolia, WV. She married Dock Lee Cisco, son of Marion Francisco and Eveline "Lina" Chafin, in 1910 in Mingo Co, WV. He was born between 27 Dec 1888-1890 in Mingo Co, WV. He died on 27 Dec 1957 in Pike Co, KY.

ii. Cora Ferrell was born in Oct 1894 in Mingo Co, Magnolia, WV.

iii. Elsie Ferrell was born in May 1897 in Mingo Co, Magnolia, WV.

iv. Joseph Ferrell was born in Nov 1899 in Mingo, Magnolia, WV.

v. Allen Ferrell was born in 1901 in Mingo Co, Magnolia, WV.

vi. George Ferrell was born in 1901 in Mingo Co, Magnolia, WV.

vii. Richard Ferrell was born in 1903 in Mingo Co, Magnolia, WV.

viii. John Ferrell Jr was born in 1904 in Mingo Co, Magnolia, WV.

ix. Anna Ferrell was born in 1904 in Mingo Co, Magnolia, WV.

14. x. William Thomas Ferrell was born on 13 Sep 1908 in Ben Ck, Mingo Co, WV. He died Feb 1989 in Barnesville, Belmont Co., Ohio. He married Mary Jane Duty on 24 Feb 1930 in Mingo Co, WV. She was born on 25 Dec 1915 in Mingo Co, WV. She died on 21 Jul 1974 in Stark Co, Ohio.

3. MARY ETTA FERRELL (Jane1 Vance) was born on 16 Nov 1871 in Logan Co, WV. She died on 22 Aug 1965 in Logan Co, WV. She married (1) Melvin Lee Runyun, son of John Tyler Runyon Sr. and Lucinda Staten, on 14 Feb 1891 in Logan Co, WV. He was born on 18 Apr 1868 in Logan Co, WV. He died in May 1900 in Logan Co, WV. She married (2) George W. Bentley in 1897. He was born in 1868 in Logan Co, WV[79].

Melvin Lee Runyon and Mary Etta Ferrell had the following children:

15. i. Edward Runyon was born on 21 Dec 1891 in Thacker, Mingo Co, WV. He died in 1967. He married (1) Rosa Cisco on 09 Jul 1912. She was born in 1898 in WV.

---

[79] Notes for Mary Etta Ferrell: Mary is listed as Mary Runyon in her mother's will dated in 1894. Mary & Edward Bentley are living next door to John & Nancy Ferrell and Miller & Amy Boon, both siblings.

16. ii. Edna "Cloa" A Runyon was born in Oct 1894 in Thacker, Mingo Co, WV. She married J S Pack. He was born in 1895.

George W Bentley and Mary Etta Ferrell had the following children:

i. Ben F Bentley was born on 20 Aug 1897 in Mingo Co, WV.

ii. Adaline Bentley was born in 1900 in Mingo Co, WV.

iii. Anna Bentley was born on 25 Sep 1902 in Mingo Co, WV. She died on 28 Jul 1998. She married William Phillips.

iv. Minnie Hazel Bentley was born on 11 Sep 1910 in Mingo Co, WV. She died on 14 Apr 2001 in Portsmouth, Scioto Co, OH. She married Benjamin Franklin Marcum.

4. RICHARD FERRELL (Jane1 Vance) born on 03 May 1874 in Logan Co, WV. He died on 14 Jul 1959 in Glen Alum, Mingo, WV. He married Lucinda Miller on 21 Jul 1896 in Mingo WV. She was born on 30 Jun 1873 in Pike Co, KY. She died on 08 Jul 1955 in Gen Alum, Mingo Co, WV.

Richard Ferrell and Lucinda Miller had the following children:

i. Irene Ferrell was born in 1892 in Mingo Co, WV.

ii. Willie Ferrell was born on 08 Dec 1898 in Mingo Co, WV.

iii. Napoleon Ferrell was born in 1902 in Mingo Co, WV.

iv. Ollie Ferrell was born on 06 Jan 1904 in Mingo Co, WV[80].

v. Jessie Ferrell was born on 18 Mar 1912 in Mingo Co, WV.

5. JOHN A FERRELL (Jane1 Vance) was born on 18 Nov 1876 in Logan WV. He died on 03 May 1962 in Mingo, WV. He married Nancy Spence, daughter of James J. Spence and Nellie 24 Apr 1900 in Logan Co. WV.

John A Ferrell and Nancy Spence had the following children:

i. Della Ferrell was born in 1903 in Mingo Co, WV.

ii. Zella Ferrell was born in 1905 in Mingo Co, WV.

iii. Nellie Ferrell was born in 1905 in Mingo Co, WV.

iv. Jane Ferrell was born in 1906 in Mingo Co, WV.

v. Everett Ferrell was born in 1908 in Mingo Co, WV.

vi. Garnet Ferrell was born in 1909 in Mingo Co, WV.

vii. Lawrence Elmer Ferrell was born in 1911 in Mingo Co, WV.

6. ELLIOTT "ELL/GREENVILLE" FERRELL (Jane1 Vance) was born in 1879 in Logan Co, WV. He died on 07 Mar 1932 in Welch, McDowell Co, WV (Browns Creek District). He married (1) Manda J. Miller in 1897 in Mingo Co, WV. She was born in May 1879. He married (2) Florence Mahan on 31 Oct 1906 in Pike Co, KY. She was born in 1882.

Ferrell and Mauda J "Amanda" Miller had the following children:

17. i. Adrian Ferrell was born in Oct 1899 in Mingo Co, Magnolia, WV. He married Emma Mahon in 1918 in Mingo Co, WV. She was born on 23

---

[80] Notes for Ollie Ferrell: Ollie was called granddaughter in 1910 census and daughter in the 1920, 1930 and 1940 census with Richard and Lucinda.

May 1900 in Mingo Co, WV. She died on 14 Oct 1998 in Danridge, TN.

ii. Lon Joe Ferrell was born in 1903 in Mingo Co, WV.

iii. Bessie Ferrell was born in 1905 in Mingo Co, WV.

Ferrell and Florence Mahan had the following children:

18. iv. Ethel Ferrell was born in 1909 in Mingo Co, WV.

v. Essie Ferrell was born in 1913.

vi. Elliott Ferrell was born in 1917 in Pike Co, KY.

vii. Pansy Ferrell was born in 1921.

7. GEORGE WASHINGTON FERRELL (Jane1 Vance) was born on 20 Feb 1880, in Logan Co, WV. He died on 25 Sep 1951 in Huntington, Cabell, WV. He married Lily Hagerman in 1906 in Pushmataha, OK.

George Washington Ferrell and Lily Hagerman had the following children:

i. Viols Ferrell was born about 1907 in Pushmataha, OK.

ii. Charles A Ferrell was born about 1909 in Pushmataha, OK.

iii. Allen Ferrell born on 20 Nov 1909 in Pushmataha, OK.

iv. Dorothy Ferrell was born about 1912 in Pushmataha, OK.

v. Mike Ferrell was born in 1914 in Pushmataha, OK.

vi. Richard Victor Ferrell was born on 21 Jan 1918 in Pushmataha, OK.

vii. Nellie Ferrell was born in 1920 in Pushmataha, Oklahoma.

8. AMY "ANNA" FERRELL (Jane1 Vance) was born in 1884 in Logan Co, WV. She died on 24 Aug 1942 in Mingo Co, WV. She married Boon Miller in 1904. He was born on 01 Apr 1884 in Logan Co, WV. He died on 13 Jul 1927 in Mingo Co, WV.

Boon Miller and Amy "Anna" Ferrell had the following children:

i. Luther Miller was born in 1905 in Mingo Co, WV.

ii. Jessie Miller was born in 1907 in Mingo Co, WV.

iii. Frank Miller was born in 1909 in Mingo Co, WV.

iv. Ernest Miller was born in 1911 in Mingo Co, WV.

v. Catherine Miller was born in 1916 in Mingo Co, WV.

vi. Bethel Miller was born in 1917 in Mingo Co, WV.

9. JANE FERRELL (Jane1 Vance) was born on 08 Dec 1884 in Logan Co, WV. She died on 28 Dec 1976 in Boone Co, WV. She married Millard Oliver Thompson on 17 May 1904 in Thacker, Mingo Co, WV. Born on 09 Mar 1873 in Boyd Co, KY. He died on 13 Mar 1960 in Boone Co, WV[81].

Millard Oliver Thompson and Jane Ferrell had the following children:

i. Lafe Thompson was born in 1907 in Mingo Co, WV.

ii. John Thompson was born in 1908 in Mingo Co, WV.

iii. Minnie Thompson was born in 1911 in Mingo Co, WV.

---

[81] Notes for Millard Oliver Thompson: 1910 Census Lee, Mingo Co, WV said he had been married twice. Ersel maybe his son since Jane said she had three children with two living.

iv. Thomas Thompson was born in 1906 in Mingo Co, WV.

v. Hildred W Thompson was born on 11 Apr 1917 in Mingo, WV.

vi. Fred C Thompson was born in 1921 in Mingo Co, WV.

vii. Millard Thompson Jr was born in 1924 in Mingo Co, WV.

10. ANDERSON FERRELL (Jane1 Vance) was born on 05 Sep 1886 in Thacker, WV. He died on 04 Nov 1964 in Man, Logan Co, WV. He married Nancy Alice Harmon in 1907 in Logan Co, WV. She was born on 05 May 1890 in WV. She died on 22 Dec 1961 in Gilbert, Mingo Co, WV.

Anderson Ferrell and Nancy Alice Harmon had the following children:

i. Pearl Ferrell was born in 1908. She died in 1934.

ii. Effie Mauda Ferrell was born in 1910.

iii. Melvin Ferrell born 27 Jan 1912 in Mingo Co, WV.

iv. Homer Ferrell was born in 1914.

v. Clate Jackson Ferrell was born in 1917.

vi. Fred Ferrell was born in 1918.

vii. Robert Ferrell was born in 1921.

viii. James Ferrell was born in 1924.

ix. Arthur Ferrell was born in 1927.

x. Oakie Ferrell was born in 1930.

xi. Irene Ferrell was born in 1932.

xii. Ruth Ferrell.

11. ALLEN FERRELL (Jane1 Vance) was born on 17 Mar 1889 in Thacker, Mingo Co, WV and died 23 Aug 1946 in Mingo Co, Magnolia, WV. He married (1) Jessie Compton on 31 Aug 1910 in Logan Co, WV. She died in Nov 1918 in Hellier, Pike Co, KY. He married (2) Katherine Erie Miller, daughter of Hosea S. Miller, on 25 Sep 1922 in Pike Co, KY. She was born on 28 Oct 1898 in Lawrence Co, KY. She died on 06 Dec 1976.

Allen Ferrell and Jessie Compton had the following children:

i. Waueka Lenora Ferrell was born in 1911 in Pike Co, KY.

19. ii. Robert Wendell Ferrell was born on 08 Jan 1913 in Pike Co, KY. He died on 02 May 1981 in Columbus, Franklin Co, OH.

20. iii. Elmer Hasel Ferrell was born on 30 Nov 1915 in Pike Co, KY. He died on 03 Mar 1993 in Alachua Co, FL. He married May.

iv. James Evans Ferrell was born on 11 Jul 1916 in Pike Co, KY.

21. v. Henrietta Ferrell was born on 04 May 1918 in Pike Co, KY. She died on 25 Nov 1991 in Houston, Georgia. She married Clifford Lyons.

Allen Ferrell and Katherine "Cathie" Erie Miller had the following children:

vi. Brooks Louise Ferrell was born on 22 Dec 1920 in Pike Co, KY.

vii. Allen Ferrell was born on 25 Sep 1922 in Pike Co, KY.

viii. Clifford Sullivan Ferrell was born in 1925 in KY.

ix. John Ira Ferrell was born in 1927 in KY.

12. GROVER CLEVELAND FERRELL (Jane1 Vance) was born between 28 Jun 1892-18 May 1894 in Thacker, Mingo Co, WV (Not sure of date). He died on 23 Aug 1926 in Wayne Co, WV. He married Amanda Ferrell in 1912. She was born in 1896.

Grover Cleveland Ferrell and Amanda Ferrell had the following children:

i. Woodrow W Ferrell was born in 1914.

ii. William Bryan Ferrell was born in 1917.

iii. Josephine Manie Ferrell was born in 1919.

iv. Geraldine B Ferrell was born in 1923.

v. Richard Ferrell was born in 1925.

vi. Edward C Ferrell was born in 1926.

Generation 3

13. ISABELLE FERRELL (James2, Jane1 Vance) was born in Sep 1893 in Mingo Co, Magnolia, WV. She married Dock Lee Cisco, son of Marion Francisco and Eveline "Lina" Chafin, in 1910 in Mingo Co, WV. He was born between 27 Dec 1888-1890 in Mingo Co, WV. He died on 27 Dec 1957 in Pike Co, KY.

Dock Lee Cisco and Isabelle Ferrell had the following children:

i. Barney Cisco was born in 1912.

ii. Woodrow Cisco was born in 1913.

iii. Allie Cisco was born in 1914.

iv. Alma Cisco was born in 1917.

v. Marion Cisco was born in 1919.

vi. Lina/Lenny Cisco was born on 20 Jan 1923.

22. vii. Elizabeth Cisco was born on 08 Oct 1924 in Mingo Co, WV.

viii. Althia Cisco was born in 1927.

ix. Okey Cisco was born in 1928.

x. Corey Cisco was born in 1931.

xi. Verna Cisco was born in 1932.

xii. Freda Cisco was born in 1934.

xiii. Louisa Cisco was born in 1936.

xiv. Goldie Cisco was born in 1938.

xv. Perry Cisco.

14. WILLIAM THOMAS FERRELL (James2, Jane1 Vance) was born on 13 Sep 1908 in Ben Creek, Mingo, WV. He died in Feb 1989 in Barnesville, Belmont, Ohio. He married Mary Jane Duty on 24 Feb 1930 in Mingo Co, WV. She was born on 25 Dec 1915 in Mingo Co, WV.

William Thomas Ferrell and Mary Jane Duty had the following child:

i. Sidney Lee Ferrell was born in 1932 in Mingo Co, WV.

15. EDWARD RUNYON (Mary Etta2 Ferrell, Jane1 Vance) was born on

21 Dec 1891 in Thacker, Mingo Co, WV. He died in 1967. He married (1) Rosa Cisco on 09 Jul 1912. She was born in 1898 in WV.

Edward Runyon and Rosa Cisco had the following children:

i. Mary Runyon was born in 1914 in Mingo Co, WV.

ii. Emmett Runyon was born in 1919 in Mingo Co, WV.

iii. Charles Runyon was born in 1923 in Mingo Co, WV.

iv. Edna Runyon was born in 1925 in Mingo Co, WV.

v. Catherine Runyon was born in 1927 in Mingo Co, WV.

vi. Mildred (?) Runyon was born in 1928.

vii. George Runyon was born in 1934.

viii. Oley Runyon was born in 1939.

ix. Opal Marie Runyon was born in 1939.

x. Donnie Runyon was born in 1947.

xi. Ronnie Runyon was born in 1947.

16. EDNA "CLOA" A RUNYON (Mary Etta2 Ferrell, Jane1 Vance) was born in Oct 1894 in Thacker, Mingo Co, WV. She married J.S. Pack.

J.S. Pack and Edna "Cloa" A Runyon had the following children:

i. Ben F Pack was born in 1913.

ii. Edith Virginia Pack was born in 1918.

17. ADRIAN FERRELL (Elliott "Ell/Greenville"2, Jane1 Vance) was born in Oct 1899 in Mingo Co, Magnolia, WV. He married Emma Mahon in 1918 in Mingo Co, WV. She was born on 23 May 1900 in Mingo Co, WV. She died on 14 Oct 1998 in Danridge, TN.

Adrian Ferrell and Emma Mahon had the following children:

i. Kansas Ferrell was born on 25 Sep 1920.

ii. Timothy Ferrell was born in 1923 in Mingo Co, WV.

iii. Cecil Ferrell was born in 1924 in Mingo Co, WV.

iv. Geneva Ferrell was born in 1926 in Mingo Co, WV.

v. Grace Ferrell was born in 1928 in Mingo Co, WV.

vi. Eugene Ferrell was born in 1930 in Mingo Co, WV.

vii. Elbert Ferrell was born in 1934 in Mingo Co, WV.

viii. Ronald Ferrell was born in 1937 in Mingo Co, WV.

18. ETHEL FERRELL (Elliott "Ell/Greenville"2, Jane1 Vance) was born in 1909 in Mingo Co, WV. She married Thomas Cisco, son of Johnson Cisco and Celia Jane Hatfield, in 1928.

Thomas Cisco and Ethel Ferrell had the following children:

i. Edward Cisco was born in 1929 in Mingo Co, WV.

ii. Thomas Cisco Jr was born in 1930 in Mingo Co, WV.

19. ROBERT WENDELL FERRELL (Allen2, Jane1 Vance) was born on 08 Jan 1913 in Pike Co, KY. He died on 02 May 1981 in Columbus, Franklin Co, OH. He married Ruth Browning.

20. ELMER HASEL FERRELL (Allen2, Jane1 Vance) was born on 30 Nov

1915 in Pike Co, KY. He died on 03 Mar 1993 in Alachua Co, FL.

Elmer Hasel Ferrell and May had the following children:

i. Betty Louise Ferrell was born in 1938 in Pike Co, Ky.

ii. Shirley Mae Ferrell was born in 1938 in Pike Co, Ky.

21. HENRIETTA FERRELL (Allen2, Jane1 Vance) was born on 04 May 1918 in Pike Co, KY. She died on 25 Nov 1991 in Houston, Georgia. She married Clifford Lyons.

Clifford Lyons and Henrietta Ferrell had the following children:

i Connie Lyons. She married Lomus Chancellor. They had children: Michael, Elizabeth, and Douglas.

ii Barbara Jean Lyons. She married a Drake.

iii Judith Ann Lyons. She married a Hodge

Top from left – Michael, Elizabeth and Douglas

Bottom from left – Lomus, Ashley (granddaughter) and Connie

Thank you Connie! Your contribution of photos proves that this family is full of love and kindness.

Generation 4

22. ELIZABETH CISCO (Isabelle3 Ferrell, James2 Ferrell, Jane1 Vance) was born on 08 Oct 1924 in Mingo Co, WV. She died on 03 Apr 2003 in So. Williamson, Pike Co, KY. She married Jesse Daniels.

Jesse Daniels and Elizabeth Cisco had the following child:

23. i. Rosetta Daniels. She married Curtis Blankenship.

Curtis E Blankenship and Rosetta Daniels had the following child:

i. Donna Blankenship.

Thank you Donna for the contribution of photos, we honor our relatives in many ways. By providing the photos, you've honored them for a lifetime.

Descendants of John Vance

Generation 1

1. JOHN VANCE was born in 1850 in Logan Co, W.VA. He died about 12 Jul 1894 in Logan Co, Thacker Hollow, WV. He married (1) Missouri Murphy, daughter of Joseph Murphy and Ruth Webb, on 24 Oct 1871. They divorced in Logan court. She was born in Nov 1851. She died on 01 Feb 1932 in Mingo Co, WV5. He married (2) Jane Chapman, daughter of Edward Chapman Sr. and Elizabeth Lou Hunt, on 20 Mar 1883 in Logan Co, WV (Listed John as divorced & Jane as single, married by Al Varney). She was born in 1845 in Pike Co, KY. She died in 1893 in WV. He married (3) Sarah Belle Mounts, daughter of Peyton Johnson and Elizabeth Mounts, on 17 Aug 1893 (Both were widowed). She was born on 19 Apr 1868 in Logan Co, WV. She died on 09 Nov 1929 in Mingo Co, WV. Notes: John married Sarah New August 17, 1893 in Logan County. Both state they are widowed. John is now 35 and Sarah is 30 years of age, both born in Logan. Married Preacher E. E. Tiller.

John Vance and Missouri Murphy had the following children:

2. i. MARY VANCE was born in 1872 in Logan Co, WV. She died after 1900. She married Charles New, son of Isaac New and Celia Daniels, on 19 Jul 1888 in Logan Co, WV. He was born in 1863 in Pike Co, KY.

3. ii. AMANDA VANCE was born in Jan 1874 in Logan Co, Logan, WV. She died after 1940. She married John A Lowe, son of J.R Browning, on 24 Feb 1890 in Logan Co, VA. He was born in Jan 1844 in Logan Co, WV.

4. iii. GROVER VANCE was born on 12 Jul 1876 in Thacker. Mingo Co, WV. He died on 24 Dec 1936 in Thacker, Mingo Co, WV.

John Vance and Jane Chapman had the following child:

5. iv. JOHN B VANCE was born in Jan 1880 in Logan Co, Logan, WV. He died on 21 Nov 1945 in Pike Co, KY. John B., was part of the mine wars in Kentucky. He may have married (1) Elizabeth Blankenship, daughter of Francis M Blankenship and Amelia Millie Phillips, on 22 Aug 1898 in Mingo Co, WV. She was born in Sep 1877. She died on 04 Jun 1964 in Huntington, Cabell Co, WV. He married (2) Amanda Mounts, daughter of Moses Mounts and Octavia/Christian Hatfield, on 03 May 1903 in Pike Co, KY. She was born on 20 Oct 1886 in Pike Co, KY. She died on 30 Nov 1973 in Vinton, Gallia Co, Ohio.

John Vance and Sarah Belle Mounts had the following child:

6. v. JULIUS VANCE was born on 02 Jul 1891 in Thacker, Mingo Co, WV.

He died on 26 Feb 1975 in Lawrence Co, KY (Died in Floyd Co, KY)[82]. He married Susie Gibson on 06 Jun 1912. She was born in Feb 1893 in Louisa, Lawrence, KY. She died in 1960 in Louisa, Lawrence, KY.

Generation 2

2. MARY VANCE (John1) was born in 1872 in Logan Co, WV. She died after 1900. She married Charles New, son of Isaac New and Celia Daniels, on 19 Jul 1888 in Logan Co, WV. He was born in 1863 in Pike Co, KY. He died in 1934.

Charles New and Mary Vance had the following children:
i.   Grover New was born in 1890.
ii.   Lona New was born in 1891.
iii. Pearl New was born in 1895.
iv.   Melda New was born in 1896.
v.   Flannery new was born in 1899.

3. AMANDA VANCE (John1) was born in Jan 1874 in Logan Co, Logan, WV. She died after 1940. She married John A Lowe, son of J.R. Browning and Lowe, on 24 Feb 1890 in Logan Co, VA. He was born in Jan 1844 in Logan Co, Logan, WV.

John A Lowe and Amanda Vance had the following children:
i.   Victoria Lowe was born in 1893 in Mingo Co, WV.
ii.   Anna Susan Lowe was born in 1895 in Mingo Co, WV.
iii. Mary Maggie Lowe was born in 1898 in Mingo Co, WV.
iv.   Greenway W Lowe was born on 28 Jul 1900 in Mingo Co, WV.
v.   Nancy Lowe was born in 1905 in Mingo Co, WV.

4. GROVER VANCE (John1) was born on 12 Jul 1876 in Thacker. Mingo Co, WV. He died on 24 Dec 1936 in Thacker, Mingo Co, WV.

5. JOHN B VANCE (John1) was born in Jan 1880 in Logan Co, Logan, WV. He died on 21 Nov 1945 in Pike Co, KY. He married (1) Elizabeth "Bettie" Blankenship, daughter of Francis M. Blankenship and Amelia Millie Phillips, on 22 Aug 1898 in Mingo Co, WV. She was born in Sep

---

[82] Julius York, 83, Louisa was dead on arrival at 3:45 p.m. Wednesday at Kings Daughters Hospital following an extended illness. Mr. York was born July 2, 1891, at Thacker W.Va., a son of the late Nathaniel and Sarah Johnson York. He was a retired coal miner and a member of Apperson Lodge No. 195 of Louisa. Surviving are his wife, Mrs. Emma Abshire York, two daughters, Mrs. Luther Tackett of Drift and Mrs. Burlin Caperton of Dayton, Oh; three sons, Earl York of Martin, Andy York, Columbus Oh, and James H. York of Grayson; three sister Mrs. Walter Ratcliff of Portsmouth, Ohio., Mrs Lillie Small of Kermit, WV., and Mrs Jack Prater of Norfolk Va.; a brother Tom York of Kermit, a half brother Andy New of Louisa; two stepsons, Allie McCallister of East Kermit, WV; 18 grandchildren; and 11 great grandchildren. Funeral Services will be conducted at 2 p.m. Saturday at the Smith Chapel Church at Point Section by the Rev. Gallie Isaacs and Rev. Junior Bevins. Burial will be in Greenlawn Cemetery. The body is at the funeral home, where friends may call.

1877. She died on 04 Jun 1964 in Huntington, Cabell Co, WV. He married (2) Amanda Mounts, daughter of Moses Mounts and Octavia Christian Hatfield, on 03 May 1903 in Pike Co, KY. She was born on 20 Oct 1886 in Pike Co, KY. She died on 30 Nov 1973 in Vinton, Gallia Co, Ohio.

John B Vance and Amanda Mounts had the following children:

7. i. Landon Vance was born in 1906 in KY. He died on 21 Oct 1991 in Pike Co, KY. He married Glenda Mae Fitch.

ii. Rosa Vance was born in 1907 in Mingo, WV. She died in 1972.

iii. Ada Adie Vance was born in Mar 1910 in Mingo Co, WV.

iv. Claude Vance was born in 1912 in Pike Co, Freeburn, KY.

v. Homer Vance was born in 1915 in Pike Co, Freeburn, KY.

vi. Pearl Vance was born in 1916 in Pike Co, Freeburn, KY.

8. vii. John B Vance Jr was born on 27 Feb 1919 in Pike Co, Freeburn, KY. He died on 31 Jul 1979 in Gallia Co, OH. He married Ruth Jennette (Faye Larkin) Dyer.

9. viii. Blaine Vance was born in 1922 in Pike Co, Freeburn, KY.

10. ix. Sidney Vance was born in 1923 in Pike Co, Freeburn, KY. He died on 08 Jul 1996 in Gallia Co, OH. He married (1) Frances about 1983. He married (2) Marie Whitt.

11. x. Jane Vance was born in 1925.

12. xi. Lawrence Vance was born in Apr 1930 in Pike Co, Freeburn, KY.

John B Vance and Elizabeth Blankenship had the following children:

xii. Infant Vance was born in 1899. Infant died in 1899.

xiii. Robert Lee Vance was born in Apr 1900.

6. JULIUS VANCE (John1) was born on 02 Jul 1891 in Thacker, Mingo Co, WV. He died on 26 Feb 1975 in Lawrence Co, KY (Died in Floyd Co, KY). He married Susie Gibson on 06 Jun 1912. She was born in Feb 1893 in Louisa, Lawrence, KY. She died in 1960 in Louisa, KY.

Julius Vance and Susie Gibson had the following children:

i. Sarah Vance was born in 1914.

ii. Mary Vance was born in 1916.

iii. Thomas Earl Vance was born in 1918.

iv. Georgia Vance was born in 1921.

v. Myrtle Vance was born in 1924.

vi. Andy Vance was born in 1927.

vii. James "Happy" Vance was born in 1932.

Generation 3

7. LANDON VANCE (John B2, John1) was born in 1906 in KY. He died on 21 Oct 1991 in Pike Co, KY. He married Glenda Mae Fitch.

Landon Vance and Glenda Mae Fitch had the following child:

i. John Vance was born in Lives in KY.

8. John B Vance Jr (John B2, John1) was born on 27 Feb 1919 in Pike Co, Freeburn, KY. He died on 31 Jul 1979 in Gallia Co, OH. He married Ruth Jeanette (Faye Larkin) Dyer.

John B Vance Jr and Ruth Jeanette (Faye Larkin) Dyer had the following children:

i. Ellen Orinda Vance.

ii. Jean Ann Vance.

9. Blaine Vance (John B2, John1) born in 1922 in Pike Co, Freeburn, KY.

10. Sidney Vance (John B2, John1) was born in 1923 in Pike Co, Freeburn, KY. He died on 08 Jul 1996 in Gallia Co, OH. He married (1) Frances about 1983. She was born in 1936. He married (2) Marie Whitt. Sidney Vance and Marie Whitt had the following child:

11. i. Riley Vance.

Descendants of Elizabeth "Betty" Vance

Generation 1

1. ELIZABETH "BETTY" VANCE was born in 1855 in McDowell Co, VA2. She died before 25 Apr 1894 in Logan Co, WV (Husband Nichols was appointed guardian of 3 children under 14). She married (1) Jacob McCoy, son of Asa Harman McCoy and Martha F "Patty" Cline, on 08 Apr 1875 in Logan Co, WV at home of Jim Vance (Record is listed in Pike Co, KY). He was born on 18 May 1853 in Pike Co, KY. He died on 09 Nov 1899. She married (2) Napoleon Bonaparte Nichols son of James J Nichols and Louisa "Levicy" Vance, on 13 Oct 1881 in Logan Co, WV (Married by Al Varney). He was born in Mar 1859 in Buchanan Co, VA. He died on 18 Sep 1929 in Mingo Co, Glen Alum, WV (Reported by Howard Nichols).

Napoleon Bonaparte Nichols and Elizabeth "Betty" Vance had the following children[83]:

i. Jane Nichols was born between 1882-1883.

ii. Lee Nichols was born between 1884-1886 in Mingo Co, WV.

2. iii. Jefferson D Nichols was born on 25 Jul 1888 in Thacker, Mingo Co, WV. He died on 26 Jul 1925 in Mingo Co, WV (Automobile accident). He married Amy Hatfield in Nov 1914 in Mingo Co, WV. She was born in

---

[83] Logan Co. Order Bk A Fiscal and Probate A pg. 86 - In Logan Co. Court Clerk Ofc. This day came N.B. Nichols and on his motion he is hereby appointed guardian for his 3 children infants under 14 years of age; Jane Nichols, Lee Nichols, and Jefferson D. Nichols, heirs at law of Elizabeth Nichols deceased (late Elizabeth Vance daughter of James Vance deceased). Where upon said N.B. Nichols together with Joseph Simpkins, his surety entered into and acknowledged a bond in the penalty of $1500 conditioned according to law, and took oaths required by law. Given under my hand this 25th day of Apr. 1894.

1898 in WV.

Generation 2

2. Jefferson D Nichols (Elizabeth "Betty"1 Vance) was born on 25 Jul 1888 in Thacker, Mingo Co, WV. He died on 26 Jul 1925 in Mingo Co, WV. He married Amy Hatfield in Nov 1914 in Mingo Co, WV. She was born in 1898 in WV. World War Draft Card stated he had wife and two children.

Jefferson D Nichols and Amy Hatfield had the following children:

i. Elias Nichols born on 10 Mar 1917 in Mingo, WV.

ii. Susie Nichols was born on 01 Jun 1919 in Glen Alum, Mingo Co, WV.

iii. Carl Nichols was born in 1921 in Glen Alum, Mingo, WV.

iv. Tommy Nichols was born in 1923 in Glen Alum, Mingo, WV.

v. Fern Nichols was born in 1925 in Glen Alum, Mingo, WV.

Descendants of James M Vance Jr

Generation 1

1. JAMES M VANCE JR was born in 1857 in Logan Co, VA or KY. He died in 1892. He married Levicia Stepp, daughter of Aaron Stepp and Parlee Jane Maynard, on 10 Dec 1891 in Martin, KY. She was born in Sep 1867 in White Post, Pike Co, KY.

James M Vance Jr and Levicia Stepp had the following child:

2. i. JAMES MONROE VANCE SR was born on 14 Apr 1892 in Nolan, Logan Co (Mingo), WV. He died on 29 Aug 1987 in Birmingham, AL.

Generation 2

2. JAMES MONROE VANCE SR (James M Jr) was born on 14 Apr 1892 in Nolan, Logan Co (now Mingo), WV. He died on 29 Aug 1987 in Birmingham, AL. He married Sarah Elizabeth Barbour on 21 Feb 1916 in Bessemer, Jefferson Co, AL. She was born on 01 Feb 1895 in McCalla, Jefferson Co, AL. She died on 10 Jun 1983 in Birmingham, Jefferson, AL.

James Monroe Vance Sr. and Sarah Elizabeth Barbour had the following children:

3. i. James Monroe Vance Jr II was born on 04 Dec 1919 in Jefferson Co, AL. He died on 23 Sep 2004 in Birmingham, Jefferson Co, AL. He married Virginia Matney.

ii. Robing Cecil Vance was born on 18 Dec 1921 in Bessemer, Jefferson Co, AL. He died on 25 May 1945 in Wildwood, Cape May, NJ (Killed in a Naval Training Mission).

4. iii. George Richard Vance was born on 08 Apr 1923 in Jefferson Co, AL. He died on 03 Sep 2005 in Birmingham, Jefferson Co, AL. 5. iv. Elizabeth Ann Vance was born on 24 Feb 1926 in Jefferson Co, AL11. She

died on 06 Dec 2010 in Birmingham, Jefferson Co, AL. She married William Lawson Sr.

v. John Louis Vance was born on 25 Jul 1934 in Birmingham, Jefferson, Alabama. He died on 12 Jan 1989 in Birmingham, Jefferson Co, AL.

Generation 3

3. JAMES MONROE VANCE JR II (James Monroe2 Sr., James M1 Jr) was born on 04 Dec 1919 in Jefferson Co, AL. He died on 23 Sep 2004 in Birmingham, Jefferson Co, AL. He married Virginia Matney.

James Monroe Vance Jr and Virginia Matney had the following children:

6. i. James Monroe Vance III was born in Birmingham, Jefferson Co, AL. He married Virginia Katheryn Slay.

ii. Charles Robin Vance was born in 1951 in Birmingham, Jefferson Co, AL. He died on 09 Mar 2013 in Birmingham, Jefferson Co, AL. He married Sheila Smith in 1985.

iii. Richard Cary Vance.

iv. Virginia K. Vance. She married Gene Milliken.

4. George Richard Vance (James Monroe2 Sr., James M1 Jr) was born on 08 Apr 1923 in Jefferson Co, AL. He died on 03 Sep 2005 in Birmingham, Jefferson Co, AL. He married Jane Zachary.

George Richard Vance and Jane Zachary had the following children:

i. Patricia Vance.

ii. Susan Vance.

5. Elizabeth Ann Vance (James Monroe2 Sr., James M1 Jr) born on 24 Feb 1926 in Jefferson Co, AL. She died on 06 Dec 2010 in Birmingham, Jefferson Co, AL. She married William Lawson Sr.

William Lawson Sr. and Elizabeth Ann Vance had the following children:

i. William Lawson Jr.

ii. Barbara Anne Lawson.

iii. Betty Lawson.

iv. Rebecca Lawson.

Generation 4

6. JAMES MONROE VANCE III (James Monroe3 Jr, James Monroe2 Sr. James M1 Jr) was born in Birmingham, Jefferson Co, AL. He married Virginia Katheryn Slay.

James Monroe Vance III and Virginia Katheryn Slay had the following children:

i. Cortney Catherine Vance.

ii. James Monroe Vance IV.

Thank you James and Virginia Vance for the precious photos provided for this book. They are, and will forever be much appreciated for all descendants to come.

Amy Vance Francisco Flynn

Descendants of Amy L Vance Generation 1

1. AMY L VANCE was born on 19 May 1860 in Pike Co, KY. She died on 24 Aug 1944 in High Point, Guilford, NC. She married (1) John Francisco, son of James Francisco and Elizabeth Lindimoed, on 09 Sep 1880 in Logan Co, WV. He was born in 1853 in Logan Co, VA. He died on 03 Apr 1889. She married (2) Charles Steven Flynn about Jul 1894. He was born on 08 Apr 1860 in Rockingham Co, NC., died on 13 Mar 1942 in High Point, Guilford, NC[84].

John Francisco and Amy L Vance had the following children:

2. i. VIOLA FRANCISCO was born on 01 Apr 1885 in Mingo Co, WV. She died on 03 Aug 1955 in High Point, Guilford, NC.

3. ii. MAGGIE E FRANCISCO was born on 17 Apr 1888 in Thacker, WV. She died on 12 Nov 1988 in Greensboro, NC.

Charles Steven Flynn and Amy L Vance had the following children:

i. James Calvin Flynn was born on 06 Jul 1894 in Thacker, WV. He died on 26 Feb 1973 in Durham, NC (at Veterans Administration Hospital). He married Bertie Ellen Hancock.

---

[84] March 14, 1942 The High Point Enterprise (High Point NC) - C.S. Flynn Taken by Death at Home – Funeral Service Will Be Conducted Monday - C.S. Flynn., well-known carpenter, passed away at his home, 202 Ennis Street, yesterday afternoon at 2:45 death following an illness of several months duration. Mr. Flynn was born in Rockingham County April 8, 1860, and had been a resident of this city for the past twenty years. About fifty years he was married to Amy Vance of Rockingham County who survives with two sons. J.C. Flynn, a member of the city fire department and S.L. Flynn of Mt. Airy: two stepdaughters, Mrs. Viola Darnell of High Point, and Mrs. J.L. Mateer of Greensboro; thirteen grandchildren and three great grandchildren. Funeral services will be conducted at the home Sunday afternoon at 3 o'clock by Rev. H.O. Miller. Pastor of Hillard Memorial at Baptist Church, and interment will follow in Floral Garden Cemetery. The body will be returned to the late residence this afternoon at 5 o'clock.

ii. Sidney Lawson Flynn was born on 30 Mar 1896 in WV. He died on 01 Oct 1979 in High Point, Guilford, NC. He married Laura Lee Frances Smith on 01 Jun 1929 in Carroll Co, NC. She was born on 04 Sep 1862 in Surry Co or Stokes Co, NC. She died on 07 Sep 1942 in Mt. Airy, Surry Co, NC (Oakdale Cemetery, Mt Airy, NC).

iii Jessie Flynn was born in Aug 1899 in NC.

Generation 2

2. VIOLA FRANCISCO (Amy L1 Vance) was born on 01 Apr 1885 in Mingo Co, WV. She died on 03 Aug 1955 in High Point, Guilford, NC. She married Charles "Charley" Ceborn Darnell about 1905. He was born on 19 Apr 1881 in Stokes. NC. He died on 14 Jul 1963 in High Point, Guilford, NC. Charles "Charley" Ceborn Darnell and Viola Francisco had the following children:

i. Edgar Lee Darnell was born on 08 Jul 1905 in High Point, Guilford Co, NC. He died on 04 Mar 1984 in High Point, Guilford Co, NC.

ii. Ethel May Darnell was born on 24 Aug 1907 in WV. She died on 09 Dec 2001 in Kernersville, Forsyth, NC.

iii Amy Ellen Darnell was born on 18 Dec 1910 in High Point, Guilford Co, NC. She died on 30 Dec 1998 in High Point, Guilford Co, NC.

iv. Edna Lucile Darnell was born in 1913. She died in 1987. She married Harold Vance Kinsey. He was born in 1903. He died in 1973.

3. MAGGIE E FRANCISCO (Amy L1 Vance) was born on 17 Apr 1888 in Thacker, WV. She died on 12 Nov 1988 in Greensboro, Guilford Co, NC. She married Jasper Lee Mateer Sr. He was born on 08 Apr 1880 in NC. He died on 09 Apr 1949 in Greensboro, Guilford, NC[85].

Jasper Lee Mateer Sr. and Maggie E Francisco had the following children:

i. Mamie Irene Mateer was born on 21 Nov 1905 in Guilford Co, NC. She died on 25 Dec 1997 in Greensboro, Guilford Co, NC.

ii. James Herbert Mateer was born on 02 Oct 1907 in Rural Hall, Forsyth, NC. Died on 29 Jul 1962 in Greensboro, Guilford Co, NC.

iii. Huell L Mateer was born on 13 Sep 1909 in NC. He died in Dec 1985 in Rockville, Montgomery, MD. He married Nora.

---

[85] Maggie Francisco Mateer dies in Greensboro at 100 – Mrs. Maggie Francisco Mateer 100, of 1910 Walker Ave., died Saturday at Moses Cone Memorial Hospital. Funeral will be 3:30 p.m. Monday at Hanes-Lineberry North Elm St. Chapel. Burial will be in Green Hill Cemetery. The oldest living member of St. Johns United Methodist Church. Mrs. Mateer was a native of Thacker, WV. Surviving are sons, Jay L. Mateer, Charles Mateer, Don T. Mateer, all of Greensboro, daughters Mrs. Mamie M. Edwards, Mrs. Aileen M. Jones, both of Greensboro, ten grandchildren. The family will be at the funeral home 7-9 p.m. today.

iv. Ruby Virginia Mateer born on 10 Mar 1914 in Guilford Co, NC. She died on 21 Apr 1982 in Greensboro, Guilford Co, NC. She married Carl Glen Godfrey Sr. on 12 Aug 1933 in Danville, VA. He was born on 15 Jun 1912 in Anderson, SC.

v. James L Vance Mateer was born on 11 Jun 1916 in Forsyth Co, NC. He died on 10 Dec 1987 in Greensboro, Guilford Co, NC.

vi. Helen Louise Mateer was born in 1921. She died in 1923.

vii. Jasper Lee Mateer Jr was born in 1923 in NC.

viii. Charles E. Mateer was born in 1926 in NC.

ix. Aileen E. Mateer was born in 1928 in NC.

x. Don T. Mateer was born in 1931.

Sources

Court case, Darnell vs Flynn.

Death Notice in Paper, The High Point Enterprise, Sat Mar 14, 1942.

Amy death certificate said she was widowed.

North Carolina, Death Certificates, 1909-1975.

1920 Census Greenboro, Gilford, NC.

North Carolina, Death Indexes, 1908-2004.

Find A Grave for Edgar Darnell, Maggie Francisco Mateer.

Social Security Death Index.

1940 Census Montgomery Co, MD

1940 Census Greensboro, Guilford Co, NC

Joel Hager

Logan Wills

1850, 1870, 1880, 1900, 1910, 1920, 1930 Census Logan Co, WV

Connie Lyons Chancellor.

Donna Blankenship.

World War I and II Registration Card on internet.

Logan County Banner, starting July 12, 1894

1850 Census, Pike Co, KY

West Virginia Marriage records, Archives on internet.

1910 Census Mingo Co, WV

Death Records, KY 1852-1953 on Internet.

Ohio and KY Death Records.

Logan Co Births & Deaths, Book # 1, 1872-1892 by Donna Brown. Logan Co WV Marriages, Book 1, 1872-1892 by Donna L Brown. KY Marriages 1852-1914.

WV Death Index 1853-1973 on ancestry.com.

Vans family Archive on Ancestry.com.

1930 Census Birmingham, Al.

APPEXDIX A – ABNER VANCE SONG AND
LETTER OF JUDGE JOHNSON

The Vance Song as copied by W.H. Lester from the Sweet Bird Song Book located at Buchanan Library; there are other versions, however this is the version recorded as the oldest version by Grace Dotson.

Verse 1
Green are the woods where Sandy Flows,
And peace, it dwelleth there,
In the valley, the deer, they lie secure,
The red buck roams everywhere;
But Vance no more shall Sandy behold,
Or drink of its crystal waves,
The partial judge has pronounced his doom,
The hunter has found his grave,

Verse 2
The judge said, he was my friend,
Though Elliot's life he had saved,
A jury man I did become,
That Elliot, he might live;
The friendship I have shown to others,
Have never been shown to me,
Humanity, it belongs to the brave,
And hope it remains to me.

Verse 3
It was by the advice of McFarlein,
Judge Johnson, did me call,
I was taken from my native home,
Confined in a stone wall;
My persecutors have gained their request,
They promised to make good,
They often swore that they never would rest,
Till they had gained my life's blood.

Verse 4
There are Daniel Horton, Bob and Bill,
A lie against me swore,
In order to take my life away,
That I might be no more;

But they and I together must meet,
When Gabriel's trump shall blow;
Perhaps I will rest in Abraham's breast,
While they roll in the gulf below.

Verse 5
I killed a man, I don't deny,
He threatened to kill me,
And for this I am condemned to die
The jury all agree;
But, I and they together must meet,
Where all things are well-known,
And if I have shed the innocent blood,
I hope there is mercy shown.

Verse 6
Bright shines the sun on Clinch's hills,
So soft the west wind blows,
The valley is covered all over with bloom,
Perfumed with the red rose;
But Vance no more shall Sandy behold,
Nor smell its sweet perfumes,
This day, his eyes in death must close,
His body conveyed to the tomb.

Verse 7
Farewell, my friends, and children dear,
To you, I bid farewell,
I love I have for your precious souls,
Nor mortal tongue can tell;
Farewell, my true and loving wife,
To you, I bid adieu;
And if I reach fair Cannans shore,
I hope to meet with you.

Letter of Judge Johnson to the House of Delegates
JOURNAL OF THE HOUSE OF DELEGATES FOR THE
COMMONWEALTH OF VIRGINIA
Begun and Held AT THE CAPITOL IN THE CITY OF RICHMOND IN
THE SEVENTH DAY OF DECEMBER, ONE THOUSAND EIGHT
HUNDRED AND EIGHTEEN
Printed by Thomas Ritchie for the Commonwealth
The Communication of Judge Johnston was read as follows;
Sir – A criminal case, attended by peculiar circumstances, and involving difficulties, which can be removed by the Legislature, only, has occurred in the county of Russell. At the circuit court held for that county in the month of April last. Abner Vance was indicted for the murder of Lewis Horton and by the jury impaneled for his trial convicted of murder in the 1st degree. Sentence of death was pronounced upon him in consideration of this conviction, but his execution was delayed that he might have an opportunity of applying to the General Court for a writ of error, because it was contented that the opinion of the court which tried him in certain points exhibited by a bill of exception for was not correct. The General Court at the last June term decided that the opinion of the Circuit Court on one question presented by the record was erroneous, directed the verdict to be set aside, and awarded a new trial of the case. In the month of September last the Circuit Court for the county of Russell was occupied until the evening of Friday, the fifth day of the term, in efforts which proved ineffectual to bring the prisoner to another trial. So great a concourse of people had attended. Heard the evidence and expressed an opinion on the trial in April, that few individuals in the county were exempt from such objections as rendered them enable to challenge for Cause, and the prisoner availed himself of his right of peremptory challenge to the greater number of those against whom a challenge for cause did not lie. Although, the court was numerously attended as long as it continued to sit. And the Sheriff every evening was required to go into the country and summon forty-eight jurors to appear on the succeeding day, it was ascertained with perfect certainty, that there is no possibility of making up a jury for the trial of this man in the county of Russell. And as no Court in Virginia passes the power of changing the venue in a criminal case, he cannot under existing laws be brought to trial in another county. For the purpose of exhibiting the character of the offense committed by Vance, give me leave to state in substance, but with precision, the testimony of the witnesses examined in his trial. The prisoner lived near Clinch river and walked down to a ford at no great distance from his dwelling on the morning of September 22, 1817, carrying his rifle, and declaring he had loaded it for the special purpose

of shooting Daniel Horton, the brother of the young man afterwards slain; and, that he would not only kill him, but three others whom he named. Lewis Horton soon appeared in view, riding along the road which leads across the river near the place where Vance was waiting, as he said, to shoot Daniel Horton. As soon as the young man came within such a distance that his person was identified, Vance said "yonder comes Lewis Horton, and I have a mind to kill him." He approached Vance and saluted him with civility. Vance charged him with having sworn his life away; language, which had reference to a deposition given a few days before by Lewis Horton, in a suit in Chancery depending before Chancellor Brown. Horton expressed his astonishment at this charge and inquired what Vance had understood to be the purport of his deposition. Upon hearing Vance's reply, Horton assured him he was mistaken or misinformed, and proceeded to repeat what he really had stated in the before mentioned deposition. Vance then expressed himself fully satisfied, declared to Lewis Horton he had nothing against him, and asked, "Have you anything against me"..."Nothing" said the young man, in a mild language and manner, "except that I do not like to see you have drawn your gun upon me." "Help yourself as you can, I believe I will shoot you now," said Vance. Horton and a certain Joseph Fowlkes (Fulks) who was present, observing from the tone and countenance of Vance, the horrid purpose which he meditated, began to implore his mercy; but he raised his gun, leveled it at Horton, while he was endeavoring to make good his flight across the river, and tried when he was not a greater distance than thirty paces, shooting the ball through the body of this victim, near the back bone, and a little below the shoulder blade. As he fell from his horse into the water, Vance poured forth execrations too bitter and horrible for repetition, and threatened with death an old man from the opposite shore, who advanced into the river, hoping that Horton's life might yet be saved. But in this, he was mistaken. Although the young man was rescued from immediate death by drowning, he survived his wound but a short time expiring on the sixth day after its infliction. It is not only probable, but certain, that other instances will arise under the present judiciary system of this State, requiring the special interference of the Legislature, unless some general law should be enacted, the provisions of which may be adequate to the prevention, of remedy of evils and difficulties, such as have occurred in the case of Abner Vance. I have made this communication from a persuasion, that if the subject appears as important to you, as it does to me, you will lay it before the General Assembly.

APPENDIX B – CONFESSION OF ELLISON MOUNTS
AND TESTIMONY OF SARAH MCCOY

1888 Nov. 5 - **No 1. The confession of Ellison Hatfield** (alias Ellison Mounts) of the Hatfield murders – Last Friday eve some detectives brought in the above prisoner & lodged him in the Pike County Jail. I was told he would make a confession and he did so as follows;

About the first of Aug 1882 about thirty of us in numbers crossed from Logan Co. W. VA & went into Pike Co. KY., and took from the guards of the civil authorities of Ky., the 3 McCoy boys. Tolbert & Farmer & Randolph Jr. We took them to Logan Co. W.Va. & kept them in an old school house & kept them there tied fast to each other with ropes that night & next day & until about 8:00 PM when me – Anse Hatfield, Johns Hatfield, Bill Tom Hatfield, Tom Mitchell, Charlie Carpenter, Alex Messer, Dan Whitt, Moses Christian, Sam Mayhorn, Joe Murphy, Jeff Whitt, & Ellison Hatfield (alias Ellison Mounts, myself). We took the 3 boys all tied together on cross from Logan Co. W.Va. over the Tug River into Pike Co., Ky. We tied them to a Paw bush all together by the arm and Anse Hatfield told the boys that if they wanted to pray to do so. We had made formal a line & hung our lantern over them to give light so as to see how to shoot them. But before the boys had time to pray Johns Hatfield shot and killed Tolbert McCoy and Anse then draw his revolver & emptied it into the dead body of Tolbert & Alex Messer leveled a double barred shot gun & blew of the head off of Randolph McCoy Jr., who was about 13 years old. The bodies of the boys were shot to pieces. The parties who did the shooting was Anse Hatfield, Alex Messer, Charlie Carpenter, & Tom Mitchell. We all crossed the river back into Logan Co. & found Wall Hatfield who at the time was at the river edge & a justice of the peace of Logan Co., was waiting for us who formed us in a line & sworn us to secrecy & asked them if their feelings was not better gratified and Anse, Cap, & Johns Hatfield & Tom Mitchell said yes. But before we went over the river from Logan Co. with the boys we signed a paper to kill all murders & to regulate all violators of the law. Charlie Carpenter done up the writing & we all signed it & agreed to it. After the oath was taken, I went to Pat Hatfield's & all the rest went to Elias Hatfield's & stayed one night. The Hatfield's roamed about in squads in arms & sold whiskey in violation of State & US laws.

The next killing was that of Jeff McCoy. Cap Hatfield told me that he took Jeff McCoy & started down the river as a prisoner on the Logan Co. WV., side & that Tom Wallace & Boney Nickels went along as guards & when they got down to Bill Ferrell, Jeff McCoy broke custody & ran through a bottom & swam Tug River to the KY., side & Tom Wallace all the time shooting at him & that Boney Nickels busted a cap at McCoy while McCoy was running & they ran after him to the top of the river bank & after McCoy got in the KY side Tom Wallace shot & killed him. The next thing that was done was the whippings of Bill Daniels wife & daughter. Cap & me that he whipped Bills wife & that Tom Wallace whipped the daughter, they whipped the woman with a calf/cows (?) tail the Daniels family lived in Pike Co., Ky.

The next thing of note done was the burning of the house of Randolph McCoy & killing his daughter Alifair & son Calvin. On the night of Jan 1st, 1888. I was at my mother's at work on the Guian (Guyan) River when John Hatfield & Tom Mitchell came to me & said that Cap had sent after me saying that the KY., authorities had warded me $500.00 & that I must stand in or I would get captured & killed & we started & came to Dow Steels on Island Creek & next Anse, Cap, & Bob Hatfield & Charlie Gillespie & me stayed next morning all of us together & came to Henry Vance's on Big Muncy Creek & stayed overnight & from there to Henderson Varney's for dinner next day on the head of Mate Creek & from there we went to Floyd Hatfield's & stayed overnight. Floyd is a cousin to Anse, we went from there to Ephraim Hatfield (Walls son) then Jim Vance Sr. met us & had a scant talk with Anse, Cap, & Johns Hatfield & he then left us that was Friday night & the next day we went to Uncle Ephraim Hatfield's (Johns son) & we stayed in his sheep pen & took our meals at the house. Then we was met by Wall Hatfield, Dock, Sam & Plyant Mayhorn, they stayed all day with us Saturday & left us late in the morning but before leaving, Anse, Cap, Johns, & Wall Hatfield & the 3 Mayhorn boys went out & had a scant talk. We went from there to Jim Vance Sr. on Sunday morning & met Jim Vance Sr. & Ferrell Ellis & on arrival at Jim Vance Sr. house Anse, Cap, Johns Hatfield & Jim Vance Sr. went out & had a scant talk & then called me to them and said some of the parties on the KY side had me warded & some of them on the KY., side must be killed in order to stop the prosecution of us on that side & told me I must stand in & Anse said here is my big gun you can take it. I told him I did not want it, that if I went I would take my own gun. Then Anse Hatfield told Jim Vance that he was not able to go & for him (Vance) to take charge of the boys & do the best he could with them. Jim Vance Sr., Cap, Johns, & Bob Hatfield (all bros & sons of Anse) Black Elliot Hatfield, French Ellis, Charlie Gillespie, Tom Mitchell, & Ellison Hatfield (alias E. Mounts myself) all went to Caps Sunday evening about 5 o'clock & stayed then until after night & went up the W. Va., side to the mouth of Peter Creek. When we got to the house of Anse Hatfield, Johns called out his mother & talked to her a few words & we then went to the Tug River & took off our shoes & waded the river & went down on the

KY side a short distance & up a branch called Pound Mill branch & over to Peter Fork of Blackberry & down it to main Blackberry Creek & up the same to Jerry Hatfield's branch & up it to the head of Blackberry Fork of Pond & down it to very near the house of Randolph McCoy Sr. when we stopped & Johns & Cap Hatfield & Jim Vance Sr. put on false faces & we then started for the house & Jim Vance Sr. told Tom Mitchell, Charlie Gillespie & French Ellis to go to the lower door of the Big House (as we called it) & told them to watch & not let any men come out with woman's clothes on & if they did to capture them. He (Vance) told Elliott Hatfield & Bob Hatfield to go to the lower door of the Kitchen. He told me (Ellison Hatfield) & Cap Hatfield to go to the upper door of the Kitchen & Johns Hatfield & Jim Vance Sr. went to the upper door of the Big House. We all slipped upon the house it was about 10:30 o'clock PM & Jim Vance Sr. changed his voice & told them to come out & surrender as prisoners of war. The McCoy family said nothing & Cap said are they coming, & Vance says no, & Cap says God Dam it Jim the house, & Cap hollowed to Tom Mitchell where are you, but Mitchell did not respond & Jim Vance went to the house & found a bunch of cotton & Vance struck a match fire to the cotton & put a part of it in a joist hole in the house & the rest of the burning cotton he placed under the shutter of the door. But before the fire began burning we shot quite a number of bullets through the two doors of the house we called the Big House & then find it we kept up a constant firing or shooting through the door of the house. Then two shots was fired through the door from within by the McCoy's. Frequent shots was fired from within & out & then Calvin McCoy went upstairs & fired on us the fire at that time had begun to burn the house considerable & Calvin McCoy called to his sisters in the other house telling them to come & put out the fire. Vance says if they come boys God D*** them shoot them & then Cap & Johns Hatfield said you boys be God D***ed certain that you obey your Captain (Vance was known as our Captain) about that time a girl came to the door dressed in dark clothes & Cap & Johns Hatfield said you big man God dam her kill her (I was called the big man) & I shot her with a 32 WC. Rifle & she fell dead or dying on the floor. I heard her sister ask her if she was dead. She muttered out something but I could not understand it but the other sister said farewell Alifair. Calvin McCoy was upstairs shooting at us at every opportunity & he asked his sister if any of them was killed and his sister answered and said yes, they have killed Alifair. We kept up the shooting, & the fire burning until Calvin McCoy shot me in the left arm the ball entered near the wrist joint & I came out just below the elbow joint & saying several pieces of broken bone, had come out. Then Aunt Sallie McCoy came out & says men for God all mighty help me put out the fire for it is burning up all we have got & spare my life. Johns Hatfield told me that he struck her with a rock & a gun. I did not see it & he left her on the ground for dead. She begged some several times. Then Calvin McCoy broke from the house & ran in the direction of a corn crib & he was followed by a volley of fire until he fell dead. Cap & Johns Hatfield both claimed the shot, but from the position of the two, I think Cap H. killed Calvin McCoy. Then Randolph McCoy Sr. made a break for life & as he came out of the burning house he had in his hand a double barreled shot gun loaded with bird shot. He shot Tom Wallace in the right hand taking off of Mitchell's fingers & almost all of the others so much so that his fingers had to be cut off by Dr. Hudgins of Logan Co. W. VA., some of the shots went into the belt of Mitchell. Randolph McCoy then shot Johns Hatfield in the top of the right shoulder. Johns had on a heavy overcoat & the shots some of them just merely penetrated the flesh of Johns. I saw the shots taken out or at least part of them. Johns was shooting at Calvin McCoy at the time Randolph shot him.

We did not know that we had killed Calvin that night. All the time Randolph McCoy left the house we shot at him several times until he escaped into the woods. Then in a few minutes we left & the house was then in good flame. The woman was crying & begging for help to put out the fire. I saw one woman come out just as we started. I do not know who drug out the body of the dead girl. We went back the same way that we came. Fainted on my way back from the loss of blood. French Ellis, Elliott Hatfield, & Charlie Gillespie helped to lead me one at a time. We all went to Cap Hatfields & stopped except Johns Hatfield & James Vance Sr. who said that they were going to Vances house. Those of us at Caps went to bed & did not get up for breakfast until 11 o'clock A.M. On Monday night we went the road down to Jim Vance Sr. & I passed the house of William Ferrell until after dark, we left Vances house the same night & went to the head of the Horse Road Fork, up Mate Creek Logan Co. WV. We went from there to the Slick Road Fork up Pigeon Creek Logan Co. we went into camp in the woods & stayed there all of us until the next Saturday when it was that Jim Vance Sr. & Cap Hatfield left us in company with Mrs. James Vance (wife of Jim Vance Sr.) who had stayed in camp with us the night before. They all started for Vances house & that was the day that Vance was killed, said to have been done by Frank Phillips of Pike Co., KY. While in camp we got our provisions from Harve Duty & Vance carried the provisions to us a part of the time & French Ellis & Elliott Hatfield the rest of the time. Dr. Bill Brown treated me for the wound. I _ he lives in Logan Co., W.Va., & I told him how I got shot. I make this statement for & of my own accord. This Nov.

170

5, 1889 at Pikeville KY. In the presence of P.A. Cline, Samuel M. King, D.W. Cunningham, T.M. Gibson, J.M. York, Col. John Dils & J. Lee Ferguson.

Ellison X Hatfield (alias Ellison Mounts)

State of Kentucky County of Pike - John Ferguson says that he is County Attorney for the Commonwealth & State aforesaid and Ellison Hatfield (alias Ellison Mounts) came into his office & in the presence of the above named parties of his own free will & accord & free from fear or favor make the above confession. This Nov 7th, 1888 - Co. Attorney

Testimony of Sarah McCoy
Sarah McCoy testimony of Aug 26, 1889 for Valentine Hatfield

I am the mother of Farmer, Tolbert, & Randolph McCoy. They are dead. They were killed on the night of Aug 9th, 1882. I saw them on the morning before that, at Floyd McCoy's while they were under arrest. I did not see Wall Hatfield there. He was not there, I next saw them on Mate Creek in Logan County, W.VA., at a schoolhouse. Wall had a double barrel shot lying across his lap. I was talking, praying, and crying for my boys.

While over at the mouth of Mate, I heard Wall say, that if Ellison Hatfield died, he would shoot the boys as full of holes as a sifter bottom.

Tolbert was shot twice in the head and there or four times in the body. Farmer was shot in the head and either nine or eleven times in the body. The __ of one said of the little boys head was shot off. Tolbert was 31 years, Farmer was 19 years of age, and Randall was 15 years old. They were hauled home in a sled and buried in one coffin.

When Wall was sitting at the head of the boys with a double barrel shot gun at the schoolhouse, they were lying on something tied together with a rope. I fell on my knees and began praying, begging, and crying for my children. Wall said there was no use of that, he would not have it. I remember seeing there at that time, Cap, Johns, Carpenter, Dan Whitt, Alex Messer, Bill Tom Hatfield, and others and they were all armed. Someone came in and said a party was coming to rescue the boys. I told them there was nothing of it. Wall said for me to leave, if they came, the house would be fired and my boys would be the first ones shot.

Cross Examined;

The conversation I had with Wall was over at Mate Creek in WV. I remember, in the conversation to have heard someone say that they had heard that my husband was trying to get up a party to rescue the boys. I don't remember that Wall tried, ordered me to try and prevent them from rescuing the boys saying that he had, had a hard time in preventing the boys from being killed. I remember a conversation I had in the town at the house of P.A. Cline with Wall Hatfield, in the presence of Andy Casebolt. I do not remember to have admitted to Wall there that Farmer had said that when Wall came up that he was afraid that Wall was going to kill him, but that he had treated them well and he wanted all his friends to remember and be kind to Uncle Wall.

Sarah on the stand in the Sentencing of Ellison Mounts on Sept 4, 1889 (note this was given more by a third party, maybe the court recorder, as the court, uses "they and her", representing third party).

Bill of Exception – Pike Criminal Court
The Commonwealth against Cap Hatfield and others} Bill of Exceptions
Be it remembered that on the calling of the cause for trial the Attorney for the Commonwealth announced ready for trial as to Ellison Mounts and the Court assigned as counsel for Defendant W.M. Connolly

Order assigning Counsel for Defendant – Pike Criminal Court August Term, 4th day of September 1889
Commonwealth vs. Cap Hatfield & others] Murder
"The Defendant Charles Gillespie having by his Attorney demurred a separate trial in his cause, it is ordered that he be allowed the same, and it appearing that the Defendant Ellison Mounts being poor is unable to employ Counsel. It is ordered that W.M. Connelly a regular practicing Attorney at this bar be appointed to defend said Ellison Mounts, who being present accepts said appointment."
After conferring with the defendant, he announced not ready for trial, and prepared and submitted an affidavit and moved the court to continue the cause for him, thereon the Atty. for the Commonwealth admitted that defendant excepted at the time and still excepts. Before the plea of guilty was entered, the Attorney for the Counsel (Ferguson) gave notice that notwithstanding the plea, he would insist on the introduction of this witness.
The witness Sarah McCoy proves that sometime in the first of January 1888, she was at home with her husband, three or four daughters, one son, and some grandchildren on the Blackberry Fork of Pond Creek in Pike County, Kentucky. Was in bed, and a crowd of men came on to the porch and demanded all to surrender and give up and open the door. Her son was upstairs got up, put on his pants, tied his suspenders around him and came to my bed and patted me, and said lay still, we will all be killed, they then said open up or we will fire the house. My boy Calvin pulled the trunk out and got his gun and cartridge and went

upstairs, and the parties on the outside fired through the door and set fire to the house and her son told her to put the fire out – and they told her that if she did, they would kill her. She threw something on it – They went unto the other house where the girls were and told them to make a light and said something to Alifair and then shot her in the breast which poured through her under the shoulder blade and killed her dead. I then went out met who I though was James Vance and said to him, have you got into this. And he told me to go back and I asked to go to any child that was shot and was told again to go back, and I begged to go, and I begged to go, and someone struck me and knocked me down, and I could not get away. Our house was burnt - and what we had, and girl and boy killed. She did not know this defendant was there.

APPENDIX C – LETTER OF SAM E. HILL

KY STATE GUARD - Adjutant Gen. Office - Frankfort, KY - Feb. 6, 1888
Gov. S.B. Buckner - Dear Sir, Pursuant to your order of the 29th Ult. I left Frankfort that night and proceeded to Pike Co. to investigate the border warfare between the Hatfield's of Logan Co., WV and the McCoy's of Pike Co. I reached Pikeville the night of the 31st and remained till the morning of the 3rd made diligent inquiry into the origin and history of the feud, and from the most reliable sources gathered the following facts viz; Sometime previous to the Aug. election 1882, the sheriff of Pike Co. appointed Tolbert McCoy a special bailiff to execute some bench warrant on Johnson Hatfield, which warrants had issued on indictments formed against said Hatfield in the Pike Circuit Court for misdemeanors and which warrants the sheriff himself had been unable to execute. Tolbert McCoy with his brothers made the arrest of Hatfield and under the warrants and started to Pikeville with their kinsmen when they were intercepted by an armed force of the Hatfield's who had been informed of the arrest by some friend, and who immediately crossed the Tug Fork of the Big Sandy and taking a nearer route than that traveled by McCoy and his prisoner intercepted them and rescued the prisoner. Afterwards at the August election 1882, several of the Hatfield's crossed over to the Kentucky side to attend the election, as was their customs where during the day "Big" Ellison Hatfield, brother to Anderson Hatfield, the present leader of the Hatfield band, and Tolbert McCoy engaged in a fight which was provoked and urged on by Hatfield who was a very large man and for overmatched McCoy who was a man of small stature. McCoy ever formed that he was overmatched and drew his knife and commenced stabbing Hatfield, notwithstanding which, Hatfield continued to have the advantage and was in the act of braining McCoy with a large stone,

which he had, where McCoy's brother come to his assistance and shot Hatfield with a pistol. The McCoy's who had participated in that fight were arrested by the Pike Co. authorities and were being detained in custody to await the result of Hatfield's wound when Anderson Hatfield and his gang took them by force from the custody of the Kentucky authorities and carried then across Tug River where they detained them till Ellison Hatfield died, some 36 to 48 hours, when they brought them back to the Kentucky side and tying them to paw paw bushes shot them to death. The McCoy's then slain were three in number, bothers and sons of Randolph McCoy one of them being but fourteen years old, whom the Hatfield accused of complicity in the wounding of Ellison Hatfield. For this murder of the three McCoy brothers, the grand jury of Pike Co. in the next term of the Pike Circuit Court returned three indictments against each one of twenty three persons. Bench warrants were repeated issued on said indictments and were as often returned "not found" notwithstanding many of the persons indicted frequently crossed to the Kentucky side, but in such occasions they were so strong and so well armed as to successfully resist arrest even if it had been attempted. These matters rested for some five years, the Hatfield's, in the meantime, taking an active interest in Kentucky elections and admonishing the sheriffs in whose hands the bench warrant might at such time happen to be to stay allow from the precinct or voting place on the east side of Pike Co. and contingencies large, which they were in the habit of visiting on election occasions, on the day of their contemplated visit, or if he showed attend to leave the bench warrants for their arrest believed and their admonitions were heeded till Frank Phillips, whom your Excellency designated as the agent for Kentucky to receive the persons named in your requisition upon the Governor of West Virginia for certain ones of said indicted parties, was appointed deputy sheriff when in one occasion, there an election was approaching they _ to Phillips to keep away from said election as they wanted to attend, or if he attended to leave the bench warrants against these behind, for if he was there with the bench warrants they would kill him. Phillips replied that his official business would demand his presence there that day and that he would be there and would have the bench warrants and if they cause he would either take or kill them. Phillips went to the election and the Hatfield's approached within gunshot and fired a volley up through the brush & stampeding all but some 8 or 10 persons, the plucky little sheriff remained till late in the evening, but, plucky as he is, he did not feel that he could accomplish their arrest. Nothing further of an eventful character occurred in history of the vendetta till last fall to him, Frank Phillips with twenty three men crossed over into Logan Co. to receive the prisoners who he said he supposed had by that time been arrested murder warrants issued by Gov. Wilson, backed upon your requisition; but learning after he had crossed the State line that no warrants had been issued, or at least that no arrests had been made, and _ with Tom Chambers, who is said to have taken a part in the murder of the three McCoy brothers, and two others, all three of who were included in the indictments, he could not resist so good an opportunity to arrest them and brought them back into Pike Co. where they were served with the bench warrants and placed in jail. To avenge that invasion and arrest, as it is supposed, the Hatfield crossed on the night of January 1st Ult., crossed the Tug Fork in force, penetrated Pike Co., a distance of seven miles till they reached the peaceful mountain home of old Randolph McCoy which they surrounded and demanded a surrender. The faithful watch dog had given warning, however, and old man McCoy and his son Calvin, about 27 years old, arose (the family had retired for the night) and made hasty preparation for the best defense possible against such heavy odds, and to the heavy volleys of the assailants returned a vigorous fire and held them at bay for some two or three hours and until the house which had been forced (fired) from without was almost ready to fall when the young man leaped out and ran towards the corn crib he would cover the fathers retreat to the same point and he believed from that retreat they could yet drive the marauders off; but when about half way from the dwelling to the crib he fell dead with a ball through his brain. The old man then seized double barrel shot gun and leaped out discharging both barrels at the enemy who somewhat disconcerted for a __, did not fire upon him till he was well out in the darkness, and although they fired several shots at him he escaped unhurt. In the meantime one of the party had commanded his unmarried daughter, who occupied a room somewhat detached from that occupied by her parents, to make a light but she replied that she had neither fire nor matches; the same was repeated and, upon her failure to comply, she was shot through the left breast and instantly killed, though she begged piteously for them not to execute their threat to shoot her for failing to make a light, assuring them that it was not within her power to comply with the request. The old mother rushed from her room to go to her daughter whereupon she was struck in the head, knocked down, and beaten with insensibility, and left for dead upon the porch, at least with part of her person on the porch. The assailants withdrew just before the house was ready to fall in at one end, first closing which little of the wood shelter which has not been shot away, with the evidence purpose of burning the remaining members of the family up, but, after they were gone, another daughter about 18 years old rescued some bedding upon which she placed the bodies of her dead sister, the almost lifeless body of her mother and two small children of Tolbert McCoy, a boy about seven years old and a little hunchback girl about five, where they remained till the neighbors arrived about daylight. The heroic girl had her feet badly frost bitten from which she has not yet recovered, and she could not avoid weeping freely as the old lady detailed to me in her presence the horrors of that terrible night. The little boy too is worthy of special mention, for when he emerged from the burning dwellings, when it was almost ready to fall, he thought of his little crippled sister who was still in the house and he re-entered and again came forth leading her by the hand, now did he even cry during the whole of the battle. Mrs. McCoy impressed me as a candid honest old lady, and was unable to walk when I saw her on account of several of her ribs being broken near the spinal column. About the 8th of January Frank Phillips, with a number of Kentuckians again crossed the Tug Fork to arrest the outlaws, and bring them to justice, when they were fired on by old man Jim Vance and Cap Hatfield, and in the fight which resulted old man Vance who is said to have been the most desperate man in the entire section and a fast friend of the Hatfield's was killed, but Cap Hatfield made his escape subsequently Phillips and party made another incurrence into Logan Co. and were again fired upon, without warning this time, and in the fight which ensued one Dempsey of the Hatfield party was killed and Bud McCoy of the Phillips party was severely wounded. In the two forays made by Phillips and party _ the present year they succeeded in capturing six more of the indicted parties, all of whom were brought safely over to Pike, served with warrants of arrest and confined in the Pike Co. jail, making nine in all of the twenty three indicted persons more confined in the Pike Co. jail and awaiting trial for the murder of the McCoy brothers. The charge that the vendetta originated during the war is "not sustained by the facts" for while it is true Harman McCoy brother of Randolph McCoy was murdered after his discharge and return home from the Union Army, his murder was attributed to old Jim Vance and none of his kindred ever attempted, so far as I could learn, to avenge his death and Johnson Hatfield, son of Anderson has since remarried his daughter. The McCoy's and Hatfield's belong to the same political party; hence the feud is and has been from the start, personal and not political. The assertion that Anderson Hatfield and his sons, Johnson and Cap, are reputable, law abiding people is not sustained, for the stories of their lawlessness and brutality, vouched for by credible persons, would fill a volume; while on the other hand old man McCoy and his boys are represented as law abiding honest people by reputable men who have known them long and intimately, and the young man Calvin, who was murdered on New Year's night, is spoken of in and of the highest conversation, and was repeated by told that Pike Co. did not contain a young man of better character or habits. I advise our people to remain upon our side of the State line and assured them of your Excellency's active sympathy for them and in all lawful mentions to uphold the law and to punish the offenders against it. Then that you were especially _ that they should _ which would give the officials of WV, cause of complaint. I took the usual step toward organizing a company of State guards at Pikeville, there being plenty of good material therefore the purpose and in which I feel confident we will secure for the State guard and I sought to impress them with the fact that their arms would be used only by command of the civil authority in maintaining the peace and dignity of our Commonwealth in the rigid enforcement of her laws.

APPENDIX D – LETTERS CONCERNING FRANK PHILLIPS

Letter urging rewards and indictments for Hatfield's on Aug. 22, 1887.
Pikeville, KY, August 22, 1887 - Hon. J. Proctor Knott - Dear Governor, The enclosed petitions in communication made copy of indictments explain why I ask & petition your Excellency to affix a record for apprehension of the parties named by Hon. P.A. Cline & S.G. Kinner (written as C.J. Kinore). Mr. Cline and Mr. Phillips and their statements is entitled to full credence.

September 10, 1887, Governor appoints Frank Phillips as agent.
KY Archives – Governors Journals - Requisitions page 7
The Governor this day issued his requisition on the Governor of West Virginia for the surrender to Frank Phillips appointed agent on the part of the state to receive and deliver them to the jailor of Pike Co. of Anderson Hatfield, Johnson Hatfield, Cap Hatfield, Valentine Hatfield, Elias Hatfield, C. Carpenter, Joseph Murphy, Doc Mayhorn, Pleasant Mayhorn, Selkirk McCoy, Albert McCoy (Kirks son), L.L. McCoy (Kirks son), Thomas Chambers, Lark Varney (Hendersons son), Anderson Varney (Hendersons son), Daniel White, Samuel Mayhorn, Alex Messer, John Whitt, Elijah Mounts Beach Creek fugitives charged with murder.
The governor this day offered rewards of $500 each for the apprehension and delivery to the jailor of Pike Co. of Anderson Hatfield, Cap Hatfield, Johnson Hatfield, and Thomas Chambers, fugitives, charged with murder.

Phillips was not the right person to make arrests on Nov. 28, 1887.
Office of S.G. Kinner, Attorney at Law - Catlettsburg Ky., Nov 28, 1887

[To] General S.B. Buckner, Governor of Kentucky

Dear Sir, I am in receipt of you favor of the 23rd instant. It is true that Frank Phillips the agent of the state to receive the Hatfields from the West Virginia authorities is a deputy of the Pike Co. Sheriff who is a relative of the refugees. Phillips has always been regarded as a good and game man, but his connection with the sheriff of Pike may so influence him that he will make no further efforts to execute his authority. Alf. Burnett is a chief of the Eureka Detective Agency of Charleston W. Va. His reputation is on a plan with that of most others engaged in his calling. I have shown your letter to Judge Rice and we agree that if Phillips does not at once take the necessary steps to arrest the Hatfields that his authority should be revoked, and Burnett appointed. I understand that Burnett has quite a number of men under his control. I met Col. Auxier on his return from Frankfort, and he introduced the subject of recalling the rewards, and his statements to me were in substance, the same as those expressed by you to me in your letter of 23rd instant. I said to him, that I was of the opinion that the Hatfields would pay no attention to any bonds they would execute to remain out of KY., and besides such bonds would not be on a legal sense, obligatory one, thence he acknowledged to me that they were guilty of willful murder and I told him to know of no way to deal with murder, but to try them for their crimes. He said he had better address to your Excellency by R.M. Ferrell and W.M. Connolly advising the withdrawal of the rewards. These two men and his law practice, and have theretofore been among the most persistent in demanding that steps be taken for the issue of rewards sufficiently large to induce men to arrest these fugitives from justice. Very respectfully S.G. Kinner.

Confirmation of the blackmail scheme perpetrated by Cline on January 2, 1888, just a couple days after the McCoy home raid.

STATE OF WEST VIRGINIA - LOGAN COUNTY, to wit; This day personally appeared before me the undersigned authority, Johnson Hatfield, Sr., who being duly sworn upon oath says: That he is acquainted with the parties who stood indicted in the Criminal Court of Pike County, Ky., for the murder of the McCoy's. That during the month of December 1887, me, together with A.J. Auxier and James York, [who were employed counsel for the parties so indicted] made a verbal agreement with one P.A. Cline, an Attorney-at-law, at Pike C.H. Ky., which was about as follows; Said Cline upon his part, agreed that if Anderson Hatfield, et.al., who stood indicted as aforesaid, would deposit with A.J. Auxier the sum of $225, to be paid to him (Cline) if he succeeded in his undertaking what he would recommend to and use all his influence with the Governor of Kentucky to have him take no further steps for the arrest of the said parties indicted as aforesaid; and this affidavit upon the part of said Anderson Hatfield et.al. agreed and did deposit with said Auxier the sum of $225, to be paid to said Cline if he succeeded in getting the Governor to Kentucky to take no further steps for the arrest of said parties. Said Cline claimed that he had spent $225. In procuring rewards and requisition upon the Governor of West Virginia for the arrest of the said Anderson Hatfield et.al. This affiant further states that it was well understood at the time of making of said agreement by all parties interested that the said Cline had not spent any such sum of money in the manner stated by him, but that it was only an excuse for him to take shelter behind. "Johnson Hatfield"

STATE OF KENTUCKY PIKE COUNTY
The affiant say he is employed counsel for some of the parties indicted in their cases for the murder of the McCoy's. And that after the rewards and requisition were offered for the arrest of Anderson Hatfield and others some money was left in my hands to pay fees and expenses in trying to get the Governor of Kentucky to withdraw the rewards. And Mr. P.A. Cline was to have of affiant members two hundred and twenty five dollars if he would recommend the withdrawal of said reward. To be paid in the event the rewards were withdrawn. Mr. Cline wrote to the Secretary of State recommending the same on certain conditions, which was taken to the Secretary and delivered to him the amount he claimed had been expended by him in procuring the rewards and requisitions. A.J. Auxier

Letter from Gov. Wilson to Gov. Buckner telling Cline and Phillips were the wrong people to be involved in the matter of the feud on January 21, 1888.
State of WV - Executive Department - Charleston, January 21st, 1888
Sir, on account of sickness in my family and necessary absence with the Board of Public Works, an unavoidable delay has occurred in answering your communication of the 9th inst. Although the indictments of Anderson Hatfield and others were found more than five years before the application to either your Excellency, or your predecessor, for a requisition, and the parties charged were continuously residing in the neighborhood of the alleged crime; and although the application for the requisition does not appear to be made or supported by any official authority of Pike County, I directed the warrants to issue as soon as the affidavit required by the statue of this State was filed, against all the parties named excepting Elias Hatfield and Andrew Varney. The may

affidavits, and statements of reliable persons showing that these two men were miles away from the place, and at the time of the killing of McCoy induced me to withhold, for the present, the warrant as to them believing that when your Excellency was made acquainted with the facts, their rendition would not be demanded.

After the warrant was directed and prepared as before mentioned, reliable information was received from various persons, [and amongst them F.D. Williams, who was appointed agent by your Excellency, in the matter of the requisition for E & L. Perdue] that the requisition and expected warrant were being used, not to secure the ends of public justice, but to extort money from the accused.

I enclose copies of affidavits of G.W. Pinson, Clerk of the Criminal Court of Pike County; Johnson Hatfield, and A.J. Auxier, an Attorney of the Pike County; also a copy of letter of Frank Williams (which is evidently in the hand-writing of Cline), and extracts from a letter of John A. Sheppard, and Attorney of Logan Co., this State.

I am sure your Excellency will conclude with me that neither Cline nor Phillips, nor any of the persons engaged in the recent violations of the law, are proper persons to entrust with process of either Kentucky or West Virginia. Considering that no move was made in this matter for more than five years after the finding of the Indictment, although the accused have continued their residence in the same locality during all that time, I would be glad if such enquiry were directed as to your Excellency may seem proper, so that warrants may issue -for those only against whom there is some evidence of guilt.

Most Respectfully & Obedient, E.W. Wilson

Letter from Frank Phillips to Governor Wilson December 13, 1887 asking for Warrants. Gov. Wilson accused Cline of writing this letter, that it was in his handwriting.

Pikeville, Ky. Dec 13, 1887 - To his Excellency Governor Wilson - Dear Sir, enclosed please find 15 dollars to pay fees due your office upon the issues of State warrants for the named parties, want for Anderson Hatfield, Johnson Hatfield, Cap Hatfield, Daniel Whitt, Albert McCoy (Kirk's son). Please send warrant to this place to Frank Phillips the agent appointed by the Governor of Kentucky as to Elias Hatfield and Varney, we do not care for. Did not intend to interrupt them. Some of the parties is dead and some gone and left the country the reason they all was named in the requisition was they were all jointly indicted and just copied the indictment, so if we want any others of the parties, we will send for the warrant hereafter. Frank Phillips

APPENDIX E – LETTER OF J. LEE FERGUSON TO GOV. BUCKNER

Jan 13, 1888 - KY Archives - J. Lee Ferguson Attorney at Law

His Excellency S.B. Buckner - Hon Sir, In 1882 what is known as the Hatfield gang came into our state, and taken from the civil authorities three of the McCoy brothers and taken them into West Virginia and kept them a day and night and brought them into Kentucky and tied their arm to arm to a tree and shot them to pieces the youngest of whom was about 14 years of age. This same gang have since that time repeatedly came into Kentucky and controlled out elections and therein was driven men home without the privilege of voting, about two years ago they came into this state and unmercifully beat Wm. Daniels wife and daughter almost to death about the same time this same gang shot from the West Virginia shore and killed Jeff McCoy who was running from them to save his life last August was a year ago they came into this state and drew their guns and pistols on a man and made him stand while on of their gang beat him most cruelly with a cane with sharp notches cut in it gashing him most brutally and this in the presence of the man's wife who at the time was in a helpless condition causing for great misfortune from the fright – The most horrible of all an last New year's night this same gang came to the home of Randolph McCoy a citizen of Kentucky and father of the three boys above spoken of, surrounded his house and demanded his unconditional surrender. He knew it was death – they called and of his daughters to the door of the room in which she was sleeping and shot her through the breast near the heart – killing her instantly she was an __ good girl so all of her neighbors say – she fell dead on the floor – They next set fire to the house Mrs. McCoy next tried to escape from the flames and begged that they would only spare her life – she was struck in the head with a gun and in the side breaking two of her ribs also struck in the back and left for dead, they then turn her back in the house and told her to burn up with the rest – In the meantime Calvin McCoy a son shot and wounded some 3 of the gang and he made an effort to run for life but a volley of at least 50 to 100 shots followed him he fell dead, fired through the brain. Then Randolph had to desert the flames that was then making for him – he made a leap for liberty and for life he met a crowd of men at the door waiting for him, he had a double barrel shot gun discharged it, both barrels all jumped behind the corner of the house save and who fill Mr. McCoy then made his escape being shot at least 50 times – He had two small daughters who escaped unburnt, but ran back into the burning house and drug out their dead sister (not being able to carry her) and also their mother who had to some extent regained consciousness but was helpless – she is now slowly improving. I give these facts as stated by the witnesses. The people of this county are greatly incensed and raised a crowd of about 30 good citizens and armed them the best so could and sent them into Logan Co., W. Va. to ascertain the names of the perpetrators of this must horrible deed, when then they captured 9 of the gang who stand indicted in our court for murder of the 3 McCoy boys and we have been able to get the names of about 8 of the parties that was in this last tragedy – Your Excellency offend a reward for 4 of these gang but his Excellency Gov. of West Virginia refused to grant a requisition after having been called upon for the same different times – The sheriff of out County is closely related to the leaders of the Hatfield gang and is useless to us in this matter – We want you to let us have 50 good guns and 100 rounds of cartridges to each gun - The guns shall be, will, can for and returned in good order and if any damage done. It shall be paid for – Please ship us at once good guns by _ the charges will be paid – the latest news is that the Hatfield gang are raising a mob to burn our town and liberate their men that we have in jail – We have a strong guard armed at jail day and night and have had for some time – but we have not got the guns to arm them as they should be – our citizens are much all armed – I hope to hear from you very soon. I am most respectfully J. Lee Ferguson Co. Attorney / Tobias Wagner J.P.C.C.

APPENDIX F – BATTLE OF POUND FORK

Headquarters District of Eastern Kentucky
Beaver Creek, July 10, 1863
Since my last dispatch, a detachment of the Sixty-fifth Illinois (Union) and Thirty-ninth Kentucky (Union), from this command, under Col. Dan Cameron, have returned from an expedition up the Tug River into West Virginia, where they routed and dispersed the enemy, under Buchanan (Confederate), killing 5 and capturing 20. The enemy took to the cliffs and mountain sides, but the brave Illinoisans and Kentuckians vied with each other in climbing the steeps under a galling fire, and driving the enemy from their mountain fastness's. Colonel Cameron and his officers and men have exhibited the utmost daring and energy, and have penetrated where no Union troops have been before. Julius White Brigadier General

Headquarters District of Eastern KY - Beaver Creek, July 11, 1863
Colonel: I have the honor to submit the following report of the recent operations of this command: On the 3rd instant, I marched from this station with six companies of the Sixty-fifth Illinois Infantry (two

Mounted), Second Battalion Tenth Kentucky Calvary, one squadron Ohio Volunteer Cavalry, one company Fourteenth Kentucky Infantry (Mounted), and two mountain howitzers, under command of Lieutenant Wheeler, of Company M. Second Illinois Light Artillery. At Pikeville, 20 miles south of this, I was joined by a part of the Thirty-ninth Kentucky Infantry (Mounted), in all about 950 men. From Pikeville I proceeded up the Louisa Fork of Sandy River with about half the entire force, directing that the Second Battalion Tenth Kentucky Calvary and the Ohio Squadron proceed by a rapid march through Pound or Sounding Gap to Gladesville, W. Va., and demonstrate upon or attack the force of the enemy at that place, under Colonel Caudill; thence to the railroad at or near Bristol, and destroy so much of it as practicable, unless it should appear too hazardous an undertaking. This command reached Gladesville (after some skirmishing the enemy on the way), completely surprising and carrying the place by storm, beating in the doors and windows, from which the enemy were firing, with axes and compelling his surrender after fifteen minutes of close and desperate fighting, during which the loss of the enemy was 20 killed and 30 wounded. Eighteen commissioned officers, including Colonel Caudell, commanding the regiment, were surrendered, with 99 enlisted men. The camp equipped, stores, arms, and ammunition of the command were destroyed. Major Brown, Tenth Kentucky Calvary (Union), commanding this detachment, then returned to camp at Pikeville, thence to this place, with his prisoners, safely, the presence of superior forces of the enemy preventing farther progress toward the railroad. Twelve hours before Major Brown marched from Pikeville, I moved the remainder of Col. Camerons command up the Louisa Fork of the Sandy River, for the purpose of attacking a regiment of the enemy under Colonel A.J. May (Confederate), said to be posted near the Stateline, and also for the purpose of diverting the attention of the enemy from the movement of Major Brown, by a demonstration in the direction of the Salt Works. After marching to a point near the State line, and finding that the enemy had retreated to a point some 60 miles distant, and within supporting distance of a force greatly superior to my own, the road being wholly bare of subsistence for me or animals, I detached Colonel Cameron, with the remaining force, to attempt the capture of a body of the enemy on the Tug Fork, some 25 miles distant, and returned to Pikeville with the infantry and howitzers, from which point I could support the movement on either flank (Colonel Cameron's or Major Brown's), should it become necessary, with facility.

Colonel Cameron was attacked by the enemy on Pond Creek, and was engaged at intervals for several hours, his men consisting of detachments from the 39th Kentucky Mounted Infantry (Union), under Lieutenant Colonel Mims, and from the Sixty-fifth Illinois Infantry (Union), under Captain Kennedy, boldly charging up the precipitous mountain sides with the greatest gallantry. The enemy was completely routed, leaving 5 dead on the field, with many more wounded, and 20 prisoners, who fell into our hands. Col. Camerons command sustained no loss.

It affords me pleasure to state that our entire loss in all these operations was but 9 wounded none severely, there being 6 of the Tenth Kentucky and 3 of the First Ohio Squadron, none of whose names have been reported to me.

The conduct of all the troops composing the expedition has been admirable. The assault of the command under Major Brown, Tenth Kentucky Calvary, supported by the gallant Major Rice and the subordinate officers and men of the Ohio squadron, upon the enemy at Gladesville, was worthy of veterans.

The courage, persistency, and endurance of the troops composing the detachment under Colonel Cameron was no less conspicuous, and would have been equally successful had the enemy been as easily accessible as at Gladesville. The spirit evinced by the infantry of the Sixty-fifth Illinois, under Lieutenant Colonel Stewart, Captain Collins, Fourteenth Kentucky, and the men manning the howitzers, under Lieutenant Wheeler, was equal to that of their comrades (who, being mounted, were able to reach the enemy), and showed conclusively that whenever their opportunity comes they will be equally effective.

Major Brown recommends for promotion, "for conspicuous and distinguished gallantry," Lieut. H.C. White and Sergeant James W. Stewart, of Company I, and Sergeant William H. Hendrickson, of Company G., 10th Kentucky Cavalry. In this recommendation I cheerfully join, and respectfully add to this roll of honor the names of Col. D. Cameron, commanding the brigade; Maj. Richard Rice, 1st squadron Ohio Cavalry; Lieut. Col. Mims and Major Ferguson, 39th Kentucky Mounted Infantry, and Captain Kennedy, 65th Illinois Volunteer Infantry.

Very Respectfully, your obedient servant, Julius White

Brigadier Gen., Commanding, Lieut. Col. Lewis Richmond, Asst. Adj. Gen. and Chief of Staff.

APPENDIX G – KENTUCKY REWARDS

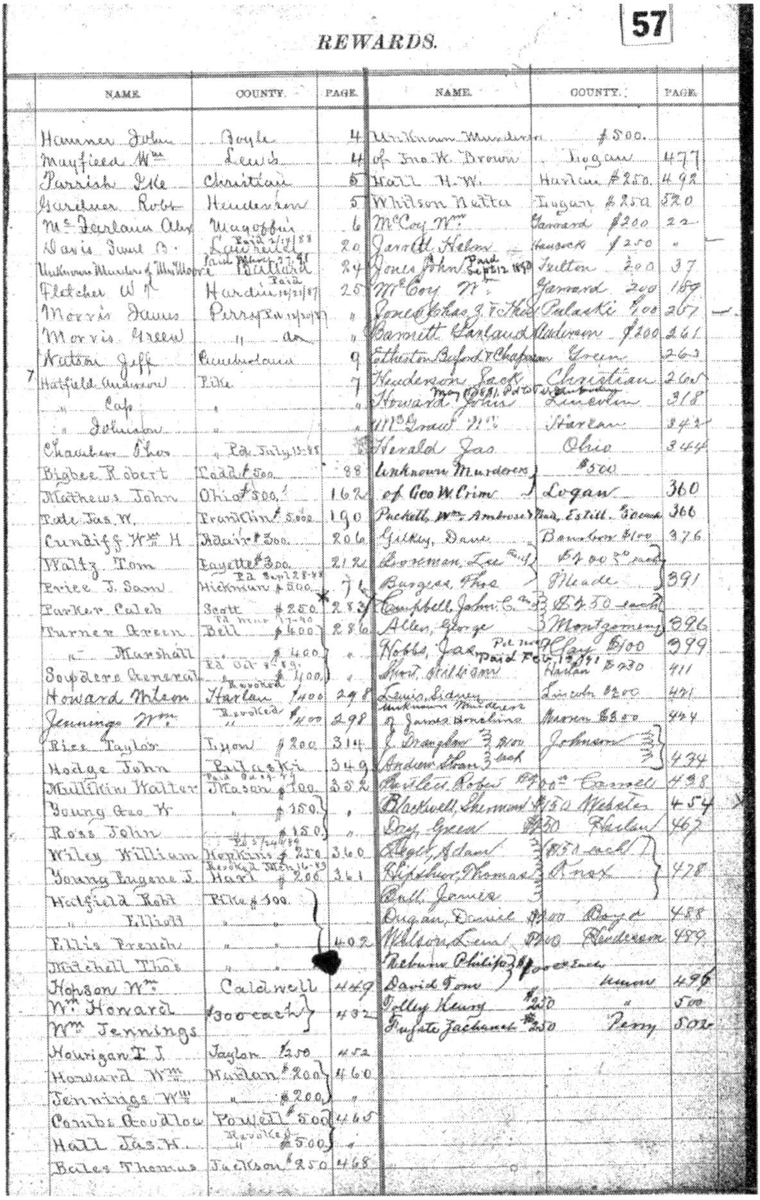

57

REWARDS.

NAME.	COUNTY.	PAGE.	NAME.	COUNTY.	PAGE.
Hammer John	Boyle	4	Unknown Murderers	$500.	
Mayfield Wm	Lewis	4	of Jno. W. Brown	Logan	477
Parrish Ike	Christian	5	Hall H. W.	Harlan $250	492
Gardner Robt	Henderson	5	Whitson Hatter	Logan $250	520
McFarland Alex	Magoffin	6	McCoy Wm	Garrard $200	22
Davis Saml B.	Laurel Paid 2/17/88	20	Jarrett Helm	Hancock $250	"
Unknown Murderers of Mr. Moore	Ballard Paid [illegible]	24	Jones John Paid Sept 12 1890	Fulton 200	37
Fletcher W T	Hardin Paid 11/21/87	25	McCoy W.	Garrard 200	187
Morris James	Perry Pd 11/20/87	"	Jones Chas J. & Thos	Pulaski $100	257
Morris Green	" do	"	Barnett Garland	Anderson $200	261
Watson Jeff	Cumberland	9	Etherton Buford & Chapman	Green	263
7 Hatfield Anderson	Pike	7	Henderson Jack	Christian	265
" Cap	"	"	Howard John	Lincoln	318
" Johnson	"	"	McGraw Wm	Harlan	342
Chambers Thos	" Pd July 13 88		Herald Jas	Ohio	344
Bigbee Robert	Todd $500	88	Unknown Murderers	$500	
Mathews John	Ohio $500	162	of Geo W Crim	Logan	360
Tate Jas W.	Franklin $500	190	Puckett Wm Ambrose	Estill $300 each	366
Cundiff Wm H	Adair $300	206	Gilkey, Dave	Bourbon $100	376
Waltz Tom	Fayette $300	212	Bowman, Lee and	$400 each	
Price J. Sam	Hickman $500 Pd Sept 28 88	71	Burgess, Thos	Meade	391
Parker Caleb	Scott $250	283	Campbell John C. and	$450 each	
Turner Green	Bell $400	286	Allen, George	Montgomery	396
" Marshall	" $400	"	Hobbs, Jas Paid Feb 19/91	Clay $100	399
Saylors General	" $400	"	Short, William	Harlan $250	411
Howard Wilson	Harlan Revoked $400	298	Lewis, Sidney	Lincoln $200	421
Jennings Wm	" Revoked $400	298	Unknown Murderers of James Hoskins	Mason $500	424
Rice Taylor	Lyon $200	314	J. Vaughan $100 each	Johnson	
Hodge John	Pulaski	349	Andrew Sloan		434
Mullikin Walter	Mason $100	352	Pastley Robert	$100 Carroll	438
Young Geo W	" $150	"	Blackwell Sherman	$150 Webster	454
Ross John	" $150	"	Day Green	$150 Harlan	467
Wiley William	Hopkins $250	360	Angel Adam	$150 each	
Young Eugene J.	Hart Revoked $200	361	Upshur Thomas	Knox	478
Hatfield Robt	Pike $500		Ball James		
" Elliott	" "		Dugan Daniel	$100 Boyd	488
Ellis French	" "	402	Wilson Lem	$100 Henderson	489
Mitchell Thos	" "		Reburn Philip	$100 each	
Hopson Wm	Caldwell	449	David Tom	[illegible]	496
Wm Howard	$300 each	432	Tolley Henry	$250 "	500
Wm Jennings			Fugate Jackson	$250 Perry	502
Hourigan T. J.	Taylor $250	452			
Howard Wm	Harlan $200	460			
Jennings Wm	" $200	"			
Combs Goodloe	Powell $500	465			
Hall Jas H.	" Revoked $500	"			
Bates Thomas	Jackson $250	468			

APPENDIX H – FOURTEENTH KENTUCKY REGIMENT

ADJUTANT GENERAL'S REPORT

ROLL OF COMPANY I, 14th REGIMENT CAVALRY

Formerly May's Battalion Kentucky and Virginia Mounted Rifles—14th Cavalry

200

	NAME	RANK	WHEN ENLISTED	WHERE ENLISTED	MUSTERED OUT When	When
1	John S. Ratliff	Captain	July 1, 1863	Buchanan Co., Va		
2	John S. Sitton	1st Lieutenant	July 1, 1863	Buchanan Co., Va		
3	Isaac Boyd	2nd Lieutenant	July 1, 1863	Buchanan Co., Va		
4	F. M. Breeding	1st Sergeant	July 1, 1863	Buchanan Co., Va		
5	R. M. Boyd	2nd Sergeant	July 1, 1863	Buchanan Co., Va		
6	R. S. Shortridge	3rd Sergeant	July 1, 1863	Buchanan Co., Va		
7	S. Ratliff	4th Sergeant	July 1, 1863	Buchanan Co., Va		
8	Joseph Rusvan	5th Sergeant	July 1, 1863	Buchanan Co., Va		
9	Jacob Lester	1st Corporal	July 1, 1863	Buchanan Co., Va		
10	J. B. Compton	2nd Corporal	July 1, 1863	Buchanan Co., Va		
11	William Ratliff	3rd Corporal	July 1, 1863	Buchanan Co., Va		
12	Charles VanDyke	4th Corporal	July 1, 1863	Buchanan Co., Va		
13	Astrop, Harman	Private	July 1, 1863	Buchanan Co., Va		
14	Boyd, Elisha	Private	July 1, 1863	Buchanan Co., Va		
15	Boyd, Alexander	Private	July 1, 1863	Buchanan Co., Va		
16	Rail, William	Private	July 1, 1863	Buchanan Co., Va		
17	Booth, William H.	Private	July 1, 1863	Buchanan Co., Va		
18	Childers, John W.	Private	July 1, 1863	Buchanan Co., Va		
19	Cook, William	Private	July 1, 1863	Buchanan Co., Va		
20	Chambers, John	Private	July 1, 1863	Buchanan Co., Va		
21	Compton, Henry	Private	July 1, 1863	Buchanan Co., Va		
22	Compton, David	Private	July 1, 1863	Buchanan Co., Va		
23	Compton, J. W.	Private	July 1, 1863	Buchanan Co., Va		
24	Dunford, Wesley	Private	July 1, 1863	Buchanan Co., Va		
25	Davis, William	Private	July 1, 1863	Buchanan Co., Va		
26	Davis, Tyree	Private	July 1, 1863	Buchanan Co., Va		
27	Davis, Chapman	Private	July 1, 1863	Buchanan Co., Va		
28	Davis, Morgan	Private	July 1, 1863	Buchanan Co., Va		
29	Davis, Wesley	Private	July 1, 1863	Buchanan Co., Va		
30	Elswick, John T.	Private	July 1, 1863	Buchanan Co., Va		
31	Gillespie, T.	Private	July 1, 1863	Buchanan Co., Va		
32	Gillespie, John C.	Private	July 1, 1863	Buchanan Co., Va		
33	Gillespie, R. S.	Private	July 1, 1863	Buchanan Co., Va		
34	Hess, James H.	Private	July 1, 1863	Buchanan Co., Va		
35	Hagg, George	Private	July 1, 1863	Buchanan Co., Va		
36	Hilton, W. H.	Private	July 1, 1863	Buchanan Co., Va		
37	Jackson, H. C.	Private	July 1, 1863	Buchanan Co., Va		
38	Jackson, M.	Private	July 1, 1863	Buchanan Co., Va		
39	Looney, John	Private	July 1, 1863	Buchanan Co., Va		
40	Looney, William	Private	July 1, 1863	Buchanan Co., Va		
41	Lester, C. A.	Private	July 1, 1863	Buchanan Co., Va		
42	Lambert, John P.	Private	July 1, 1863	Buchanan Co., Va		
43	May, Isaac	Private	July 1, 1863	Buchanan Co., Va		
44	Moore, John M.	Private	July 1, 1863	Buchanan Co., Va		
45	Music, Elevion	Private	July 1, 1863	Buchanan Co., Va		
46	Maglantham, David	Private	July 1, 1863	Buchanan Co., Va		
47	Napper, W. H.	Private	July 1, 1863	Buchanan Co., Va		
48	Napper, G. W.	Private	July 1, 1863	Buchanan Co., Va		
49	Presley, Isaac	Private	July 1, 1863	Buchanan Co., Va		
50	Presley, Sampson	Private	July 1, 1863	Buchanan Co., Va		
51	Presley, James	Private	July 1, 1863	Buchanan Co., Va		
52	Puckett, Squire	Private	July 1, 1863	Buchanan Co., Va		
53	Ratliff, Julius	Private	July 1, 1863	Buchanan Co., Va		
54	Ratliff, Moses	Private	July 1, 1863	Buchanan Co., Va		
55	Stillwell, Elias	Private	July 1, 1863	Buchanan Co., Va		
56	Sullner, Charles	Private	July 1, 1863	Buchanan Co., Va		
57	Stevens, Isaac	Private	July 1, 1863	Buchanan Co., Va		
58	Street, Simon	Private	July 1, 1863	Buchanan Co., Va		
59	Street, John	Private	July 1, 1863	Buchanan Co., Va		
60	Street, William	Private	July 1, 1863	Buchanan Co., Va		
61	Vance, A. H.	Private	July 1, 1863	Buchanan Co., Va		
62	Vance, Elijah	Private	July 1, 1863	Buchanan Co., Va		
63	Vance, James H.	Private	July 1, 1863	Buchanan Co., Va		
64	Vance, W. H.	Private	July 1, 1863	Buchanan Co., Va		
65	Ward, A. P.	Private	July 1, 1863	Buchanan Co., Va		

NOTE—The only roll of this company on file is dated Buchanan County, Va., July 31, 1863 and marked Company "X" May's Mounted Riflemen. There are two rolls marked Company "It", and this latter roll is designated Company "I", as it appears to be the junior company.

APPENDIX I – ESTATE DEBTS FOR JAMES VANCE

Lawsuits for James M. Vance son of James M. and Mary Collins Vance (these are just a few of the entries from Logan Court Books.

Logan Chancery Book C pg. 314 Oct 4, 1888 - H. Krish vs. J.M. Vance et al} In Chancery - Special Commissioner Jn. A. Sheppard this day tendered his report of sale of the tract of land mentioned in the plaintiffs bill and proceed discharge herein as 1500 acres on Grapevine Creek on the 2nd day of October 1888 at public auction in the manner prescribed by said decree of sale. At which sale J.D. Sergeant became the purchaser of said lands for the sum of $5025.00. And appearing from said report that the purchaser has complied with the terms of sale in said decree in of sale mentioned by paying to said Commissioner the sum of $161.64. That being sufficient to pay cost of suit and expenses of sale, and executed his bonds for the two deferred payments each for the sum of $2431.68 due in 12 and 24 months respectively with interest from date and that on each of said note be given J.A. Nighbert as security. There being no exception to said report and to the sale therein mentioned and the court being of opinion that said lands sold for its fair value. The same is in all things approved and confirmed. The purchaser desiring to obtain a deed for said land at once. The court being satisfied that the security given is amply sufficient said Special Commissioner is directed to make and deliver for record an apt and proper deed to said land reserving a vendors lien therein for the balance of purchase money for which he shall be allowed the sum of $10.00 to be paid out of the fund.

Logan Co. Chancery Bk D. page 27-28 – Oct 14, 1889 - H. Krish vs J.M. Vance] In Chancery - This day Frank De La Lane and Jno. E. Lawson executors and Jennie Lawson executors of M.B. Lawson deceased tendered and asked leave to file their separate petitions herein and here being no objections to the filing thereof the same are ordered to the filed whereupon this defendant James M. Vance by counsel appeared and waived the issuing and service of matters in each of said petitions and is appearing to the court that there is more due and unpaid upon his judgment in favor as said executor and executrix in their petitions including principal and interest and cost to this date this sum of $1314.15 and that there is due the said Frank D. La Lane including principal interest. And costs to this date the sum of $257.40 and that satisfied out of the proceeds of the sale of lands old herein special commissioner Jno. A. Sheppard

It is therefore adjudged ordered and decreed that the said Jno. E. Lawson and Jennie Lawson executrix of M.B. Lawson deceased recover of he said James M. Vance this said sum of $1314.15 and that he said Frank D. La Lane recover of this said James M. Vance the sum of $257.40 with interest on each of said sums from this date, and John A. Sheppard Special Commissioner herein is directed to pay the said sum of $1314.15 and $257.40 to said petitioners respecting out of his surplus of any of the proceeds arising from the sale of land of the same James M. Vance heretofore made by said Commissioner after paying off and satisfying the decree of sale herein and that if there is not sufficient surplus in his lands arising from said law that their said petitioners shall share pro-value in said surplus if any their said Judgment being of equal dignity.

Logan Co. Chancery April 23 1890 Book D. page 107 - H. Krish vs James M. Vance} In chancery - Jno. A. Sheppard the Special Commissioner who made sale of the real estate mentioned in the proceedings in said cause this day tendered and asked leave to file his report showing the collation and disbursement of the amount due on the first deferred payments, and is appearing from said report - that the whole of principal and interest of said not which was $2576.88 was collected by said commissioners and paid over to the parties thereto entitled as follows;
To H. Krish in full his Judgment $388.02
To Hurst Miller & Co., in full $914.82
To Frank D. La Lane & Co., in full $261.25
To M.B. Lawson Exec., in part payment $1012.79 and there being no exceptions to said report the same is in all things approved and confirmed and said Commissioner so far as related to said first deferred payments is released from further responsibility.

APPENDIX J – DEEDS AND OTHER

James M. Vance et al to Clay & Headley} Contract – Know all men by these present that we James M. Vance and John Francisco of the County of Logan and State of West Virginia have this day sold and by these present do bargain and sell to Samuel Clay Jr. and George W. Headley of Fayette County KY. A certain tract of land situated in the County of Logan and State of West Virginia. On the waters of Grapevine, Thacker, and Pigeon Creek waters of the Tug Fork of Sandy River and bounded as follows; beginning on the beeches at the mouth of Wolf Pen Fork of Grapevine Creek thence southward to the top of the ridge between Grapevine and the River. Thence with said ridge the dividing ridge between Grapevine and Beech Creek. Thence with the said ridge to the head of Thacker Creek. Thence with the dividing ridge between Grapevine and Thacker Creek to the head of Wolf Pen Fork of Grapevine Creek. Thence with the dividing ridge between Wolf Pen Fork and main Grapevine to the beginning. Also with tract on Thacker Creek beginning on a beech tree near the creek and running with the calls of the deed to the beginning. Known as the Mounts tract. Also another tract on Thacker Creek beginning on a beech and sycamore near the creek thence running with the calls and courses of the deed to the beginning. Known as the William S. Ferrell tract. Also another tract on Pigeon beginning on a maple and Lynn near the creek running with the calls and courses to the beginning. Known as the Jake Ferrell tract. Also another tract on the Big Branch of Pigeon Creek bounded on the north by Gurley and wife on the south by James Starr on the west by Dempsey's heirs known as the G.B. Goff land all the walnut timber from 16 inches and up on the 1338 acre tract on Grapevine is hereby excepted in this tract. It is further agreed that the said Clay and Headley agrees to pay the above named parties one dollar per acre for the mineral rights of the house tract of land. Which is supposed to be 500 acres more or less the same survey at the same time said land above specified are measured and paid for and supposed to contain (5000) five thousand acres more or less the same to be subject to survey. The price of said land is to be $2.85 two dollars and eight five cents per acre. Of which the sum of $110 one hundred and ten dollars is this day paid in cash the receipt of which is hereby acknowledged. The remainder of the purchase price to be paid within twelve months from this date at which time and upon receipt of the balance of the purchase money we bind ourselves to make to said Samuel Clay Jr. and Geo. W. Headley of Fayette County a good and sufficient deed to said boundary of land. With relinquishment of dower and homestead claims and with covenants of general warranty thereto witness our hand and seal this 7th day of May 1888. James M. Vance & John Francisco Attest J.C. McNight and Joseph Hatfield

Feb 15, 1889 James M. Vance et. als to J. Dickinson Sergeant} Contract – Know all men by these present that we James M. Vance agent for Mary Vance, Jno. Francisco and Amy his wife, N.B. Nichols and Eliza his wife, Evan Ferrell and Jane his wife do hereby covenant and agree…..to grant bargain sell and convey to J.D. Sergeant and his heirs, with general warranty of title covenants of quiet possession and freedom from incumberments for the price of $4.00 per acre. All of the following real estate 1900 acres of land; 400 acres lying on pigeon creek in Logan County and the balance lying on Thacker Creek and joining the lands of the said J.D. Sergeant, divided amongst the different parties as follows.

Jno Francisco & wife 800 acres
Mary Vance 500 acres
N.B. Nichols & wife 400
Evan Ferrell & wife 200
These land to be surveyed and deeds made on or before 20th of May 1889. (Money paid on contract Void)
Now the conditions of the foregoing are as follows; should Clay Headley come here and comply with their contract on or before the 7th day of May 1889 they this obligation to be null and void, otherwise it is to remain in full force and virtue and we are not to be held liable for any damage. Witness our hands and seals this 15th day of Feb 1889.
James M. Vance for himself & agent for Mary Vance
John Francisco, Anne Francisco, N.B. Nichols, Eliza Nichols
Witness as to Nichols & wife} James M. Vance

Other Deeds
1884 Jan 9 - James M. Vance to Elizabeth Nichols} Deed – This deed made this 9th day of January 1884 by and between James Vance and Mary his wife and James M. Vance of the first part and Elizabeth Nichols and the heirs of her body of the second part all of the County of Logan and State of West Virginia, witnessed that for and in consideration of the sum of $200.00 to them in hand paid by the party of the second part before the sealing and delivery of these present the receipt whereof is hereby acknowledged hand this day bargained and sol and by these present do bargain and sell unto them the said Elizabeth Nichols and her heirs forever the following tract or parcel of land situated lying and being in said County of Logan and Thacker creek of Sandy River beginning on an oak trees at the top of the point between the ? fork and the Prater fork running down the point to _ tree at the mouth of the Prater Fork thence down the creek with the bed of the creek to a large rock thence up the north side of the creek to the top of the point and the upper side of what is known as the Traft Hollow thence with said point to the dividing ridge between Grapevine Creek and Thacker Creek thence down said ridge to a corner on chestnut oak tree between Moses C. Chafin and Mary Vance thence with Moses Chafin line back to the beginning corner supposed to contain 100 acres to be the same more or less to have and to hold the said tract of land with its appurtenances except the mineral rights which they preserve for themselves unto them the said Elizabeth Nichols and her heirs forever and the said James Vance his wife Mary and James M. Vance will warrant all the right title and interest in said tract of land to the said Elizabeth Nichols and her heirs forever in witness whereof the party of the first part has here unto

set their hands and affixed their seals this day and year first above written. James Vance, Mary Vance, James M. Vance 9th day of Jan. 1884

1884 Jan 9 - James M. Vance to Jane Ferrell} Deed - This deed made this 9th day of January 1884 by and between James Vance and Mary his wife and James M. Vance of the first part and Jane Ferrell and the heirs of her body of the second part all of the County of Logan and State of West Virginia, witnessed that for and in consideration of the sum of two hundred dollar to them in hand paid by the party of the second part before the sealing and delivery of these present the receipt whereof is hereby acknowledged hand this day bargained and sol and by these present do bargain and sell unto them the said Jane Ferrell and her heirs forever the following tract or parcel of land situated lying and being in said County of Logan and Thacker Creek of Sandy River. Beginning on a beech tree near the branch below the peach orchard thence running up the north side of the creek to a chestnut oak tree and the point thence with said point to the dividing ridge between Grapevine Creek and Thacker Creek thence with the dividing ridge between Mates Creek and Thacker Creek to a hickory on a nob thence down the fork ridge of Thacker to a hickory thence a square line back to the beginning corner supposed to contain one hundred acres be the same more or less to have and to hold the said tract of land with it appurtenances except the mineral rights which they reserve for themselves unto them the said Jane Ferrell and her heirs forever and the said James Vance his wife Mary, James Vance will warrant all their right title and interest in vested in said tract of land to the same Jane Ferrell and her in witness whereof the part of the first part have here unto set their lands and affixed their sealing this day and year first above written. James Vance, Mary Vance and James M. Vance. 9th day of January 1884

James M. Vance to Amy Francisco} Deed This deed made the 10th day of Mar. 1886, by and between James M. Vane of the one part and Amy Francisco and her heirs of the second part all of the County of Logan and State of West Virginia. Witnessed that for and in consideration of the sum of $380.00 unto him paid in hand by Amy Vance and her heirs before the sealing and deliver of these present. The receipt whereof is hereby bargain and sell unto Amy Francisco her heirs forever the following tract or parcel of land situated lying and being in said County of Logan on Thacker Creek of Sandy River bounded as follows. Beginning on three beeches and a sycamore in the bottom near James Vance shanty. Thence running a square line to the top of the ridge between Middle Fork and Main Creeks. Thence running square line across creeks to a sweet gum in the bottom. Thence a square line to the top of the ridge between Thacker creek and Grapevine Creek. Thence down the top of ridge so as to make, a square line to the beginning corner supposed to contain 150 acres more or less to have and to hold the said tract of land with all its appurtenances unto said Amy Francisco and her heirs forever. And the said James Vance will account the title to said tract or parcel of land specially to the said Amy Francisco and being forever do witness whereof the party of the first part hereunto set his hand affixed his seal this day and grants first above written.

Mary Vance to C.H. Taylor} Title Bond – Thacker Creek Logan Co. W. Va. Nov 10th 1891 – Know all men by these present. That we Mary Vance and James M. Vance are held and firmly bound unto C.B. Taylor, L.M. Hall, John Rapelje, Joseph Powell Jr. in the full and just sum of ten thousand dollars. In lawful money of the United States for which we bind ourselves our heirs and our administrators jointly and severally with our seals and date this 10th day of November 1891. The condition of the above obligation is such that Mary Vance and James M. Vance have this day sold unto Chas. B. Taylor, Louis M. Hall, John Rapelje and Joseph Powell Jr a certain tract of land situated on Thacker Creek, Logan County, West Virginia. Supposed to contain about five hundred acres being the land covered by a deed dated Feb 27th 1869 recorded March 3rd 1870 in Deed Book E, page 253, of the records of Logan County. Deeded by Alex and Michael Mounts to Mary Vance. And also land covered by deed dated Dec 9th 1878 recorded June 10th 1879 in deed Book G page 177 in the records of Logan County from Moses Chafin to Mary Vance. And also all the coal and mineral rights on a tract of land covered by deed dated Jan 9th 1884 recorded Feb 8th 1886 in Deed Book "I" page 340 from Mary Vance and others to Elizabeth Nichols and others. And also the coal and other mineral rights on a tract of land covered by deed dated about Jan 9th 1884 and recorded about Feb 8th 1886 in the records of Logan County from Mary Vance and others to Jane Ferrell and others lying in the head of the main fork of Thacker Creek. For the price or sum of ten dollars per acre for the five hundred acre tract first mentioned to which both surfaces and mineral right are to be conveyed. The price or sum of five dollars per acre for the said mineral rights on property herein described by a surveyor to be mutually agreed upon at the expense of C.B. Taylor, L.M. Hall, John Rapelje (sp) and Joseph Powell Jr. The payments for said land are to be made as follows. Fifteen hundred dollars ($1500) paid in hand. The receipt for which is hereby acknowledged. One thousand to be paid in six (6) months from this date. One thousand dollars at intervals of six months each from the time of the proceedings payment with interest on the amount unpaid at the time of each payment until the whole amount is paid. The said Mary Vance reserving the right to live upon & till the soil of said land for the terms of her natural life if she so desires. To take such fuel as she may wish for her own use and such timber as may be required to repair fences and buildings provided. However, that the parties purchasing said land or their successors shall have the right to use such parts of said land as are necessary to the operation of coal or other mines if they desire so to use them. Provided however that if they interfere with the house of said Mary Vance they shall remove the same to such a place as she may designate on said premises not interfering with such at their expense. Now if the said Mary Vance and James M. Vance shall make a good and sufficient title to the said tract of land and the mineral rights before mentioned then this obligation to be void other wise to remain in full force & virtue. Given under our hands and seal this 10th day of November 1891. Mary Vance and J.M. Vance Witness Amy Francisco

Dec 1, 1893 this deed made this first day of December 1893 between Amy Flynn and Charles S. Flynn her husband of the Magnolia District of Logan Co, W.Va., of the first part and Louis M. Hall, Henrietta P. Powell, John K. Newell and John Rapelje of the second part. Witnessed that for and in consideration of the sum of $1832 dollars in hand the receipt whereof is hereby acknowledged the said parties of the first part do grant unto the parties of the second part with covenants of general warranty the following described property to wit. A certain tract of land situate on the main fork of Thacker Creek a tributary at a beech tree on the bank of said creek on line of W.S. Ferrell land. Thence up the hill north 14 degrees and 30 ½ half minutes east, 800 feet. Thence black oaks a sourwood and black gum on the ridge between the main fork and middle fork of said creek. Thence up the same with the center thereof to a small beech for a corner, thence down the hill south 29 degrees east 223 feet to a second gum in line of land lately owned by Allen Chafin and others. Thence containing the same count up the hill 2692 feet to a red oak and hickory on a corner on top of the main dividing ridge between said creek and the _. Thence down the same with the _ thereof to two white oaks as a corner thence down the hill north 22 ½ degrees east 1178 feet to the place of beginning containing 183 2/10th acres be the same more or less. Whereas on 26th day of December 1891 Amy Francisco (then a widow, now intermarried with Charles S. Flynn) made and entered into a certain title bond with the said L.M. Hall and Joseph Powell Jr., for the conveyance of the above described lands. Whereas the said Joseph Powell Jr had since died and all his interest in said title bond passed to his father Joseph Powell Sr. Then to the said and then to the said Henrietta Powell. And afterwards the said John K. Newell and John Rapelje have each paid on one-fourth part of the payments of said land. The said Joseph Powell Jr. and L.M. Hall being trusties for them. Now this deed is made and accepted as a full and complete performance of all the conditions of said title bond and same in forever discharged said title bond being of record in County clerk's office in and for the County of Logan in deed book Q at page 329.

Amy Flynn & Husband} deed to G.W. Taylor – This deed made this 23rd day of February 1894 between Amy Flynn and C.S. Flynn of the first part and G.W. Taylor of the second part. Witness that for and in consideration of the sum of $6000 in hand the receipt of which is hereby acknowledged the said parties of the first part do hereby grant unto the party of the second part with covenants of general warranty the following. Situate in Logan County West Virginia on Grapevine Creek....a certain tract of land supposed to contain fifteen hundred acres which was conveyed to one John Francisco the former husband of the female grantor from James M. Vance by deed bearing date of the 24th day of June 1887 now of record in the clerk's office .....deed book J. page 357 to which reference is land for a more particular description of the property hereby conveyed and whereas the said Francisco depart this life intestate in the year 1889 leaving the female grantor his widow and his two infant children Viola and Maggie his heirs at law and the said female grantor having since intermarried with male grantor further covenant for and on behalf of said infants that they will cause to be conveyed as soon as possible the interest of the said infants in and to said land. Witness the following signatures and seals. Anna Flynn C.S. Flynn the 23rd day of Feb. 1894

C.S. Flynn to Lucy Flynn} Deed – This deed made this 2nd day of October 1894, between C.S. Flynn of Cabell County W.Va. of the first part, and Mrs. Lucy Flynn of Nolan, Logan County West Virginia of the second part. Witnessed that for and in consideration of one hundred dollars cash in hand paid said C.S. Flynn, hereby, grants sells and conveys unto said Lucy Flynn the following described town property to wit. One lot situate in said town of Nolan in Logan County W.VA. It being the same lot conveyed to C.S. Flynn by B.A. Duncan. It being situate between a lot owned by said Duncan on lower side and by lot owned by Thos. Alley on upper side said lot fronting fifty feet and two hundred and twenty feet...to have and to hold to said Lucy Flynn her heir and assigns forever with the appurtenances thereto belonging with covenants of land. Witness the following signature and seal. C.S. Flynn

Deed for Vicey Vance to Parlee Stepp regarding the Store in Nolan, in the Duncan Addition, after Jim Jr. died. 028-00055

COURT CASE OF VIOLA AND MAGGIE FRANCISCO

Case 079_00054 Viola Francisco vs Little Kanawha Lumber Company
Bill of Complaint of Viola Francisco and Maggie Francisco infants under the
age of 21 years, who sue by their next friend C.S. Flynn, plaintiffs against the
Little Kanawha Lumber Company, a corporation Charley Stephens, Levi
Stephens, Jacob Spaulding and Amy Flynn defendants filed in the circuit court
of Logan County, West Virginia.
To the Hon. Thomas H. Harvey Judge of said Court: The plaintiffs, complaining,
says that on or about the 5 day of April 1890 their father, John Francisco late of
said county departed this life intestate leaving, surviving him, as his only heirs,
his two children the plaintiffs herein who now then, as well as infants under the
age of 21 years, and his widow, the mother of the plaintiffs, Amy Flynn, who has
currently intermarried with the said C.S. Flynn.
The plaintiffs further allege that their father at the time of his death was seized
and possessed in fee simple of a tract of 150 acres of land, more or less, situate on
Pigeon Creek in said county. The same having been conveyed to their father,
from Jacob Ferrell and wife by deed, dated Jan.15, 1878 and now duly recorded
in the clerk's office of the county court, as will more fully appear from a duly
attested copy of said deed herewith filed as part of this bill marked exhibit A.
That upon the death of their father the title to said tract of land descended to,
and vested in, the plaintiffs, as his next of kin under the laws of descent and
distribution of this state. That the plaintiffs are now the owners in fee simple
thereof, subject to their mothers' dower therein which has never, in any manner
been laid off and assigned to her.
That neither the plaintiffs nor their mother, are now in the possession of said
tract but that the right and title of the plaintiffs, thereto on so far as is known to
them are disputed in any manner. That about 150 acres of said tract of land have
been cleared and fenced, and that a good portion of the cleared land is level and
productive and that the said tract of land is valuable mainly as farming land for
which it was cleared and fenced as aforesaid.
That the defendant, the Little Kanawha Lumber Company is a foreign
corporation organized, created and existing as the plaintiffs, are informed, that
believe and so charged under the laws of the state of Maine. And is now, and has
been for some time past, extensively engaged in the lumbering or saw logging
business in said county, in various streams therein. That said company has now
about 5000 saw logs (being trees cut into logs of convenient lengths) lying above
and back of the said tract of 150 acres of land, ready to be, and now being hauled
to said Pigeon Creek in which they will them be floated out to Tug River, Thence
onto market. No part of which were cut or taken from off the said 150-acre tract
of land of the plaintiffs. That said logs above the back of said tract of land would
have to be, or are expected to be, brought out over and through the same. That
the said company for this purpose of reaching and removing said logs have

without any lease or license from the plaintiffs, entered upon said tract of land and has constructed a tram road through the same for a distance of about one mile that he same passes through the level and most valuable part of said cleared land. Has torn down the fences around the same. Has taken timber and stone for the construction of said tram road, which is about five feet in width, constructed of timber placed cross-wise, a few feet apart, as ties, and timbers laid end to end or lengthwise. On said ties, as rails, on which said company expects and intends to haul said logs, which are loaded on trucks in cars and drawn by mules or horses. That said tram road is almost, if not wholly completed. That said company has already dug up and destroyed the soil and earth of the plaintiffs belonging to said tract of land in constructing a roadbed for said tram road. That it has beaten and expects to continue beating stone in the earth through said cleared and level land of the plaintiffs. In under and above said tram road for the purpose of making solid and securing said rad bed thereby rendering it difficult, if not, impossible to plant and cultivate said cleared land after said tram road shall have been removed therefrom. That said company is now using and expects to continue to use a portion of said cleared and level land for the purpose of a log yard, that is a place where logs are dropped or dumped off and allowed to remain until ready to be removed by tide or otherwise. That in the use of said log yard the sold and earth will be so beaten and trodden down, as to greatly injure and destroy it for farming purposed. That the said company has been, and expects to continue, hauling said logs on and over said tract of land with r leaves thereby cutting ditches or branches through said cleared land and trodden the same down. Whereby the free hold is, and will be permanently injured and rendered almost, if not quite, worthless. That the said company has entered upon said tract of land and arrogated to itself the exclusive use and control of said land, for its own private interests. And expects to continue to use and control the same for one or two years. Yet to come, that being the time estimated to be necessary to enable it to remain said timber by said tram road ox teams and otherwise. That by the instruction of said tram road and the use intended to be made thereof in the future, including the harm to be done to therein on the way of bedding timbers and stones under and along the same for the purpose of keeping the same in repair. Together with the constant use of a portion of said cleared land as a log yard, and the like construct driving the said mules or horse, and ox teams on and over the said cleared land. Well as the plaintiffs are advised believes and so charge work on irreparable injury to their said tract of land. And that if the several acts of trespass aforesaid, already committed by said company, and by it intended and threatened to be continue for one or two years aforesaid, are allowed to go on it will become a nuisance and a common grievance to the plaintiffs, calculated to produce and producing irreparable loss injury and damage to the plaintiffs. Who have already sustained at least $500 damages by the acts aforesaid.

The plaintiffs further allege that they are informed that the said company caused to have some kind of lease from their mother, the defendant Amy Flynn by which they entered and took charge of said tract of land. In the manner and for the purpose hereinbefore stated. Plaintiffs charge that their mother has no interest in said land, except her right of dower therein. Which has never been set apart to her as before stated. That she has never qualified as guardian of the plaintiffs and as the plaintiffs are advised has no legal authority whatsoever to bind the plaintiffs by said lease. Nor any authority to lease the said company or anyone else to damage and destroy the free hold of the plaintiffs in said tract of land in the manner herein complained of or otherwise. The plaintiffs further allege that the said company as plaintiffs are informed believe and so charge is wholly insolvent. And that the defendants Charley Stephens, Levi Stephens and Jacob Spaulding have been employed by the said company as the plaintiffs are informed believe and so charge to use and operate said tram road and ox teams for the purpose of removing said saw logs. And continue with the same in removing the same, unless prevented by injunction from so doing.

The plaintiffs thereof being without adequate remedy at law, come into your honors court of equity. Where alone full and complete justice can be done in the premises, and to the end pray that the defendants, the Little Kanawha Lumber Company, Charley Stephens, Levi Stephens, and Jacob Spaulding, all other agents and employees of said company, be perpetually inhibited, restrained and enjoined from hauling or otherwise removing the saw logs, herein complained of over. Or through the said 150 acres of land herein mentioned by means of horse, mule or ox teams or said tram road or elsewhere, through said tract of land. And that upon a final hearing of this cause the plaintiffs may recover of the said Little Kanawha Lumber Company the damages already done to said tract of land. And that the plaintiffs be afforded such other, further and general relief as the court may see to grant. And as in duty bound, they will ever pray. Viola Francisco, Maggie Francisco, by C.S. Flynn their next Friend. J.B. Williamson Sol. 20th day of Feb. 1894.

APPENDIX K – ASA HAMAN MCCOY 1890 SPECIAL CENSUS

This is hard to read, line 15 shows Patsy (Martha) McCoy as wife of Asa H. McCoy, moving down to the explanation in the lower line 15, showing the post office of Phelps, and Asa's disability was frost bite, matching the Adjunct Generals report of the men in the 45th Kentucky.

APPENDIX L – RECORDS FOR VANCE, BROMLEY, AND VANCE

Two pages from the case of James Vance vs. John B. Bromley.

Made in the USA
Lexington, KY
26 November 2015